Anger

Anger

The Unauthorized Biography of Kenneth Anger

BILL LANDIS

HarperCollins*Publishers*

HarperCollins books may be purchased for educational, business, or sales promotional use. For information please write: Special Markets Department, HarperCollins Publishers, Inc., 10 East 53rd Street, New York, NY 10022.

FIRST EDITION

Designed by Nancy Singer

Library of Congress Cataloging-in-Publication Data

Landis, Bill, 1959–
 Anger : the unauthorized biography of Kenneth Anger / Bill Landis. — 1st ed.
  p. cm.
 ISBN 0-06-016700-9
 1. Anger, Kenneth. 2. Motion picture producers and directors— United States—Biography. I. Title.
 PN1998.3.A54L36 1995
 791.43'0233'092—dc20   95-10886
 [B]

---

95 96 97 98 99 ❖/HC 10 9 8 7 6 5 4 3 2 1

For my wife, Michelle Clifford, with love

The Great Oz has spoken! Pay no attention to that man behind the curtain!

L. Frank Baum
The Wonderful Wizard of Oz

Nothing is true. Everything is permitted.

Aleister Crowley

Contents

Acknowledgments   xi
Introduction   xiii

Part I: The Child

Chapter 1. Reflections of Youth   3
Chapter 2. A Magickal Escape   16
Chapter 3. Camera Obscura   36
Chapter 4. A Bed Less Empty Than Before   51
Chapter 5. Dancing with One's Own
    Madness . . .Welcome!   65
Chapter 6. Gall Wasps   82
Chapter 7. Single-Room Occupancy   91

Part II: The Father

Chapter 8. Sting Me   99
Chapter 9. Kustomized   114
Chapter 10. Beautiful Son   130
Chapter 11. The Mad Hatter   161
Chapter 12. Invocations   169

Part III: Decadence

Chapter 13. Bootlegged Babylon   187
Chapter 14. The Gossip   197
The Public Humiliation of Jimmy Page: An Interlude   208
Chapter 15. A Swastika of Desire   210

Chapter 16. I Love Lucifer   219
Chapter 17. The Budweiser Boys   239
Chapter 18. Going Home   254

Sources   265
Index   277

Photographs follow page 146.

Acknowledgments

The following individuals provided a great deal of information and support: Ed Earle, Curtis Harrington, Bob Anglemyer, the late Maxine Peterson, Marilyn Granas, Billy Barty, Amos Vogel, Dennis Hopper, Robert Dean, John Calendo, Bruce Byron, Nigel Finch, Herb Caen of the *San Francisco Chronicle*, Gerard Malanga, Kit Fitzgerald, Charles Henri Ford, William Klein, Mike Mideke, Jamie Gillis, George Payne, Scott Covert, Robert Hawkins, Rocco Malce, Frater Clayton Patterson, M. Henry Jones, Sylvia Plachy, Gavin Smith, Harlan Jacobson, Robert Campbell, John Stackpole, and John Le Moss—and several individuals who would rather remain anonymous. Thanks to Bobby Beausoleil, who managed to give some very good interviews under very difficult circumstances, and his wife, Barbara Beausoleil, for supplying photographs.

The following individuals at various institutions were very helpful: Sam McElfresh of the American Federation of the Arts; Roland Hansen of the Chicago Art Institute Library; Nancy Robinson of Walker Arts Center; the staff at the Museum of Modern Art, New York City; and Lou Maletta, for generously sharing his archive of films.

Robert Jones was a wonderful and perceptive editor who always gave cogent pragmatic advice. I must thank certain other individuals who were integral to this project:

My ever-supportive literary agent, Robert Cornfield;

Robert Christgau, of the *Village Voice*, for his early support of my writing;

Matt Martin, Esq., who did an astute legal read;

Chip Kidd, for his startlingly original cover artwork;

Craig Nelson, my first editor at HarperCollins, who began this project at the company;

John Le Moss, a true friend and someone I'd always want in my corner;

Marcia Felix, for her assistance with computers;

Willie Sanders, who's a wonderful guy who never let me down; and

Thanks also to Frank Martinez, Bruce Yaffe, and Richard B. Sherman.

Last but foremost, as the Moonglows sang it in "Most of All," I'd like to thank my wife, Michelle Clifford, for endless discussions about topics ranging from early underground film to the sex magick of Aleister Crowley; for her assistance in discovering some wonderful chapter titles and their introductory quotes, and in editing and rewrites; for the interviews she conducted with Bobby Beausoleil; and for her great patience in living with an obsessive writer during the four years of this project. Michelle actually initiated the whole thing by asking me, when we first met eight years ago, "What was Ken Anger like? Are there any books about him?"

Introduction

Kenneth Anger is an extremely private individual. This is understandable, since he so mercilessly revealed the sexual and addictive foibles of his movieland icons in his *Hollywood Babylon* books. Anger also wears a mask of threat, for he is a footnote in every crime book concerning the Manson Family because of his association with convicted murderer Bobby Beausoleil.

Anger resisted this project from the outset. When my wife, Michelle, interviewed Beausoleil via phone from prison, Anger issued a proclamation on his special "magical" Puck Productions stationery stating that I was "an avowed enemy" of his and my book was a "purported" biography. Copies of this letter were sent to Michelle, Craig Nelson, who was then my editor at HarperCollins, and numerous other individuals. Curiously, Beausoleil had nothing to do with this proclamation, since he had ceased speaking to Anger and had designed the Puck Productions letterhead well over a decade ago. Anger then followed up with a plethora of blustering lawyer letters, concluding with the Mohammedan declaration that no photos of him—a public figure—be used in this book.

I met Kenneth Anger on April 30, 1980, when I interviewed him for the *Soho Weekly News*. Anger was also the subject of a PBS documentary at the time, and he was premiering his first film in years, *Lucifer Rising*, a work he had initiated with Beausoleil back in the mid-1960s. I found Kenneth Anger to be a brilliant, vital man.

Underground film had fascinated me since I first read Parker

Tyler's *Underground Film* and Amos Vogel's *Film as a Subversive Art* as a teenager. Anger's outrageous achievements in this avant-garde mode of filmmaking led me to believe that he was its most outstanding exponent. At the same time, his aesthetic innovations were more readily absorbed into mainstream film-making than any other underground artist's. I felt that a study of Anger's career could provide a microcosm of the phenomenon of American underground film.

While still associated with Anger in 1982, I saw him become entangled with *Hollywood Babylon II*, a project he was admittedly executing for the money. During a benefit function in which he was supposed to read a chapter of the book, our relationship went completely awry. Later, I found out that this, unfortunately, was frequently the case with associations with Anger.

As his self-chosen surname indicates, and as his brother Bob has stated, "Ken's just an angry guy. He was angry at everything and everybody." Yet I still feel that Kenneth Anger has a great deal to teach students of filmmaking and occultism.

Bill Landis
New York City
September 8, 1994

Part I

The Child

Chapter 1

Reflections of Youth

Men have a fantasy about this and it often is implanted by either mother, a nurse or big sister or something from their childhood, just like the homosexual thing may be father, big brother or the priest or the rabbi or who knows what. You know, it all has to start somewhere.

KENNETH ANGER

A male child of perfect innocence and high intelligence is the most satisfactory and suitable victim.

ALEISTER CROWLEY
"OF THE BLOODY SACRIFICE: AND MATTERS COGNATE,"
MAGICK IN THEORY AND PRACTICE

the sound of thunder heralds a lightning bolt. A title card announces FIREWORKS, with the letters bordered in red against a brown background, making the word sparkle like a firecracker. A flame comes to rest on a photograph lying in silvery water.

A blond Apollo sailor, his eyes dramatically lit by a streak of light, dispassionately holds the dreamer, an emaciated, seemingly unconscious man, in his arms.

The dreamer and his Apollo savior fade farther and farther into the black, starless universe surrounding them . . . the dreamer picks up a well-worn matchbook saying UNITED STATES NAVY . . . he passes a room, walking by a hanging tinfoil object, to a door with GENTS tacked on . . . into the blackness of initiation.

A shot of cars cruising illuminates the night highway. The dreamer enjoys a cig. He turns around. Five maniacal sailors, joined by three others, are staring at him, swinging heavy chains, one of these chains holding a rock.

The sailors take off to make war with the dreamer, running over dirty newspapers on the street. They circle him. He falls to his knees, dropping his cigarette. The sailors attack like barracudas. They tear off his clothes, rip at his nostrils. Blood spurts into his eyes, which look blackened and swollen. His mouth is open in a silent scream that you sense would be deafening if you could hear it.

The sailors look down, their faces obscured, and they swing the chains and wail on his ass some more. One digs his fingernails into the dreamer's wrists and twists them repeatedly. While he writhes in agony, they smile with sadistic affection. Naked and bloody, the dreamer crouches on his knees, cowering. White liquid explodes on the pavement in close-up.

His chest is heaving. There are drops of blood on his cheek. His tormentors eviscerate him, digging through the gory meat of his chest to reveal a ticking clock. Milky white fluid falls on the dreamer's chin, into his mouth, on his Adam's apple, pouring down his body, passing his bloody nipple in a ritual.

Through the blackness, the first sailor-savior is seen, slowly unbuttoning his pants. Out pops what looks like a cock in black and white, but, lo, it's a Roman candle that fires in every direction . . .

*   *   *

Kenneth Anger never volunteers details about his immediate family, and he has never publicly stated his given name. If questioned, Anger professes to despise his father, will not discuss his mother, and holds a longstanding antipathy toward his brother and sister.

Anger was born Kenneth Wilbur Anglemyer on February 3, 1927, in Santa Monica, California. His father, Wilbur, was a mechanically inclined fellow from Troy, Ohio, who during the First World War worked for Kellogg, which was then developing machine guns for the war effort. One of Wilbur's many hobbies was the history of his lineage, and he claimed descent from an Aunglemeyer family of German immigrants who arrived in America some time around the Revolutionary War.

Wilbur attended Ohio State College, where he met an older coed, Lillian Coler, the product of a divorced family—a social distinction that set her apart at the time. In addition, Lillian had taken a terrible fall in a horseback accident as a child, which left her permanently crippled and stooped. Lillian Coler could trace her lineage back to England and Lord Townsend, the British official who imposed the tea tax on the American colonists.

Wilbur and Lillian married and, in 1918, had their first child, a daughter, Jean. About that time, Lillian's mother, Bertha Coler, purchased a home and set up Coler Studios, an interior decorating business, in Pacific Palisades, slightly north of Santa Monica. In 1921, Wilbur and Lillian followed Bertha west, moving into Bertha's old-fashioned Spanish-style house. That same year Lillian gave birth to a son, Robert, nicknamed "Bobby" until he was ten. For a time Wilbur Anglemyer worked for a Flying Circus, an amusement park ride in Ocean Park on the Santa Monica pier. Eventually he found work at Douglas Aircraft as an electrical engineer, remaining there well past retirement age.

Bob Anglemyer was six years old when his mother gave birth to his younger brother, Kenneth Wilbur. "Ken was brought home in a fog," he recalled. "We had a Model A and my grandmother drove. It was so foggy that my father walked in front of the car to guide it."

Bob remembers Wilbur as a good father who was always around: "He and I were very close." Wilbur worked with all the children, was good with his hands, and had a lot of hobbies. One hobby that particularly interested him was the Boy Scouts.

Ken would never get along with his father. He has contemptuously spoken of Wilbur as having "a lot of hobbies." Although Anger has referred to his father's abusiveness as being more psychological than physical, Wilbur Anglemyer did have a preference toward disciplinary spankings and could be intimidating. "He had a German temper," remembers Bob. "He wasn't that way very often. We all had our spankings—let's put it that way."

Anger describes his father, Wilbur, as puritanical, although this puritanism was not religiously motivated. The Anglemyer clan would pay lip service to the church, switching back and forth between Methodist and Presbyterian to whichever minister they found most appealing.

Anger inherited his mother's dark coloring and hair rather than his father's, whose hair was light brown. As an adult, Anger would stand six feet, while his father was 5'9", his sister Jean 6', and Bob 6'3".

Bob felt that his parents had a good marriage, but Ken has spoken of family disharmony his entire life. The intense bitterness between Ken and his older brother has always been mutual. Bob remembers that Ken was "sort of a bratty brother. Not particularly friendly. He and I never did get along. Part of that's probably my fault, but we never did. Six years at that early time of life is quite a bit of difference. His interests were entirely different from mine. My interests were not along artistic lines whatsoever.

"Ken's from the same family I was, but our lives were entirely different. He was closer to our mother and our grandmother than my father. I think my mother and grandmother spoiled him. They were overpowering to a certain extent. They thought he was a genius—even before school. Anything he wanted he got. That was part of the problem between us, because I couldn't get away with *anything*."

In 1929, when Ken was two years old, the stock market crashed, ushering in the Great Depression. People who supported families and held longtime jobs were reduced to breadlines and food rationing. Homelessness and hoboism became widespread. One of the few cheap diversions were Hollywood movies, which offered fantasy escapism such as Busby Berkeley musicals.

Ken's grandmother, Bertha Coler, saved her family during the Depression by purchasing and holding on to real estate. Bertha was relatively well off, but she also had a lot of familial responsibility. Besides the Anglemyer family, she assisted several siblings.

Bertha had virtually no friends. Her family was her main concern and pleasure. As she entered her late sixties, she began to express outwardly her taste for the arts. She painted in oil and watercolor—landscapes, cityscapes, and portraits—and dipped into clay sculpture. She frequently sketched family members. These little artistic fugues widened Bertha's social circle. She met Miss Diggy. Diggy became part of Bertha's family. In 1932, Bertha left Pacific Palisades to move in with her ladyfriend on Holly Drive in Hollywood, a house since razed by the L.A. freeway.

Wilbur and Lillian also moved, taking fourteen-year-old Jean, eleven-year-old Bob, and five-year-old Kenneth to 437 10th Street in a pleasant, predominantly white Santa Monica suburb. Their house was a typical California adobe affair, circa 1915.

Ken was upset that his grandmother had left the household. She had taken him to his very first movie, a double bill of Al Jolson in *The Singing Fool* and Sol Lesser's *Thunder Over Mexico*, his cut of Sergei Eisenstein's *Que Viva Mexico!* "I remember being very disturbed and riveted by it," Anger states, "but I never hid under the seat or anything. I remember watching it."

At this young age Ken was exposed in *Thunder Over Mexico* to two aesthetic approaches that would become hallmarks of his own cinematic techniques: Eisenstein's editing montage, which utilized cross-cutting of diverse scenes to bring out the interior meaning of events and personalities, and a blatant focus on sadomasochistic eroticism, which reached its zenith in death.

In its present form—still only an approximation of Sergei Eisenstein's unfinished film—*Que Viva Mexico!* is divided into three sections. One documents Mexico's Day of the Dead holiday, a paganistic festival that euphorically celebrates terminal iconography. Miniature skeleton ornamentation abounds, and participants ecstatically consume candy bones. Another portion depicts semi-clad Mexican peasants lounging in Eden-like tropical splendor. The final sequence provides the central focus of *Thunder Over Mexico*. It comes the closest to straightforward narrative and concerns an uprising on a plantation by the Aztec-looking peasantry against a feudal, Europeanized landowner. The conclusion shows the three muscular, bare-chested rebel leaders executed in a scene alluding to Christ's martyrdom. They are buried waist-deep in sand and horses trample them to death.

Although Ken missed his grandmother terribly, he enjoyed her new friend Diggy. She furthered his interest in film with stories from her days as a Hollywood extra and wardrobe girl. Years later, after Kenneth Anglemyer had reinvented himself as Kenneth Anger, magician-filmmaker, he would apply the editing shears to significant portions of his early life. Diggy's characteristics would be grafted onto Bertha. "When I was growing up," Anger has said, "old enough to understand fairy tales—to listen to them, not read them—my grandmother, instead of telling me stories about Little Red Riding Hood and Sleeping Beauty, would tell me bedtime stories of Fatty Arbuckle, what Clara Bow used to do with her football team, Rudy Valentino's strange sort of dominant wives, and things like that. I didn't quite understand everything she was talking about, but I was absolutely fascinated."

It may seem odd that a woman who wasn't even a family member would be telling a preschooler stories that were then considered immoral and perverse. However, they may have been presented in the form of morality plays derived from topical gossip. Just as Ken's lifelong idol, English occultist Aleister Crowley, was captivated as a child by the devils and demons in the biblical readings by his puritanical family, Ken was obsessed at an early age by hedonists who defied conventional norms.

The thrills, spills, and suicide chills in these Hollywood stories provided Ken with a constellation of movie stars that would become fetishes for the rest of his life. While the stars were virtually mythological figures to the general public, they were also human beings with sexual and narcotic problems. The obsessional pleasure Anger would derive from watching their performances and collecting memorabilia associated with them would reach its height with the *Hollywood Babylon* books he'd write as an adult.

The world of Hollywood was so magical to Ken that later he'd insist that Bertha Coler was a costume mistress during the Silent Era, a fact he greatly values in his personal mythology but which has more connection to the facts of Diggy's life than his grandmother's. Today, Anger's sister, Jean Anglemyer Roof, who refuses to discuss him, is adamant that Bertha Coler had no relation to the movie industry. Bob is equally firm about this matter.

Around the time Bertha moved in with Diggy, six-year-old Ken began sneaking up to their Holly Drive attic to dress in beaded silk flapper gowns that his "grandmother" kept as souvenirs from her "seamstress career." He refers to this as his transvestite period.

Since his grandmother was less available to give him attention and his siblings were so much older, Ken commenced a rich fantasy life of his own invention. Taking off from Bertha's artistic inclinations, he began creating puppet shows. He would orchestrate Chinese legends, which he wrote himself. "They were always Oriental," Anger recalled during his seventies *Hollywood Babylon* period. "One was called 'The Banana'—that was my first script. I may still be making it. I think you're doomed to repeat yourself in that department. The first love somehow lingers."

Ken also indulged a passion in reading Big Little Books. An early form of movie tie-in books, they were aimed at children under twelve. They were small, three-by-four-inch books, an inch and a half thick, printed on pulp paper, with the narrative alongside the film stills. A Shirley Temple edition, one based on a Bela Lugosi movie, or a movie western are examples. In *Classics Illustrated* fashion, Big Little Books followed the plot of the movie instead of the original source material. For example, *Moby Dick* is based on a silent version that has John Barrymore as Captain Ahab triumphantly slaying the white whale and returning to the arms of his sweetheart, who's aptly named Faith. The Big Little Books would initiate Ken's lifetime hobby of collecting movie memorabilia.

Ken's favorite comic strip was "Flash Gordon," whose hero was also incarnated by blond Apollo prototype Buster Crabbe in a long-running movie serial. Flash was superhuman in his tolerance of pain. "Flash Gordon" had the dual female natures: a dominant evil princess with a severe bobbed and black-banged Betty Page [the S&M icon and cheesecake phenomenon] hairdo, and Flash's girlfriend, who inevitably gets tied up for her troubles. Presiding over all is the sadistic paternal figure, Emperor Ming, who makes Flash go through hell and back to rescue his submissive girlfriend. Flash's heroic masculinity framed within masochism had a special appeal for Ken.

Also included in his beloved kiddie library were the original Oz books by L. Frank Baum, such as *The Wonderful Wizard of Oz*, *The Land of Oz*, and *Ozma of Oz*. Hugely popular around the turn of the century, these books have retained their popularity until the present day. However, this is not the Oz of Dorothy as popularized by the movie with Judy Garland; this Oz is predatory and as vengeful as an Old Testament parable. Children are continually mentally and physically menaced by adults. Inventions of the children's imagination are brought to life as henchmen to aid their powerless creators.

Considering his early exposure to Diggy's Hollywood tales, Ken immediately connected with the sexual threat and terror contained in the Oz books. Sexuality is enforced by adult figures with the end result often being gender reversal. For example, the boy protagonist of *The Land of Oz*, Tip, metamorphoses at its conclusion into Princess Ozma, who carries the narrative through the next sequel, *Ozma of Oz*. The Oz books also provided Anger with his first exposure to occult, specifically Rosicrucian, philosophy. The themes of divination, transformation, and alchemy are essential components of the text, with the Rosicrucian key primary colors of red, blue, and gold used as a mantra throughout. They laid the groundwork for Ken's attraction to Crowley, the occultist who would rework Rosicrucian thought into his own magical system.

For books intended for children, jarring illustrations abound in the Oz books. An all-girl army carrying knitting needles. Stickmen in disjointed, uncomfortable positions. Children wielding axes. Patterns of coital positions of odd complexity, such as a child enjoying lifeless passion with a sawhorse as a pumpkin-head man bends over in the background. The caption under this curious troika reads: "Do Keep Those Legs Still."

At the same time, Ken began attending dance classes. They were taught by Russian émigré Maurice Kosloff, a former Diaghilev dancer trying to earn a living in Depression-era California. Ken quickly developed an inclination toward tap and interpretive dancing.

After Shirley Temple became a child star, Ken danced with her at the Santa Monica Cotillion, where it was considered democratic to let the movie royalty mix with ordinary kids to keep them from getting fat heads. "She was exquisite," Anger recalled, "but she wasn't overwhelmingly friendly. In fact," he elaborates, "at one point she was quite irritated at me because I blew one of the contests which she would have won if she had any other partner but me. I insisted on putting in sort of a surreal caper in the middle of one of the steps, and the judges frowned on it."

Anger talks of appearing in some of the Baby Burlesks made during the 1930s. Many dancing schools supplied talent to these grade-B independent productions, which gave Shirley Temple her start. These parodies of hit movies starring diaper-clad children had titles like *War Babies*, *The Runt Page* (a takeoff on *The Front Page*), and *Glad Rags to Riches*. With their toddler cast they seem vaguely lewd today, even pedophiliac. In *Polly Tix in Washington*, Temple plays a gold-digger sporting a black lace bra. For a Tarzan spoof, a bunch of black boys were trip-wired so that they fell into a heap, their legs cut. "They took risks in those days, perhaps more than they do now," Anger bemusedly recalled. Not as popular as the *Our Gang* comedies, the Baby Burlesks were shown as backup for double bills. Depression-era audiences were lured into sitting through them by giveaways of kitchen dishes.

The biggest keystone of Anger's personal mythology, and his permanent love-hate link to Hollywood, is his appearance as the Changeling Prince in the 1935 MGM Max Reinhardt–William Dieterle version of *A Midsummer Night's Dream*. Anger has maintained that Bertha Coler's movie industry connections got him this role, but the reality probably has more to do with Diggy and his dancing school.

Ken's part does not appear in the cast or credit listings. His propensity for mythmaking has caused individuals to doubt that he even appeared in the film. This doubt extends from the remnants of the microscopic underground film world, where opinion may be colored by bias, jealousy, or a combative encounter with Anger, to the beacon of conventional movies, as manifested by the Academy of Motion Picture Arts and Sciences. Academy workers cannot confirm or deny Anger's presence in *A Midsummer Night's Dream* because of his absence from the cast listing but do mention that "there have been rumors that he was never in the film."

The Changeling Prince in *A Midsummer Night's Dream* is, in fact, Anger as a child; visually, he's immediately recognizable. Dressed like a little genie out of *Arabian Nights*, he chases after pixie girls who magically take off and fly through the air, just out of reach, and wanders through a forest occupied by newts. A beautiful, long-tressed Amazonian goddess, Titania, lifts him aloft, kisses him, and looks upon him with maternal wonder and excitement. In the story, Titania had been quarreling with her husband Oberon for the affections of the Changeling. The black and white monochrome glitters, like diamonds shining in the sun. Although the film seems rather static now, its best scenes, such as those with Anger as the Changeling, turn William Shakespeare's occult-mythological comedy into an ethereal fantasy world.

On the *Midsummer* set, the difference between reality and the fantasy world of motion pictures was made quite vivid to Ken, and its impact was both lifelong and rapturous. The film crew had arc beams playing on a staircase made of steel, which was wrapped around a plastic tree. The staircase was covered with cellophane to hide the steps in the structure. With filters on the camera, the cellophane looked like a moonbeam wound around the great big oak tree. To the eye it looked like a bunch of cellophane—but that's the magic of movies.

The forest in *A Midsummer Night's Dream* was a complete fantasy. The trees were plaster, but they were sprayed with shellac and highlighted with silver paint. The heat from all the lights on the shellac released fumes, and Ken experienced the first glue high he'd ever had. Billy Barty, who played Mustard Seed, found being on the set a wonderful experience for a kid and also recalls the overpowering shellac odor.

Magic and reality collided on the set, creating for Ken some sadistically amusing fireworks. One particular scene required a group of children playing elves to climb up the cellophane moonbeam. The girls were almost nude under their cellophane dresses. The arc lights on the soundstage were placed very close so the moonbeam would glow, but suddenly the cellophane caught fire. The flames raced everywhere and the children became hysterical as their dresses also caught fire.

Anger later said, "Oh, gee, I would have done that on purpose, because it was so thrilling to me. They felt genuine emotion. They felt genuinely afraid. There was a genuine feeling of something real happening. That impressed me very much."

Mickey Rooney, as Puck, enjoyed in *Midsummer* what is probably his finest film role. His little boy-satyr/devil, complete with horns, is sexually forthright and startling. Naked except for a tiny loincloth, he looks like he stepped out of the pages of a chicken magazine or fantasy sequence in *Pink Narcissus*, a pastiche of gay pornography itself highly influenced by Anger's films.

Offscreen, Mickey Rooney was a nasty, horny, cigar-chomping, gambling, limb-busting tough guy in a child's body; he speaks candidly of his unbridled childhood in his autobiography. He and Anger became good friends. Rooney obtained a neon violin from *Gold Diggers of 1933* for Anger. The prop man was sure the child would shatter it, but Rooney finagled it for his young chum; he was that kind of a kid. *Hollywood Babylon II* refers to Mickey affectionately as "Puck Forever."

There would never be another Hollywood part for Ken after *A Midsummer Night's Dream*. He would remain forever bitter about not being a child star, and it would fuel the antagonism toward Hollywood that would manifest itself in his *Hollywood Babylon* books. As Anger reflected years later, "I have developed a case of enormous, petrified, extremely sour grapes over the subject of Hollywood."

He turned inward and tried to create the moviemaking experience as best he could. In 1937, at the age of ten, he shot his first film, *Ferdinand the Bull*. The Anglemyer family had gone on a two-week vacation to Yosemite National Park. They took their 16mm wind-up camera, the medium for home movies at this time. When they returned home, Ken begged his parents for the short ends of the 16mm reversal stock. Two fellow Boy Scouts incarnated the bull. Anger recalls that "In *Ferdinand* I had the bull—two boys under the skirt—play effeminate." His brother Bob remembers him borrowing their father's camera and running around with a cape.

Anger downplays *Ferdinand the Bull* and frequently states that *Who Has Been Rocking My Dream Boat* was his first film. According to his own synopsis, this 1941 film was an atmospheric montage of children at play in the summer before Pearl Harbor. A similarly titled song by the Ink Spots, along with other hits of the time, provided Anger's first use of popular music as an ironic counterpoint to the visuals, a technique that would later reach its ipsissimus in *Scorpio Rising*.

About this time the Anglemyer family began to split up. Upon leaving high school, Ken's big sister Jean had left to work as a tutor for an American family in Japan. Bob was attending the University of California in Berkeley, studying forestry. At the outbreak of the war, Jean returned home and married, Bob joined the Navy, and their father went to work on bombers for Douglas Aircraft. In this tumultuous atmosphere Anger continued making short films.

In 1942 Ken made his own variant on *Flash Gordon—Prisoner of Mars*, what he calls a "science fiction rendering of the Minotaur myth." Anger constructed the major prop—a small volcano—in his backyard. For the first time, he played his own hero onscreen and began to integrate classical mythology into the narrative. Unfortunately, like all of Anger's pre-*Fireworks* films, *Prisoner of Mars* remains inaccessible to the general public.

Maxine Peterson, a friend from grade school, came across Ken again at Santa Monica High. "It was a three-year school. He was a semester behind me. He was sort of a loner. Weird. I don't think he was very friendly. 'Aloof' would be the adjective. I don't remember him with a group of kids. Even way back then one could see he was either homosexual or headed that way."

While at Santa Monica High, Ken first began researching the

work of Jean Cocteau, the French artist-poet-writer who would provide him with significant aesthetic and, later, personal influence. In 1943 he made his own variant on Cocteau's *Les Enfants Terribles*—*The Nest*, a half-hour study of incest and narcissism. Anger summarizes it as "a brother and sister relate to mirrors and each other until a third party breaks the balance; seducing both into violence. Ablutions and the acts of dressing and making-up observed as a magic rite. The binding spell of the sister-sorceress is banished by the brother who walks out." Fellow Santa Monica resident Dare Harris played the boyfriend catalyst. He grew up to be Hollywood's John Derek. Meanwhile, Ken was starting to metamorphose himself, as he struggled for artistic and intellectual maturity.

Chapter 2

A Magickal Escape

n 1944 Ken moved, with his parents, to his grandmother's home on Holly Drive. She was aging, and alone, now that Diggy had moved out. He transferred from Santa Monica High to Beverly Hills High where he met Marilyn Granas in art class. Granas had been Shirley Temple's stand-in. She was shy about it, keeping it a secret, and thought that nobody knew. By that time Shirley Temple was no longer active in movies.

Like Maxine Peterson, Granas remembered Ken as "very much a loner. But he was enormously talented. Everybody knew it then, but they just thought he was weird. He was a genius! He was so far advanced over any of the rest of us in the art class." Ken would make plaster of paris creations with razor blades jutting out, very way out for his classmates' taste, very much influenced by the surrealists.

Granas remembers Ken as a tall, slender, attractive young man with dark hair and fine bones. He came up to her one day in class and said he was making a film. Most of the kids thought he was weird and weren't at all friendly with him. "Would you like to be in my film?" inquired Anger. Granas thought he was interesting and creative and was just flattered to be asked. "There were so many really pretty girls at Beverly High and he really could have had his pick of them.

Granas's costar in what Ken first titled *Demigods* was her classmate Bob Jones, who had been in *The Nest*. Jones, a student in the art class, was quite short but highly attractive, popular, and outgoing, very much in the in-crowd.

Granas and Jones were the only actors cast in the original film except for the character of the gray-haired lady. For the film's set, Anger used a spooky old castle in Hollywood, which he claimed once belonged to Japanese-born actor Sessue Hayakawa.

Ken did everything in relation to the production of *Demigods*. He did the lights; he photographed it; wrote it; directed. Even for a novice filmmaker, Anger was extraordinarily inventive. He shot over a period of months because he didn't have the money to do it all at once.

The film was shown under the title *Demigods* (it was later called *Escape Episode*) at the Coronet Theater on North La Cienega in

Los Angeles, one of the few theaters to show independent films. Granas first viewed it at this screening, which was presenting a collection of experimental films. "Our film was the least way out of all those movies that showed that day. There was a film of kaleidoscopes with weird music that went on and on for a whole reel. Ours was the only one that made sense at all. I was offered a film contract by Michael Curtiz on the basis of that film."

Lewis Jacobs, later producer of *It Won't Rub Off, Baby* with Dick Gregory, critiqued *Demigods* in the book *Experiment in Film*. He found it "less concerned with the cinematic form and more with human conflict . . . begins with a boy and a girl parting at the edge of the sea. As the girl walks away she is watched by a woman from a plaster castle. The castle turns out to be a spiritualists' temple, the woman a medium and the girl's aunt. Both dominate and twist the girl's life until she is in despair. Finally, in a gesture of defiance, the girl invites the boy to the castle to sleep with her. The aunt is informed by spirits, becomes enraged, and threatens divine retribution. The girl is frustrated, becomes bitter, and resolves to escape. The quality of the film is unique and shows extreme sensitivity to personal relationships."

An especially moving sequence in *Demigods* used a caged canary as a metaphor for the girl's situation. "She wanted to escape," Anger said. "It was the first film that had any kind of statement of what I was about. It was a reflection of my own desire to break away from my family." Ken was feeling that desire more strongly than ever.

In Hollywood, Ken began escaping into the world he loved the most—the big movie studios, the dream factories surrounding him. He loved discovering the supposedly secret lives of the stars, a hobby fueled by the widely syndicated gossip rantings of Hedda Hopper and Louella Parsons.

The movies that enthralled Ken the most were the silents in which the stars he'd heard about from Diggy appeared. "The silent period," he stated, "has a kind of extra magic. You don't hear the people's voices. A silent image is more like a ghost or a dream." It was a concept he would apply to his own filmmaking. He began attending screenings of silent films at Clara Grossman's art gallery.

At these screenings Ken saw Valentino as the Sheik. Ken's narcissism was piqued; he saw a refraction of himself in this swarthy, exotic, sensual splendor. The Sheik was a dark, dominant, romantic character—yet Anger recalled the gossip of his childhood that portrayed Valentino as a sexual submissive who preferred dominant women. Rudolph Valentino had long been ensconced in his minimalist mausoleum at Forest Lawn by the time Anger became obsessed with him. As is the case with many of those who fixate on dead celebrities, the unfulfilled love only fueled Anger's unrequited obsession.

Major figures in the silent genre, such as D. W. Griffith and Lillian Gish, appeared at the Grossman gallery screenings in person. Anger loved the lavishness of Griffith's pictures: complete orgiastic worlds unto themselves, outrageously sexual and paganistic, with huge majestic sets populated by thousand of extras in minutely detailed costumes. He held Griffith's editing innovations in as much esteem as Eisenstein's.

Ken watched Griffith, who lived near the Grossman gallery in a cheap hotel, with particular fascination. This master filmmaker was bitter about the studio system for the control it exercised over his projects. Anger recalled with disquiet that Griffith was "always dignified, always a gentleman, always supplied with bourbon—you could smell him ten feet away. Never sloppy or messy, but you could smell that he was drinking."

At the Grossman screenings Ken also met Curtis Harrington, himself a young budding filmmaker. They were drawn into a close friendship by their intense interest in cinema.

To the shy, brooding Harrington, Ken's parents were just people in the background. He thought Ken's mother, Lillian, was a terribly sweet woman. Harrington was most impressed by the distinguished-looking, white-haired Bertha Coler. "She was the strong personality in the house. A very strong-willed old lady. He [Anger] was quite fond of her and she was very supportive of Kenneth. He got a lot of his best qualities from his grandmother.

"His family was just very ordinary. I think he came from a very nice, middle-class family, as did I. I suppose there were conflicts because he was an artist; they're exceptional people. And nobody can explain how they appear, where they come from—ever."

In a burst of youthful enthusiasm, and an initial attempt to professionally assert themselves, teenagers Ken and Curtis founded a company called Creative Film Associates, which advertised in *Partisan Review*. There was a group of American filmmakers working outside the studio system since the 1920s who used nonnarrative structures to explore myth, mysticism, personal sexuality, and the unconscious mind. This group would form the inner core of the aesthetic movement that would popularly be known as "underground film." There were no national distributors, so these films were either self-distributed or handled through small collectives like Creative Film Associates.

The first American underground film of note, Robert Florey's *Life and Death of 9413, A Hollywood Extra*, was released in 1928. Resolutely antistudio and highly influenced by the surrealists, its theme concerns an artist who aspires to become a Hollywood player and is branded on the forehead with the number 9413. His dreams are shattered by the reality of NO CASTING TODAY signs. An actor who wears a cardboard mask over his real face becomes a success and the hero dies. He ascends to heaven, where the number on his forehead is wiped away and he travels through a celestial landscape. *Life and Death* made extensive use of tabletop models and animation, and is a much admired early work of underground film.

In the same year, Melville Webber and James Sibley Watson collaborated on *The Fall of the House of Usher*, an adaptation of the Edgar Allan Poe short story that blended animation, superimposition, and expressionistic sets. This duo's 1934 film, *Lot in Sodom*, was the first to establish underground film as a vanguard for outfront sexuality. *Lot in Sodom* is best summarized by pioneering film theoretician Parker Tyler in his 1972 book on homosexuality in the cinema, *Screening the Sexes*:

WHILE OBEYING THE BIBLICAL ACCOUNT CONCERNING LOT AND HIS FAMILY AND THE FUNCTION OF THE TWO ANGELS WHO INVESTIGATE SODOM AT THE LORD'S BEHEST, THE WATSON-WEBER WORK USES ALL ITS CREATIVE ACCENTS TO DEPICT THE SENSUAL RESPONSES OF THE MALE HOMOSEXUALS OF SODOM TO THE PHYSICAL BEAUTY OF THE FOREMOST

ANGEL. THE ACCENT OF THE LARGELY CHOREOGRAPHED HOMOSEXUAL
ORGY IS ON EROTICISM AND WHILE NEVER "OBSCENE" IS QUITE LITERAL.

Abstract animators were painters who used film as an instrument. They were major forces in opening up new aesthetic possibilities for the underground. Norman McLaren painted objects directly onto the actual film frame in such works as *Stars and Stripes* and *Dots and Loops* (both 1934). In *Dots and Loops* McLaren painted a dot running along the edge of a 35mm filmstrip causing the film's soundtrack to become a function of the size and thickness of the dot as it runs through the projector.

Harry Smith was a bizarre cat with serious links to the occult and drug subcultures. Smith gave his films numerological titles in the format of *No. 1, No. 2*, ad infinitum. *No. 1*, made in 1939, by Smith's own account, is "hand-drawn animation of dirty shapes— the history of the geologic period reduced to orgasm length (approx. 5 minutes)." The overwhelming effect of Smith's films on the viewer is a hypnotic trance induced by repeated and refracted geometric patterns and hermetic symbols.

John and James Whitney, a pair of West Coast twins, continued in this tradition in 1943 with their numerically titled *Film Exercises 1* through *5*. These films were similar to computer animation before such a thing was invented. Another technical innovation, original electronic scores, provided the soundtrack.

Anger and Harrington's Creative Film Associates distributed the Whitney Brothers' films and those of various East Coast filmmakers. Among the most important of the latter was Maya Deren. An archetypical bohemian from her early involvement in socialist causes to her aggressive pre-feminist stance, she was a formative influence in underground film's polemics. Deren was fiercely anti-Hollywood and considered bending to commercial motion picture formats aesthetic treason. Like later similarly self-created popular culture movements such as punk rock and fanzines, which intrinsically and blatantly attack the hand that could finance them, this attitude would ultimately cause the majority of underground film to be exclusionary and without mass commercial acceptance.

Extremely confrontational, Deren was obsessed with Haitian

culture in general and voodoo in particular. Like many under-grounders, she frequently appeared in her own films. Her films, however, have a very proper art museum air. Deren's best-known film, *Meshes of the Afternoon* (1943), utilizes the dream format of surrealism. An incident in a dream becomes the leitmotif for what later kills the protagonist (Deren). In one sequence in *Meshes of the Afternoon* Deren envisions her doppelgänger as a mirror-faced nun. Past, present, and future intermingle.

Another major force among these early filmmakers was Willard Maas, who worked out of New York City. An alcoholic poet, Maas had learned to use the camera in the Signal Corps during World War II. His 1943 film, *Geography of the Body*, juxtaposed extreme close-ups of the male and female anatomy. Poetry by George Barker comparing nipples and buttocks to mountain peaks and landscapes supplied the commentary.

Around this time Maas made *Images in the Snow*, in which he boldly examined his own homosexuality. The hero is tormented by daydreams of muscular young men. He runs into a cemetery where he identifies his mother with the Virgin Mary and his own suffer-ing with Jesus Christ's and numbs himself in the snow.

Although he was homosexual, Maas married Marie Menken, and the marriage would last throughout their lifetimes. She began her own experimental filmmaking in 1945 with her haiku-patterned *Visual Variations on Noguchi*, which opened up more possibilities for the hand-held camera.

The avant-garde tradition in Europe had inspired many of the American underground filmmakers. One of the earliest films in this tradition and a peak in German Expressionism was *The Cabinet of Dr. Caligari* (Robert Wiene, 1919). The free-floating plot took the form of a nightmare in which the head of an insane asylum directs his hypnotized somnambulist victim to murder. The aesthetic hall-marks of *The Cabinet of Dr. Caligari*—handmade sets utilizing painted backdrops; severe black and white photography that beauti-fully integrated shadows; stylized movements of the actors; opiated quality of the dream-contained narrative—all left their imprint on the American underground. Conrad Veidt's memorable, strangely moving somnambulist was revered as an underground icon.

Entr'acte (1924) provided students of avant-garde film with a cinematic encyclopedia of French Dada. Made by René Clair as a ballet intermission short film and scored by composer Erik Satie, its influential style included the use of varying film speeds, wildly displaced camera angles, superimposition, and animation.

Major artists of many schools then began experimenting brilliantly with film. In 1928 Luis Buñuel and painter Salvador Dali collaborated on what is perhaps the most famous avant-garde film ever, *Un Chien Andalou* (An Andalusian Dog). From its opening scenes of Buñuel smoking and a woman's eyeball being slashed, it is a furious surreal optical assault on the viewer. Shocking and discomforting sexual images emerge out of an internal dream logic instead of conventional narrative; fondled buttocks turn into breasts, a cow suddenly appears on a bourgeois man's bed. The authoritative presence of the filmmaker in his own work, which would become an underground modus operandi, was initiated here by Buñuel.

Buñuel's 1930 film, *L'Age d'Or*, is a surrealist attack on societal oppression of the libido. A couple try to make love and are constantly separated by enforcers of the status quo. The violently hedonistic hero kicks dogs and throws a Cardinal out a window; the heroine greedily sucks a statue's toe. *L'Age d'Or* has a powerful anticlerical charge at its conclusion, when the leader of the orgies in de Sade's *120 Days of Sodom* is revealed to be an incredibly tacky Sunday school version of Jesus Christ.

Anger would later integrate Buñuelesque autobiographical and anticlerical elements into his work, but he would also reconceive the surrealistic autobiographical mode established by Jean Cocteau's 1930 film, *The Blood of a Poet*, which had its roots in French decadence and romanticism. The self-searching hero is a poet who wanders through a dreamscape of a hotel, where suggestions of homosexuality and narcissism abound.

Eisenstein's *Que Viva Mexico!*, even in poorly cut versions like *Thunder Over Mexico*, demonstrated to artists such as Anger the use of montage applied to documentary footage to bring out the filmmaker's own subjective reality. Buñuel's 1932 documentary *Land Without Bread* is another important film in this realm. It depicts a remote Latino village whose inhabitants are stunted by inbreeding, mental illness, and extreme poverty. Scenes such as scorpions crawling across barren dry land take on a frightening and larger-than-life dimension.

Besides gravitating toward these overtly surreal models, the early French filmmakers Lumière and Méliès, who were working before motion pictures had clearly delineated genres, were tremendous inspirations to Ken. One of the most unknown filmmakers in the United States is Lumière, who in the 1890s had a group of anonymous cameramen working under his direction. They went out all over the world, to the courts of China and Japan, and filmed in absolute wonder. Seeing some of the processions and ceremonies they captured on film is like looking into a crystal ball and watching something from another age. Ken loved Méliès's delightful 1902 film, *A Trip to the Moon*, which was complete with Parisian showgirls and an amusingly irascible moon face that clearly isn't thrilled about the visitors that land on it. Anger has stated that "Méliès has always been my mentor." Méliès demonstrated how he could create a world of imagination with limited means and very little cash. His sets and costumes were just canvas and paper, but for Anger the trip to the moon is a thousand times more fabulous than *2001*. "The man in the moon is there; he's the guy we really want to meet."

Ken's other aesthetic icons included Aubrey Beardsley, a Victorian prodigy who died at age twenty-five. Known as the "imp of the perverse," his fantastical, pre-psychedelic, heavily phallic illustrations were used to adorn Oscar Wilde's *Salome*. Beardsley's strong graphics, a pervasive use of black, highly compressed perspective, and hints of sexual ambiguity gave his art power and threat.

Ken idolized Jean Cocteau, the French writer, poet, filmmaker, and artist. Cocteau often combined high art and pornography, an aesthetic he found congenial. Ken especially enjoyed a privately circulated collection of Cocteau's drawings that included French sailors with enormous genitals and a priest holding a cross in one hand and an altar boy's crotch in another. Cocteau often wrote thinly disguised autobiography, notably his "anonymous" book, *Le Livre Blanc*, which detailed his own homosexual development.

Ken closely identified with Jean Genet's erotic sensibility. Since Genet had not yet been translated widely into English during the 1940s, reading him gave Ken the opportunity to expand his knowledge of French vernacular in a tantalizingly erotic way. Genet talked of rough trade and men in prison in an unabashedly sexual manner. Personally, Genet had the traits of a paranoid hermit, living anonymously in cheap hotels, caring little for his physical appearance, and turning bellicose with the intellectuals who would support him.

Ken introduced Curtis Harrington to the French decadent writers of the nineteenth century, particularly J. K. Huysmans, whom Harrington found more suitable to his personal taste than Genet. Huysmans's *À Rebours* (variously translated as *Against Nature* or *Against the Grain*) is one of the quintessential books of the symbolist movement in turn-of-the-century France. Though he ended his life as a pious Catholic monk, Huysmans dabbled in satanism. His book *Là Bas* (*Down There*) had a very exact detailing of a black mass, complete with a great deal of sexual blasphemy.

Bob Anglemyer recalled Ken's interest in the occult, particularly in Eliphas Levi. The primary philosopher of all the French decadent personalities, Eliphas Levi Zahed captivated Anger. Levi was the Karl Marx of occultism, an armchair theorist whose ideas had far-reaching consequences. Born Alphonse Louis Constant, the son of a poor shoemaker, he was trained for the priesthood but refused to accept the vow of chastity. Levi was involved in fringe politics ranging from monarchism to socialism, for which he spent some time in jail. He supported himself through hack writing jobs, including an encyclopedia of the Christian religion.

His books on occult subjects, however, have become classics: *The History of Magic*, *The Dogma and Ritual of High Magic* (generally referred to as *Transcendental Magic*), and *The Book of Splendors*. For these hypnotic tapestries of purple prose, he adopted the pseudonym of Eliphas Levi Zahed, a kabbalistic translation of his French name. Immersed in the Judeo-Christian mysticism of the Rosicrucians and Freemasons, Levi derived his theories from interpreting the Kabbalah, a commentary on the Old Testament passed down by Hebrew scholars of the Middle Ages. Levi's theories laid the cornerstone for modern occultism. In his formulation, the universe and man—the macroscopeia and microscopeia—are reflections of one another. The Will manifests itself as a virtually physical force to be harnessed. Other planes of consciousness besides the physical exist. Ritual magic, therefore, could enable the practitioner to invoke the elemental forces of the cosmos externally or, more important, internally. The most disturbing of Levi's kabbalistically derived theories is that the devil is the inverse of God, thus evil could be used as a means to a good end. Spiritualists at their most extreme and distasteful put this theory into practice in a myriad of executions.

Ken was also fascinated by the beliefs behind the practices documented in J. G. Frazer's *The Golden Bough*. A classic of myth and folklore, it is as bloody as a *Mondo* movie in its documentation of pagan behavior. *The Golden Bough* has an underlying Darwinistic survival-of-the-fittest thrust.

But the writer who epitomized all of Ken's philosophical interests, who combined the intellectualizing of Eliphas Levi with the physicality of the pagan religions of *The Golden Bough* was Aleister Crowley. Crowley became Ken's lifetime idol and messianic paternal figure. Ken no longer needed his biological father, Wilbur Anglemyer.

It was not by accident that Ken would adopt a theology that extensively spoke of the "dying father." Crowley's life's work encouraged the rejection of patriarchal and matriarchal authority and role models. His motto, from his theological *Book of the Law*, was "DO WHAT THOU WILT SHALL BE THE WHOLE OF THE LAW. LOVE IS THE LAW, LOVE UNDER WILL." The id ruled all. The child within you was "crowned and conquering." One's own will manifested one's being, with love being the most potent of emotions, roughly defined as the inverse of hatred.

Arguably the most important occultist of the twentieth century, Crowley's *magick*—to use his spelling—filtered the sexual psychology of Freud through the Jungian concept of the collective unconscious. Crowley has been the subject of several biographies. The most hostile yet richly personally detailed account is *The Great Beast* by John Symonds, his literary executor. Symonds interprets

Crowley as a man who built a religion out of his own weaknesses. The most accessible biography in both occult and human terms is Francis King's *The Magical World of Aleister Crowley*. King, an occult scholar of impeccable repute, calls Crowley "a man in whom good and evil were as mutually existent, and as closely blended, as in the human race itself." Crowley was truly an individual who lived out Eliphas Levi's theory that the devil was the inverse of God.

Often mislabeled satanic, yet a huge influence on contemporary satanism, Crowley went to great lengths to say he was no messiah, taking this stance to the extreme of proclaiming himself the Antichrist.

Aleister Crowley was born Edward Alexander Crowley on October 12, 1875, in Leamington, England, near Stratford-on-Avon. His father had studied to be an engineer but never practiced that profession. A family fortune established by a brewery afforded Crowley's father the time to be a Plymouth Brethren minister. The Plymouth Brethren, direct descendants of the Puritans, believed in a literal interpretation of the Bible. "Get right with God" was their rallying cry. They believed that Jesus was returning imminently and the wise course was to be among the chosen ones—join now, or it would be too late.

As a young man Crowley became relatively wealthy when his father's death provided him with a trust fund. He attended Cambridge and aspired to be a poet. A turning point in his career occurred in 1898, when he joined the Hermetic Order of the Golden Dawn, one of the most influential mystical societies that ever existed. Many contemporary artists, Anger included, continue to apply in their work the Golden Dawn's hermeticism—the concept that certain symbols are recognizable to all humans and that people's actions and emotions can be manipulated by using these symbols. Present-day occultists ranging from the innocuous to the obnoxious all hark back in some manner to the Golden Dawn system.

The Golden Dawn was organized into a Masonic system of degrees and inner circles complete with elaborate rituals with colorful ceremonial robes, incense, and dramatic oaths. A friendly alliance existed between Madame Blavatsky's Theosophical Society and the Golden Dawn, and they shared the doctrine that Lucifer is the light-bearing god, not the devil of conventional Christianity. This was a doctrine that Crowley embraced, and which Anger would incorporate into his aesthetic.

At the time of its inception, the Golden Dawn also functioned as a celebrity social club, an outgrowth of intellectuals reacting against the soulless rationality and modernization of the Industrial Age. It lacked the sexual bias of Freemasonry by admitting female members. Important personalities of the time were among the Golden Dawn members: poet William Butler Yeats, author Algernon Blackwood, actress Florence Farr, and Constance Wilde, Oscar's wife. There were also a fair share of combative cranks, like writer Arthur Waite and Golden Dawn cofounder S. L. "Mac-Gregor" Mathers. As they passed through various initiation degrees, the members studied the Kabbalah and practiced astral projection (letting the mind leave the physical body). They employed the use of such arcana as the tarot, Egyptian hieroglyphics, and Masonic symbols to manipulate people and analyze life situations.

Naturally, in a society of dominant egos, not all the Golden Dawn members got along. Crowley eventually quarreled with his prior mentor Mathers. W. B. Yeats often bored Aubrey Beardsley to tears, and there was an outright hatred between Yeats and Crowley. Yeats strongly disapproved of Crowley's hedonistic and homosexual tendencies, complaining that he was a wild hooligan. Crowley later mercilessly caricatured Yeats in his novel *Moonchild* as "Gates," an Irish poet of slovenly personal appearance who is used as a dupe by black magicians.

Crowley was the bisexual hedonist that Yeats complained of, but Crowley lived his life to the fullest, without shame. He lived for self-exploration and pleasure, with pleasure giving him his greatest challenges.

Crowley enjoyed women not as sexless madonnas, but as what he termed "scarlet women," meant in the most sophisticated, enticing sense of the word. His wives and scarlet women would change frequently throughout the years. He preferred highly intel-

ligent, curious women with whom he could feel comfortable raising some hell. For a time he was married to Rose Kelly, sister of
the painter Sir Gerald Kelly, until Rose fell into total dipsomania.
Mary D'Este Sturges, mother of Hollywood director Preston
Sturges, had an involvement with Crowley. Leah Hersig, a Swiss
woman who worked for a time as a New York City public school
teacher, was among the most loyal and cherished of his scarlet
women. The bohemian pair spent time in London and Greenwich
Village. Crowley would get loose with a heroin-cocaine speedball
or opium and dictate his writings to Leah. As Crowley grew older,
his scarlet women grew younger, including relationships with
teenage German and English girls.

Yet Crowley also had a number of homosexual relationships, in
which he almost always played the passive role. He had affairs with
a female impersonator friend of Beardsley's and the poet Victor
Neuberg as well as casual pickups. This was an aspect of Crowley's
personality with which Ken would feel a special identification.
Crowley, like Ken, had an effete voice that belied his masculine
physical appearance.

Apart from sex, chess, mountaineering, and big game hunting,
Crowley's notable pursuit was drugs. He embraced them as a way
of life, at times elevating them into a sacrament, using hash, grass,
peyote, mescaline, opium, heroin, and cocaine.

Crowley's gift was for words; he was a brilliant, hypnotic con-
versationalist and refracted his experiences and philosophy
through his writings. He left behind a voluminous amount of literature, much of which continues to influence contemporary artists.
Though now sold in mainstream bookstores in the "New Age"
sections, Crowley's writings were difficult to obtain when Ken first
gravitated toward them; they were often accessible only through
private collectors. Like the underground filmmakers, Crowley was
forced to operate outside of normal distribution channels, using
self-publishing or small presses.

Never has an occultist left behind such a treasure trove for the
perverse imagination. Shot through with his tremendous sense of
dark humor, Crowley's works are self-referential yet traverse every
genre. Crowley unashamedly entered socially taboo realms with an

audaciously candid autobiographical sensibility that was readily embraced by Ken and influenced such other writers such as Henry Miller. *Diary of a Drug Fiend*, one of his most popular novels, filtered his speedball experiences through an aristocratic couple's agony. The first-person narrative switches from the hero to his wife's diary entries and back to the hero for the climactic third. Although there's a lot of Aleister Crowley in both the hero and heroine, he explicitly based the character of King Lamus, the misunderstood genius/mystic who helps change the couple's perception of drug use, on himself. On a darker level, *Drug Fiend* depicts cult living situations. The literary achievement of *Drug Fiend* would be dismissed at the time of its release because of Crowley's sinister personal reputation, but the novel stands out today as predating both William Burroughs and Hunter Thompson in depicting the drug subculture and its surrounding psychology.

Ken idolized Crowley because he, like Cocteau and Genet, filtered his sexual experiences through erotica, much of it anonymous and privately produced. The value of recording the subjective reality of one's own sexuality was another Crowley aesthetic that Ken would embrace in his life's work. Crowley's notorious *White Stains* is still circulated in mimeographed form by private collectors. Dealing with his homosexual experiences, it is a long poem about a poet whose sexual enthusiasms lead him into degeneracy, madness, and death. A typical example of Crowley's humor can be found in his comment that the conclusion of *White Stains* would be approved of by any Sunday school. Ken loved this sort of jesting, and he would later employ a variety of entertaining japes when discussing the making of his films.

Crowley asserted philosophical beliefs that Ken would put into practice in books like *Magick in Theory and Practice*. He defined magick as "the art of causing change in accordance to will," distinguishing it from the magic of stage conjurors and placing the libido at the center by the addition of the *K*, the first letter of the Greek word for a woman's genitals. The key to executing magick would be the union of pairs of opposites. *Magick in Theory and Practice* is elegantly written and employs extensive footnotes to create a parallel text.

The cornerstone for Crowley's theology is *The Book of the Law*. He used it to place himself in a prophet role, not unlike Mohammed or Moses, even writing extensive comments on the subject in his own publication, *The Equinox*, a bulky volume that came out twice a year. With three short chapters of prose poetry, and the occasional rhyming couplet, *The Book of the Law* uses the Egyptian gods of Isis, Osiris, and Horus as a mock-up of the Christian Holy Trinity. Crowley asserts that Isis represented the maternal phase of religions; Osiris, like Jesus Christ, was part of the paternalistic cult of the "dying father"; and Horus, the son of Isis and Osiris, was the hawk-headed, vengeful god of the new aeon. Thelema—Greek for will—would be the religion for this new aeon. *The Book of the Law* contained much aggressive neo-Nietzschean sentiment concerning individual strength and contempt for those weaker. It also makes veiled reference to sexual magick, using alchemical terminology for the mysteries of procreation. *The Book of the Law* builds to an explosive conclusion as it blasphemes against Christ, the Virgin Mary, and Mohammed while holding up the merciless "scarlet woman" as the new feminine ideal.

Crowley's extensive use of hermetic symbolism makes *The Book of the Law* particularly powerful, as if it were a series of tarot cards flashed at the reader, each evoking a specific association. It is no surprise that one of his finest works, *The Book of Thoth*, written in 1944, would concern this visual arcana. Crowley utilized the tarot as the pivotal point for a discussion that connects Thelemic theology, Christianity, and pagan myth in Jungian terms. The deck designed by Crowley and drawn by his friend Lady Frieda Harris over a period of five years is the most highly pleasing aesthetically, and its focus on a visual medium would be especially inspiring to Ken.

Crowley looked upon secret societies as a stage where he could act out his theories in human terms. After completing *The Book of the Law* he was sought out by the quasi-Masonic O.T.O.—Ordo Templi Orientis—to head its British division. Composed of several German high-grade Freemasons and occultists, the O.T.O. grooved with the Nietzschean "love under will" ethos of *The Book of the Law*, along with its sex magick underpinnings. Like many

Masonic orders, the O.T.O. claimed descent from the Knights Templars. The Templars were a Masonic group of military men known for their strategic exploits during the Crusades who were later destroyed by the Catholic Church.

Crowley relished the Templar myth and reworked the O.T.O.'s rituals into a series of nine levels as an analogue to Freemasonry's thirty-three initiatory degrees. The first three offered his unorthodox interpretations of Masonic symbolism. The fifth concerned his analysis of Rosicrucian iconography, the cross, and the rose. Upper degrees delved into sex magick. He issued two manifestos for members, *Liber Agape* (*agape* is Greek for "love") and *De Arte Magica*, which couched sex magick instructions in allegorical alchemical terms. In these writings Crowley broke down the systems of belief that had influenced him—pagan, Masonic, Rosicrucian—into a macroscopeia of Ancient Egyptian sun worship, which had its microscopeia analogue in the phallus. This is the "solar-phallic religion" that Ken would personally and publicly worship throughout his life.

Crowley wrote that all religions were obsessed with the mysteries of sol, luna, and terra—the sun, moon, and earth of the macroscopeia—which find their microscopeia equivalent in the penis, vagina, and anus, respectively. Even though the enigma of procreation is heavily addressed, no sexual thrust is excluded. The upper degrees concern sexual magick, so that there would always be a particular degree to appeal to one's sexual persuasion or fantasies. Certain individuals can find comfort in the tripartite seventh degree, in which initiates are sworn to abstain from gross sexual acts. The eighth degree concerns masturbation, not in the Christian spill-of-seed-waste sense, but as a spiritual and talismanic charger. Members are instructed on how to masturbate onto cutout truncated paper pyramids. The ninth degree focuses on heterosexual magick. It reveals the Great Secret, known variously as the fabled Universal Medicine, Elixir of Life, or Great Work of the Alchemists. It is the mingled male and female genital secretions after at least an hour of vigorous sex. When consumed by the participants, the gates of heaven are opened and the magickians are able to obtain what they desire.

Crowley did not exclude homosexuals from this Great Work. Crowley added the eleventh degree—concerning homosexual practices. This degree was regarded as so secret that it had no instruction manuals, though there are ambiguous references to it in Crowley's other writings. *Rex De Arte Regia* (King of the Royal Art, Crowley's sex diary) has instances of Crowley doing eleventh-degree workings on unknowing partners in a Manhattan bath-house. He even pulls a few characteristic pranks in his tarot-card book *The Book of Thoth*, implying that the Egyptian hieroglyphic of the eye in the triangle and the Indian eye of Shiva were known as the asshole to eleventh-degree initiates.

Ken always found Crowley's dirty japes of this nature amusing, and *De Arte Magica* is permeated with them. Crowley obliquely refers to fellatio as vampirism, in which the "victim" lapses into a comatose state. Oscar and Constance Wilde, as well as Mathers and his wife, are cited as examples of practitioners. *De Arte Magica* also dealt with the terminal zenith of sex magick—Erotocomatose Lucidity. More allegorical than practical, sex is prolonged through drugs and the courtesan's touch until the initiate is literally fucked to death.

Crowley had recast religion into a sexual mold that was not so much specifically sexist as male oriented. The phallus is every-thing, the all giver, the all begetter of life and human behavior. This system of exalted penis worship was a school of thought that Ken felt comfortable with.

All religion is the search for a big daddy, the true father who will always love you, always take care of you; for the masculine comfort that is powerful without hurting the worshiper. Despite his stated antipaternalism, Ken found this in Aleister Crowley.

As he was starting to delve into Crowley, Ken began to seek out other like-minded individuals. Crowley's more fervent American supporters were located at nearby Pasadena O.T.O. headquarters, the Agape Lodge, which was headed by Jack Parsons, a brilliant, handsome, and erudite chemical engineer who was inclined toward sex magick. Parsons operated the lodge out of his mansion at 1003 South Orange, Pasadena's millionaire's row. He also opened his doors to boarders, advertising for atheist tenants and attracting a motley crew of artists, writers, and occultists. Parsons would evolve into one of the most remarkable of Crowley's disciples in ensuing years, and would prove to be the true believer who would have the most mythical impact on Ken personally.

The sad reality of Crowley's life at this time is that of an old, high-dose heroin addict living in furnished rooms in locations like Piccadilly, London's Times Square, and at Neatherwood, a boarding house near Hastings. A 1937 libel suit he brought against artist Nina Hammett for her portrayal of him in her novel *The Laughing Torso* turned into a farce that left him bankrupt. The trial cemented his public image as "the Great Beast 666." On the one hand, he liked the fame, but it also painted him as a shady character who few took seriously. He was appreciative that his American followers regularly sent him correspondence and money. Still, Crowley never lost his sex appeal. Although he had alienated virtually all of his friends, associates, lovers, and girlfriends and was physically deteriorating from drug use, Crowley still had the charisma to attract a nineteen-year-old girl at this trial who volunteered to have his baby, an offer he accepted.

In 1944 Ken met the abstract animator Harry Smith. Ken was becoming more immersed in Crowley, and Smith occupied a legendary position in that occult realm. He claimed it was in his blood. Smith gave two stories to explain this. One was that his great-grandfather founded a branch of the Masons modeled on the Knights Templar. The other was that he was Crowley's illegitimate son, conceived during one of Crowley's American jaunts. Then again, Smith said that his mother claimed to be Anastasia of Russia. Smith remembered meeting Crowley when he was a little boy "at least once; he showed me a clam neck hanging out of a cliff; he had a black turtleneck sweater on. He was not any kind of sissified character."

Ken picked up a few tricks from Smith about building an image and telling stories that people would like to believe could be true. Physically small, Smith had a propensity for huge drug consumption: heroin, speed, acid, and, even in his sixties, smoking crack and huffing Liquid Paper with young apprentices. He cared not at all what people said about him—the more ominous the better—but, in general, everyone got along with him.

Ken graduated from Beverly Hills High in winter 1945. He does not appear in the yearbook; he is listed as a camera-shy senior.

At the close of World War II, with his brother Bob on active duty in the Navy, Ken made a five-minute record of sexually charged crowds on V-J day. By his own description, *Drastic Demise* was "a freewheeling, hand-held camera-plunge into the hallucinatory reality of a hysterical Hollywood Boulevard crowd celebrating War's End. A mushrooming cloud makes a final commentary."

In 1946 Ken tightened up *Demigods* from thirty-five to twenty-seven minutes and retitled it *Escape Episode*. He added an atmospheric soundtrack consisting of bird, wind, and surf sounds, along with Scriabin's "Poem of Ecstasy." In effect, it was his first real sound film. He continued to show this Kenneth Anglemyer film for several years after he had become Kenneth Anger.

Chapter 3

Camera Obscura

For some, sex leads to sainthood; for others it is the road to hell . . . it all depends on one's point of view.

HENRY MILLER
THE WORLD OF SEX

At last there must come a moment when his whole being is swallowed up in fatigue, overwhelmed by its own inertia. Let him sink (when no longer can he strive, though his tongue be bitten through with the effort and the blood gush from his nostrils) into the blackness of unconsciousness; and then on coming to himself, let him write down soberly and accurately a record of all that hath occurred: yea, a record of all that hath occurred.

ALEISTER CROWLEY
MAGICK IN THEORY AND PRACTICE

"**Y**ou know what a camera obscura is?" asked Bob Anglemyer. "It's an entertaining device. There was one in Pacific Palisades Park, which is on the bluffs overlooking the ocean. You walk into this darkened room. There's a big lens right over-head on top of the building and it shines down. It projected on a big, flat, white table type of thing, which was the screen. You could turn the camera—it was sort of a camera—manually, with the wheel, to various angles and things. You can see the immediate vicinity around the building; quite a ways away, too. You can see the ocean, all the trees, people and everything. Very fascinating. It was in that vicinity—whether in the restroom or there—that Ken was caught."

Ken was busted in a homosexual entrapment set up by the police. His father was extremely upset, bailed his son out of jail, and proceeded to humiliate him by turning the incident into a topic of discussion with other family members, including Bob. This increased the already large emotional distance between the brothers. To this day, Anger has never discussed the incident.

Entrapment of homosexuals in cruising areas was common dur-ing the 1940s. Ed Earle, a filmmaker and actor who was a close friend of Ken's at this time, recalled that "there was a great deal of entrapment going on. There was a vicious circle. People were used like quislings to help entrap others, as decoys. You'd go into a movie theater on Hollywood Boulevard or Sunset Boulevard and all of a sudden some very pretty trick would sit down next to you and start playing kneesies with you. He'd ask you if you wanted to go to his place. After all the little initiations and groping and car-rying on, he headed off. Across the aisle two burly policemen would jump up and handcuff you.

"It was a death penalty in that it could be the end of your career, your reputation. Serious imprisonment. You could be incarcerated if you were caught in the act of doing anything, and it was the scarlet letter. There were very, very few people who were openly homosexual in those days. You really did live a clandestine life."

Ken was so ashamed and devastated by the camera obscura inci-dent that, with his grandmother's help, he moved out of the Anglemyer household into a small, dungeonlike apartment in the

Hollywood Hills. Its furnishings were spartan: a bed, a desk, a projector, and a screen.

Ed Earle recalled that "Kenneth was an extreme. He was in a
state of almost abject poverty. He would have these bursts of energy
and then he would disappear for two or three days, and you'd go
over to see if he was alive or not or whether he had eaten or not or
whether he had shacked up with somebody who'd beaten him up."

According to Earle, Ken had become a known quantity among
his friends. "All his friends were continuously inviting him over to
dinner or supplying him with his favorite peanut butter because
they knew, instinctively, out of almost bitter experiences, that
whenever he borrowed money from them or pleaded for rent or
whatever he was using it to buy shards of film. He was a soda straw
when I knew him. A scarecrow. A tiny person. And that's why a lot
of people got worried about him. Is he emaciated by genetics, by
choice, or just poverty?

"I vaguely recall we suspected that there was some sort of
stipend coming from his family because it seemed totally impossible for him to survive the way he did. He never mentioned too
much about his family other than the fact that they caused a lot of
manic-depressive fits—discussing them, or being with them, or
being away from them."

Ken still played the role of *enfant terrible*. Since he aspired to be
an artist, he refused regular employment. His grandmother would
supply just enough money for him to pay rent and basic expenses.
A lifetime pattern of financial support through family allowances
and bursts of money, and no steady income, was created.

Ken and Earle attended the University of Southern California.
Earle was in the drama department while Ken took cinema classes
in which he learned how to operate a Moviola, to do editing, and a
few technical things, especially concerning lighting: keylights,
backlights, and spotlights.

Ken was beginning to explore the self he'd been forced to
repress under his family's roof. Like Sigmund Freud, Aleister
Crowley, and Aldous Huxley, he enlisted the aid of "mind-altering
substances," as he put it to Earle, who remembers that Ken would
smoke pot and "talk about peyote constantly."

Magazines like *Physique Pictorial* and *Dance*, along with mail-order film loops from the Athletic Model Guild, were the most ubiquitous and accessible of what was then considered homosexual pornography. Their formula featured musclemen in tiny posing straps, accented with sailor caps and genie headdresses, poised against fake backdrops in photographers' studios. The models would build up a mystique that would attract interested patrons from the magazine's readership. They used names with connotations of aggressive domination, like Ed Fury.

Kenneth Anglemyer chose the new name Kenneth Anger at age twenty to fit his new persona. Bob Anglemyer found his younger brother's name change apt in the sense that "Ken isn't so much combative as angry. That's his personality. He was angry at everything and everybody."

Motivated by a desire to create, to embrace a new set of values, and to dramatize his own psyche, Anger made one of his finest and best remembered films, *Fireworks*. He found the muscular models in the posing-strap material attractive but woefully inadequate for his own erotic imagination. "When I made the film, I made it for myself." He was also publicly embracing the beliefs of Aleister Crowley. By way of alchemy, of turning excrement into gold, he would transform the shattering, traumatic camera obscura incident into an ecstatic magical experience.

Both Anger and his friend Curtis Harrington were simultaneously working on films that were statements of their identity. Harrington appeared in *Fragment of Seeking* and Anger in *Fireworks*. "We did not discuss these projects with each other," Harrington recalls. "We simply went out and made them. Independently. But we made them approximately the same so that we were sort of exploring similar paths." The audience was not jarred by *Fragment of Seeking* because it showed nothing overtly sexual, but *Fireworks*, with its obvious phallic references, shocked them.

In making *Fireworks*, Anger had the help of a circle of relatively, for that time, out-front homosexuals. Chester Kessler, the photographer, had made a very fine film of Kenneth Patchen's "Sleepers Awake on the Precipice." Chester was not only an important aesthetic influence on Anger, but he also took superb portrait photos of him. Harrington also knew Kessler "quite well. He was very, very thin and like someone at the time of the witch hunts in Salem, with long fingernails. He was a young intellectual. Very nice fellow."

With Kessler's encouragement, Anger's aesthetic bloomed, combing the stark confrontational quality of German Expressionism, the balletic flow of French Romanticism, and the violation of his own life, which is surrealism in the most Sadean sense. In a reference to the French surrealists, specifically to Buñuel's *Un Chien Andalou*, he'd tell friends that "I had my razor blade in my eyeball and I was able to do something spectacularly existential." Filtering these high cultural influences through pornography, Anger transformed that genre into a reflection of the collective unconscious.

Anger could either have fun or make a serious statement. He did both. The nervousness of his first autobiographical performance in *Fireworks* feeds the emotional realism of scenes such as the inevitable beating Anger receives from the sailors he's been cruising. Anger placed the Crowley idea of sexual self-analysis in a cinematic format that, like *The Cabinet of Dr. Caligari*, utilized a dream structure to encompass brief, self-encapsulated incidents.

Over the years *Fireworks* has undergone many different permutations. People recall scenes that others haven't had the pleasure of witnessing. Fragments of voice, optical effects, or music have been added and removed. Anger was already performing the magician's role of shuffling his deck. Every few years the film changed—as all of his later movies would. This is one of the traits that mark him as a deeply feeling perfectionist, a committed artist on a continual quest of explaining himself best.

Fireworks has remained stable since 1980. This version was committed to videotape in 1986, which, unfortunately, seals it off from Anger's personal touch on individual film frames. The movie opens with "A Film by Anger" spelled out in Cocteauesque white script against a black background. The sound of thunder heralds a lightning bolt onscreen. A modern title card announces fireworks, with letters bordered in red against a brown background, making the word sparkle like a firecracker. It seems a tacky seventies effect to place on such an antique, posing-strap era film, yet one remembers it because it suits the film's self-parodying elements.

A flame comes to rest on a photograph lying in silvery water. A blond Apollo of a sailor, his eyes dramatically lit by a streak of light, dispassionately holds a limp, seemingly unconscious Anger in his arms. The scene is exquisitely lit in high contrast. The sailor (Gordon Gray) is seen in a series of poses—front, side, three-quarter profile. His face is remarkably kind and serene. The sequence is a predecessor of the marbleized style of portrait photography of Robert Mapplethorpe, who was influenced by Anger's films. Below Anger's body, the sailor's well-lit crotch is marked with a shadow on the fly, which resembles an enormous penis hanging down to the sailor's knee level. The shot analyzes the "Daddyism" inherent in the savior fantasy of this type of sadomasochistic activity: the sadist—the object of desire and emblem of physical violence to the masochist—also provides him with a paternal figure who grants him emotional release.

Anger and his dream savior fade farther and farther into the black, starless universe surrounding them. Cut to Anger lying motionless in bed, his head hanging off the edge in a receptive position. A scar, etched into his left eyebrow, is defined by a streak of missing hair. The camera pans down Anger's body. His hand grips the sheets in frustration; his sleep is troubled. A statuette of a hand by the bed is missing its middle finger. Anger pulls the sheets down almost to his genitals and a huge erection wriggles under the sheets, but comically, it turns out to be a cheap tiki doll, which Anger whips out and eyes with obvious disappointment.

He gets up, covering himself with the sheet. He looks at photos scattered around the floor, shots of himself vulnerable and bloody in the sailor's arms. Disgusted, he gathers them up, and begins to dress. Pulling up his jeans, he appears emaciated. His head looks wider than his body.

A painting of a ghostly figure dancing in an eclipsed moon hangs in the background as Anger buttons his shirt in front of a totem. Here Anger used a subliminal trick that was a shared secret among people using 16mm cameras in which the film is rewound. A private image could be superimposed on the film. If *Fireworks* is slowed down at this point, you'll catch a glimpse of a guy reaching for another guy's cock.

Anger adjusts his fly. For what seems like a long time, he gazes at himself in the mirror in one of the most seductive stares film has ever documented. His hand movements, the camera's framing suggests, imply that he's jerking off while looking in the mirror.

Anger rifles through his offbeat stills collection once again, then picks up a well-worn matchbook saying UNITED STATES NAVY. He passes a room, walking by a hanging tinfoil object, to a door with a GENTS sign tacked on it. Inside, it's all black and he's all alone. There's a light shining to his right. Anger looks around as headlights cruise a freeway. He strolls, making himself available, until he arrives before a painted backdrop of a bar, which looks like a prop from the pages of *Physique Pictorial*, where he eyes his prey.

The sailor (Bill Seltzer) turns out to be a good-natured lunk who accommodatingly whips off his shirt and makes every muscle in his upper body rumba; his biceps flex, his stomach contracts, like a male belly dancer.

Anger is pleased, but the sailor is just starting. He pushes Anger aside and walks on his hands. This narcissist is delighted that he's found an admirer. Anger silently mouths "Got a light?" The brute is offended at such a blatant advance. He whacks Anger in the face, sending the cigarette flying.

The next *pas de deux* is with a different sailor, darker and more Mediterranean-looking, who twists Anger's arm behind his back. Suddenly, Anger and Bill Seltzer are in front of a fireplace. The sailor trick takes no offense at all at Anger's attention. He picks up a burning palm and lights Anger's cigarette. Anger inhales deeply and with satisfaction. The sailor throws the palm down, nods approvingly, and adjusts his cap—signaling the job's finished and it's time to go.

A shot of cars cruising once again, illuminating the night highway. Anger enjoys a cigarette. He turns around. Five maniacal sailors, joined by three others, are staring at him as if they mean business, swinging heavy chains. One has a rock on a chain. There's repeated emphasis on these menacing swinging chains.

The Respighi music on the soundtrack suddenly sounds a battle cry with a naval motif. The sailors take off to make war on Anger, running over dirty newspapers on the street. They circle him. In a geometrically composed shot Anger falls to his knees, dropping his cigarette. The sailors attack like barracudas. They tear off his clothes, rip at his nostrils. Blood spurts into his eyes, blackened and swollen. His mouth is open in a silent scream that you sense would be deafening in its excruciating pain.

The sailors look down, their faces obscured, and they swing the chains and wail on Anger's ass some more. One sailor digs his fingernails into Anger's wrists as he twists them repeatedly. While Anger writhes in agony, the sailors smile in sadistic satisfaction. Naked and bloody, Anger crouches on his knees, cowering. White liquid explodes on the pavement.

Anger's chest is heaving. There are drops of blood on his cheek. His tormentors eviscerate him, digging through the gory meat of his chest to reveal a ticking clock. This Cocteau-Buñuel joke suggests the heartless objectification that Anger's physical masochist/mental sadist feels toward his quarry.

Milky white fluid falls on Anger's chin, into his mouth, on his Adam's apple and pours down his body, passing his bloody nipple in a ritual that's both symbolic of purification and a metaphor for the sexual climax. Music builds to a triumphant crescendo as the camera pans a row of YMCA type urinals. Anger lies on the toilet floor, wearing an impish sailor cap, slightly tilted, signifying his initiation. He is nude, with one leg coyly pulled up to hide his genitals.

The GENTS door swings open. From the blackness emerges the troublemaker who started it all—big Gordon Gray. He slowly unbuttons his pants. Out pops what looks like a cock in black and white, but lo, it's a Roman candle. It fires in every direction and Gray massages his thighs, as if he's having an orgasm.

The flaming United States Navy matchbook drops into water. And . . . Toro! It's Anger wearing a Christmas tree on his head, complete with silver balls, garlands, and a lighted candle on its tip. He points at the camera, then slowly marches through his house and carefully puts the tree into a fireplace on top of his photo packs of the sailors, which are already burning. Anger has asserted his independence and attacked the societal dogma that partially triggered his conflicts.

Anger is next seen lying in a bed again, neck arched back, prone. An out-of-focus pan reveals a man lying next to him. The fire behind them rages. The guest's face is glowing from the handmade scratches on the film frames there ostensibly to obscure it. The statuette is beside him, its middle finger restored. The ritual has been completed.

Anger has often quipped that "this flick is all I have to say about being seventeen, the United States Navy, American Christmas, and the Fourth of July."

It was about the time he made *Fireworks* that Anger would begin manufacturing Crowleyesque anecdotes that refashioned the facts of his life to fit his own idealization of events. Casting himself in the role of boy genius, which had been so familiar to him from birth, and establishing his first lie about his age, he recalled the making of the film:

"I was a world-weary seventeen-year-old. The only way I made the film is my family went away for the first time in my life and left me alone, which was unusual, because there were always too many other people around."

Bob Anglemyer, however, contends that *Fireworks*, was not shot in the Anglemyer house on Holly Drive but instead in a Hollywood Hills residence.

Anger manufactured outrageously entertaining anecdotes to surround *Fireworks*. He relished saying that the cast was "real sailors, but they were studying at the University of Southern California cinema department to become film technicians for the Navy. I explained I was making an unusual film and would they like to play in it free because I didn't pay them. They had stolen the 16mm negative from the Navy." He chuckles over the cast being "my first government grant."

Ed Earle comments, "That's a wonderful illusion. I never heard the sailor story because I was too close in the schoolroom to believe that kind of nonsense. They were people dressed up. They were tricks who had no inhibitions, because in those days very few

people were into being involved in pornography. He talked everyone into doing it because it was almost as though he was going to
make the ultimate porno film. They all got high and instead of
having an orgy they made a movie.

"When I knew Ken *everything* was a fantasy to him," says Earle.
"I mean, sex was the ultimate drug in those days. He would have
three variations of every story—Column A or Column B or
Column C—so you never knew which was the truth. You never
knew unless it was a personal experience."

The "government grant" quip is another one of Anger's
Crowley-like puns on a personal experience, but Anger's real need
for money would create an even greater schism between him and
his older brother Bob. While Bob was attending Navy flight
school in Maryland, Anger wrote him a letter in which he asked to
borrow money to buy film. Bob said, "Look, Ken, I don't have a
lot of money, but I'll be glad to loan you some money, but it's
going to be a *loan*. I can't afford to give it to you." Bob was a
Lieutenant Junior Grade, had two children, and had recently
moved. He knew Ken had access to money through their parents
and grandmother.

"It wasn't a huge sum of money at all. But he never acknowledged that he had gotten it. I never even got a thank you. I got
back a canceled check. I never heard from him as far as it being a
loan or anything else. He never gives any money back."

Anger would not show *Fireworks* publicly until 1949. Ed Earle
saw the original in private screenings. "He always referred to
Fireworks as his own autobiographical fantasy. For the time, it was
shocking. It was pornography. I saw the film two times at his
apartment. There were only three of us the first time and only
myself the second time. It was one of those things you sneak out of
a brown paper bag, you know, the *Lady Chatterly's Lover* syndrome
or a *Playboy* under the mattress. He really took a delight in the fact
that he had done something naughty. And when he first showed it
to you, it was like flashing a centerfold at an adolescent.

"The first time I saw the film he said something about 'it was
such a delicious experience' because these guys were people he
couldn't have sex with. When he explained to them that he wanted

to make this film and that they could beat him up, they got off so much that it was like having sex with them.

"Another time, he said the fellow with the Roman candle was one of the best tricks he ever had, but he was so bashful. Kenneth really wanted it to be an act of urination and degradation, and this guy was shy and embarrassed about exposing his privates on film. The idea suddenly occurred to have the Roman candle and Kenneth said it was like *Un Chien Andalou.*

"Kenneth would say, 'Whenever I get blue and whenever I can't get high on anything else and whenever I can't find anyone else to enjoy, I turn this on.' And, as I recall, the two times he showed the film to me were virtually masturbatory experiences for him."

Earle spotted the footage missing from the current print of *Fireworks.* After Anger is poised on the toilet floor like a model in a physique magazine, he writhed around for quite some time. The sailors charge in, surround, and mock him. Earle was shocked to see Anger lying nude in a urinal. "The sailors did a whole fag-bashing routine on him, kicking and beating him as he was lying in a urinal."

Earle remembers that "Ken scratched his genitals off each of those frames by hand because he wanted to sell prints of it by mail and was afraid he'd get in trouble." Earle was especially jarred because "Ken didn't like to make a public display of his body. Kenneth was not particularly proud of his body. He was one of the few people I ever knew that much preferred to do whatever they did in the dark." Earle also recalled that the unbuttoning of Gordon Gray's fly to reveal the Roman candle was slower and more euphoric.

Anger told the gay publication *The Advocate* in 1981 that "I am homosexual—all of my lovers have been male. Some of them think they're straight, but that's my problem." However, he would make claims and intimations of bisexuality throughout his life. Earle remembers that "Kenneth was into playing the female role. He loves women like hairdressers love women. He likes to play with them like Barbie dolls. I can certainly imagine him fantasizing about having a bisexual ménage à trois or some kind of orgiastic Greco-Roman feast, but I can't possibly imagine him being alone with a woman sexually."

According to Earle, the period's conventions of gay life held little appeal for Anger. "I mean, going to a gay bar in the forties was the progenitor of the way they describe things in *The Boys in the Band*. Everyone stands around with attitude for days. Nobody wanted anything to do with an effeminate man. It was one thing to see a female impersonator doing an act, because that was a show, an entertainment. That was not a show of personal preference. There was also the whole butch mystique of if you're a man, a homosexual, you're a man who wants to sleep with a man, not a sissy or an imitation woman.

"Kenneth was one of those people who did not fit into either mold. He did not like to dress up in drag. People saw Kenneth as obviously homosexual, with that willowy body and that kind of oily personality and soft voice that never rose above a semi-whisper. He was like a shadow on the wall. I cannot recall Kenneth ever being in a bar. Everything he did and the people he met were always through a kind of grapevine effect. I do recall him hovering on streets around people he had seen and going after them."

Earle lived on Western and Pico before his family moved over near USC. Anger stayed at his home a couple of times when they were having late-night discussions about music and philosophy and film. One day he came over and said, "Do you know there's a leather bar within two blocks of this place?" Earle had lived there all his life and didn't know it. "He took me down the street on the *opposite* side of the street. 'That little place over there.' He pointed it out to me. But he wouldn't cross the street and go near it. So, I got the image of him hiding behind a trash can watching people go in and out and seeing someone he would like and then sidling up to them on a dark street saying, 'Hi sailor, got a match?' kind of thing."

When Anger reached middle age, when homosexuals were extrovertedly out of the closet, he said that he thought sex would become more exciting again if things went back to the pre-gay-lib days. Earle described that period as "a far more particularly exciting world in its own way. We all grew up under the scary death penalty of being arrested or being caught. The vice squad was incredible. That's also why a lot of people, like Kenneth, were entranced by Nazi society. They all thought of the Los Angeles police as virtually part of the SS troop."

USC would provide Anger and Earle with their first high-voltage exposure to Nazi cinematic imagery. World War II had only been over three years. Ed recalled that "Kenneth, Curtis [Harrington], and my close friend Bobby, who studied Germanic languages, sponsored a film festival at school based on [Siegfried Kracauer's 1947] book *From Caligari to Hitler*. We got all these films from the Museum of Modern Art in New York. It was at least a thirteen-week series, starting out with *The Cabinet of Dr. Caligari*. We had *Metropolis* and all these classic films, once a week.

"It ended with Leni Riefenstahl's *Triumph of the Will*. When we got there that evening, Kenneth was a nervous wreck because he had heard rumors that there were a lot of Nazi sympathizers and FBI people in the audience. So it was a very electric evening. We all sat around obviously waiting for a few people to jump up and scream *Sieg Heil!* and wondering if we were all going to get arrested. Finally, when the evening was over and nothing had happened—but it was a vibrant night in this little screening place we had—we all toasted each other and thanked God it was over.

"The next night, at about midnight, my phone rang. I was still living with my parents. It was Kenneth. He said, 'Get over to school right away!' I said, 'What for?' He said that the fellow who was doing our projection had agreed to break into the cinema department of USC. A man had approached him who had been at the screening. This man had come to most of the screenings out of nostalgia. He had worked with Leni Riefenstahl and when he came to America from Germany he smuggled out the only uncut print of *Olympiad* in the United States. The entire eight-hour film was ours to see. If we could do it now.

"There were about five of us altogether. We snuck into the cinema department and saw the complete, uncut version of *Olympiad*. It was morning when it was over. People were wondering what we were doing there. We said, 'Oh, we came in early to clean up.'"

When Anger was attending college, he was already manifesting the eccentric behavior patterns that would continue for the rest of his life. He would inexplicably show up at Earle's door in the wee hours of the morning, perhaps after a night spent hovering around the after-hours leather club across the street. Earle's mother would feed him and they would drop him off, since Anger never drove.

Anger also wanted to continue improving *Escape Episode*. He wanted Earle to do the music for *Escape Episode* because Earle was in the music and drama department. Harrington was more involved with it and he had shown it to someone who could give Anger a stipend. Originally, Anger had wanted to do it as a full-length color feature. He was experimenting with color and had done a couple of test episodes with an actress from school. Anger talked of doing *Escape Episode* as a twenties amalgam of Aubrey Beardsley. He was fascinated by the twenties.

At this time the homoerotic fiction of Tennessee Williams was circulated in brown wrappers. Among everything that Anger turned Earle on to—Beardsley, German Expressionism, Fascist cinema—this was one offering that really stood out. Williams's "One Arm" was eerily prophetic of one of Anger's later involvements. It's the story of a stunning, statue-perfect hustler who used to be a boxer until he lost his arm in a car accident. His aggression no longer has an outlet. He eventually kills a trick who was using him to fuck a girl in a stag film. To pay for this crime he is sentenced to death. While grieving in prison over the fleeting glimpse of salvation a boxing career had offered, he starts receiving letters from johns all over the country. "You don't remember me, but . . . " Faceless bodies from bus stations, parks, toilets.

One Arm winds up in the electric chair. The guards are unable to pry the letters out of his hands, and he dies clutching them. Williams ends the tale with a mention of the beautiful, chiseled corpse.

Earle recalled that "Ken by nature was attracted to people who were either well endowed or the Arnold Schwarzenegger type. Or the story of the "Black Masseur," which I read because of his insistence. For him, that was the ultimate fantasy he'd love to make a movie of."

Williams's "Desire and the Black Masseur" is about a passive, repressed businessman masochist. In a steambath he finds the stereotypical big black man as the masseur. The businessman has an orgasm on his towel as he gazes at him. The massage quickly escalates from bruises to broken bones. He's eventually beaten to death and devoured by his cannibal inamorata, who moves on to the next town and again gains employment as a masseur.

Despite Anger's later Crowleyesque joke that he was "somewhat to the right of the KKK" with regard to blacks, Earle found that Anger "had a definite hunger for black men and for big— Well, for the brutal. Strong black males. Ken was a size queen and where in the forties and fifties do you turn for the largest size—at least mythologically? Ken was a mythologist. Need I say more?"

Much of Anger's behavior and thought patterns at the outset of his adulthood were fixated on a masochistic death wish. It both motivated and was the subject matter of his first major work, *Fireworks*. However, Earle best described it as "a death wish that a lot of us have. It is not a *death* wish, it's a phoenix-rising-from-the-ashes wish of 'I wish I am not the way I am, that I don't look the way I do.' I wish I could have the things I want. I wish I could have the people I want. It's that 'if only I were' or 'the grass is greener' kind of death wish."

Chapter 4

A Bed Less Empty Than Before

Kenneth lived entirely in a world of his own. Who entered into it, who inhabited it, who did he love or trust or confide in?

ANAÏS NIN

Shortly after *Fireworks* was completed, his grandmother, Bertha Coler, passed away. In 1948 Anger commenced work on a new film that would express his feelings for the era that he had learned so much about through Bertha and Diggy. *Puce Moment*, according to Anger, was conceived as a "film on the women in Hollywood in the 1920s." It was to be a study of their lifestyles, their clothes, their cars, their houses, their social patterns, and, like the play *The Women*, it would have an all-woman cast, not a man—not even a male cat—in it.

"I did make drawings of the whole movie, like Hitchcock or William Cameron Menzies for *Gone With the Wind*. I made a production sketch for each setup." Curtis Harrington described this as "a very elaborate, detailed scenario. Not a shot breakdown, but a sequence of sequences. He had a great gift for the use of words and the writing was wonderful."

The one segment that was shot begins with "A Film by Anger" in puce-colored art deco letters, followed by the title, *Puce Moment*. Dress after rhinestone-beaded dress wriggles at the camera. Jonathan Halper's soundtrack blasts with Pink Floyd–style feedback broken by his folkie voice singing lyrics of omnipotence.

Yvonne Marquis's face fills the camera. Her eyes look glassy under long, black lashes. Huge black deco earrings swing herky-jerky. She wears heavy dark eye makeup and coral lipstick.

Yvonne raises her dress to fill the camera frame. She's naked and laughing, looking up through the dress at the sky. She drops it over her head and it falls to her toes. Her steps seem unsure and unsteady, and she puts on shoes laid on a pillow. More soundtrack feedback highlights a shot of her makeup table, with its enormous bottle of perfume.

The Puce Woman, Yvonne, strikes Nazimova (Rudolph Valentino's wife) poses in front of a mirror as she applies the perfume. She looks at herself again in the mirror to Jonathan Halper's lyrics. She throws her head back, striking a glamour pose on her puce day bed. The day bed moves. She sighs.

The day bed is being taken on a trip. Her eyes roll back in ecstasy and sexual anticipation. Shadows turn light and dark again as though the bed is moving though a passageway. Then she's lying on her porch outside.

In the background are the Hollywood Hills. Now holding the leashes of her six Rashimov hounds, the Puce Woman surveys her kingdom. From the camera angle, the hounds are on the level of her house. The camera pans up the leashes for a close-up of her hand.

The Puce Woman has a petulant and bored expression, like Clara Bow, as her dogs lead her down the steps. Her face fades into the camera as *Fini* appears in deco lettering.

Puce Moment has a unique visual style in that all movement seems slightly off-kilter. It appears as if Yvonne Marquis is performing the movements backward and that the resultant film is played in reverse. This is due to Harrington's photography and a technique that happened by chance. Since they didn't have enough light and the film was to be in color, they shot it at a slow eight frames per second for more exposure. Anger had Yvonne move very slowly, which gave that slightly odd quality to the movement and made her pendant earrings swing very fast.

Anger outfitted Marquis in authentic flapper gowns that he'd later say belonged to his "costume mistress" grandmother. Marquis was a friend of both Harrington and Anger. She was dark and androgynous, exactly as she looks in the film, and came from a well-off Jewish family in Beverly Hills. Marquis wrote free-form poetry that was definitely pre-beatnik, although she had nothing to do with the Beats.

Anger discovered a house in the Hollywood Hills that was perfect for the exteriors in *Puce Moment*. The interiors were shot at the home of Samson De Brier, who became a lifelong friend of Anger's. De Brier was a slender, fey, continental type. His old-fashioned air led people to believe that he was much more advanced in years than he was. De Brier had been part of the Atlantic City homosexual milieu depicted in the 1933 novel *The Young and the Evil* by Charles Henri Ford and Parker Tyler. In the 1940s De Brier left Atlantic City for Los Angeles, and during the Second World War he worked in a defense plant, sinking his wages into real estate. The rental income from his properties enabled him to stop working and pursue a new career—artistic social butterfly, taking tea and exploring avant-garde scenes.

At the time he was working on *Puce Moment* Anger was still

attending the screenings at Clara Grossman's gallery, where he met wealthy Hollywood stars, including Gene Kelly and his then wife, Betsy Blair. Anger attempted to interest them in financing *Puce Moment* when they expressed an interest in the art of classic and avant-garde cinema. To secure their backing, Anger presented his extensive pre-production work, including drawings and scene descriptions, and *Puce Moment*. The Kelly interest alone was an accomplishment for the twenty-one-year-old unknown student filmmaker. Anger immediately slated his USC classmate Ed Earle to do the music if the film would be expanded. Sadly, the Kelly funding was not forthcoming.

Anger said that "I really regret I didn't make it in the sense [of being] more ruthless about hustling money. I didn't know how at the time and I still don't know how. My grandmother had unfortunately died the year before and she would probably have given me the money. [*Puce Moment*] was one of the most charming ideas I've ever conceived and I only made a little tiny piece of it. I just get to the point where she's going down the steps and that's it. I mean, for the scene that followed I would have had to rent an old 1925 Rolls-Royce, which I had found, but it would have cost me $200 or something, which I didn't have."

In 1948 Anger traveled to San Francisco because Harry Smith had managed to arrange a showing of *Fireworks* at the San Francisco Museum of Art. "He came to the showing," Harry recalled, "and embarrassed everyone. After the clapping at the end of the film, I thought he was putting his hands up like a prize-fighter. But he explained that that was a sign having something to do with the Aleister Crowley cult—I forget what, perhaps Shu holding up the sky."

The experience with Gene Kelly and Betsy Blair did not deter Anger from seeking out other important personalities in the arts. During his San Francisco excursion he sought out Anaïs Nin, who had just published *Under a Glass Bell and Other Stories*. Nin was special to Anger not only for her diaristic writing—Anger himself was a personal and aesthetic diarist—but for having met Aleister Crowley. In *Incest* she recalls Henry Miller falling under Crowley's spell in 1934. Crowley, who was then living as a painter in Zurich, came to see them in Paris. He found Nin's aura so powerful that he could not look directly at her.

Anger told Nin that he was part Cuban. She thought he was handsome. He took her out for flaming shish kebab. Nin subsequently went to one of the private screenings of *Fireworks*. She was revolted, but found it powerful and aesthetically perfect: "It has a nightmare quality. Everyone has mixed feelings, horror and recognition of Kenneth Anger's talent." Anger, Curtis Harrington, and their mutual friend Paul Mathiesen went on beach excursions with Nin. They'd discuss film history. She was familiar with the avant-garde film world through her husband, Ian Hugo. He had cast her in his surrealistic film *Bells of Atlantis* (1953).

Anger's next project was *The Love That Whirls*, in which the depiction of the ritual sacrifice of an Aztec prince involved a great deal of nudity. The project reflected Anger's admiration for Eisenstein's *Que Viva Mexico!* With its naturalistic Mexican peasants and exotic Latino mysticism, it had always been an inspiration for him. Unfortunately for the *The Love That Whirls*, film labs then assumed greater power than they do today; when the film was sent to Eastman Kodak for processing, it was deemed obscene and the only print destroyed.

At this point underground film still lacked national distribution. The filmmakers either distributed their work themselves or formed collectives such as Creative Film Associates. But for artistic individuals who had trouble dealing with business transactions, the inherent problem remained the same even with these makeshift situations. And at this point underground film was starting to gain fans, who enjoyed the films for the relatively forthright depiction of sexuality that far exceeded Hollywood norms. These fans, who often kept private film collections, were entering into distribution by arranging small, members-only screenings. In these cases the distributor was frequently motivated by a desire to dupe prints or snip scenes and frames for their own collections.

The first national distributor of avant-garde films, Cinema 16, came none too soon. Founded by Amos Vogel in 1947, Cinema 16 became the central force that transformed underground film into a movement. It grew to be the largest film society in

America, with seven thousand members. Well known for his ethical treatment of artists, Vogel had what he described as "a very unusual idea about programming which was not shared by many people and which, on the other hand, was very popular. Namely, we would show any kind of an independent non-Hollywood film that I thought was of value, be it documentary, experimental, or anything. We made absolutely no distinctions. Very often in one program there might be six or seven shorts. Some of them were documentaries or political films. And others were the wildest kind of avant-garde you can think of. Now, that created an interesting problem because there were people that loved documentaries, but not avant-garde, and vice versa. So there was a tension in the audience, but that was okay with me. We did that for sixteen years."

Cinema 16 started with screenings at the Provincetown Playhouse in Greenwich Village. Parker Tyler, one of the pioneers in turning film writing into an art, supplied the program notes.

By the 1950s Vogel moved the screenings to "regular movie theaters with 16mm arc projection for the first time. We showed at the Beekman, the Paris Theatre, the Murray Hill Theater—which has since been torn down—on Sunday mornings from eleven to one prior to the regular showings. Between five and six hundred people came to each of these shows. In addition to that, we had the Fashion Institute's auditorium, with sixteen hundred seats on Twenty-fourth Street. We had two performances in one day. We had two, three thousand people come just for that.

"Theoretically, it could have been possible even with a membership setup for the police to intervene if they wanted to, but we had very good lawyers working with us, civil liberties lawyers who were totally opposed to censorship. Ephraim London, for example. So it couldn't have been a problem."

Vogel contacted Kenneth Anger. "I was very much taken by *Fireworks* the first time I saw it. In those days, people didn't go around making films about being gay or about their nightmares. So I thought that was a very important and very valid, very private statement. I thought it ought to be shown. There was a lot of anxiety and trauma in that film. He was willing to put that on film and that was a great, important step. The intensity, the tragic feelings he had within himself came through very clearly.

"Ken was not younger than any of the other filmmakers. He had a very controlled public persona. He didn't want you to get too close to him. I didn't get the kind of feeling from him that he was capable of doing that—at least with me.

"He was not one to be intimidated. He felt superior to the audience. He didn't like it when people didn't like his work, but he had a strong enough ego to overcome that. That wouldn't stop him from going on with his work. It would spur him on. However, I must say the films I showed by him had a much more positive than negative reaction.

"Whatever the tensions were in his own life, they were multiplied, if not caused, by the sexual problem. In those days you couldn't come out, or you could, but it wasn't the same as now.

"[Ken was] a very complex and really unhappy human being, but that can make some of the best artists. There's a lot of very interesting writings by Freud and some others that artists are people who can't adjust to normal life. I'm not asking you to accept that, but I've found, in people I know, that's it's quite accurate sometimes. The most important way he dealt with his conflicts was through his films, through his work as a filmmaker. He could make the conflicts more manageable by putting them on celluloid."

Fireworks was finally unveiled by Cinema 16 for the general public in 1948 with a premiere at the Coronet Theater in Los Angeles. Critical reaction was extremely favorable. Lewis Jacobs, who had positively received *Escape Episode*, Anger's first public film effort, in *Hollywood Quarterly*, felt that "despite the difficulties of 'forbidden' subject matter, the film's intensity of imagery, the strength and precision of its shots and continuity, produce an effect of the imaginativeness and daring honesty which on the screen is startling. The objectivity of the style captures the incipient violence and perversion vividly, and the film becomes a frank and deliberate expression of personality. Consequently, the film has a rare individuality which no literal summary of its qualities can communicate."

Parker Tyler astutely captured the film's Freudian symbolism: "The vision of a sailor holding the beaten-up youth in his arms, Pietà fashion, is not realistic, however, but pure fantasy. So is the sailor's supposed seminal stream, spraying the victim's mouth as if it were milk fountaining from the maternal nipple. The simulated evisceration of the victim, in turn, is a demonstration of emotion, not literal except as it stands for the penetration of the anus as a kind of rape, an appalling destruction of the male's figurative maiden-head."

"I always wanted to meet my idols as an equal." This was an aspiration Anger had held since he was a child on the *Midsummer* set. *Fireworks* accomplished this. Artists and public figures whom Anger had admired responded with overwhelming enthusiasm to the film. Tennessee Williams, for instance, hailed it as "the most exciting use of cinema I have seen."

Anger sent a copy of *Fireworks* off to Biarritz, France. Jean Cocteau was sponsoring the Festival of Damned Film, which was comprised of films that were not allowed to be shown or were shown in drastically cut versions because of their controversial subject matter. This was a special occasion where films were shown in their original form. Jean Genet's lyrical evocation of prison sexuality, *Un Chant d'Amour*, which summarizes in fifteen minutes the sensibility of his novels, would premiere in this setting.

Cocteau was so taken with Anger's effort that he bestowed the festival's Poetic Film Prize on *Fireworks*. He said, "This film comes from that beautiful night from which emerge all true works. It touches the quick of the soul and this is very rare."

Anger got a fan letter from Jean Cocteau. "This letter made me want to go to Europe. I figured, I'll go to Europe where they'll appreciate me."

For all Anger's complaints of receiving no domestic attention, he was rapidly becoming the first celebrity of the underground. His sensibility, however, had always been steeped in French decadence, so it seemed the logical move to go to France at this time to grow humanly, intellectually, and artistically.

In a fit of enthusiasm, Anger moved to Paris to go "looking for and hoping I would find a sympathetic producer." He enjoys saying he "hocked the family silver" as a joke on the fact that his parents were actually financing the excursion. One of the first things he did upon arrival was to meet the author of the praise that was so magical to him, the man who had been the chrysalis for his journey, Jean Cocteau.

Not one to be restricted to a single mode of expression, Cocteau wrote poetry, diaries, novels, plays; painted; sketched; directed his own work cinematically and theatrically. Cocteau had infuriated people left and right and didn't care. It was just five years after the Nazi occupation of France, which had severely traumatized and divided its citizenry, and Anger applauded artists who remained during the occupation. "Cocteau was perverse in that he rather enjoyed the whole thing. Look at Oscar Wilde. People would ask him, 'How can you go have dinner with these very pretty hoodlums,' and he said, 'I love feasting with panthers.'"

Meanwhile, *Fireworks* was arousing considerable continental interest. It was presented at the First Experimental Film Exposition at Knokke-le-Zoute in Belgium and awarded the Prix Henri Chomette in Paris. It was shown at the Royal Film Society in London in 1950. The screening caused a minor brouhaha that Anger loved. Halfway through, the wife of the Indian ambassador shouted, "That film should be burned," and stormed out of the theater.

Cocteau gave Anger permission to make a movie of his ballet *The Young Man and Death*, and Anger was eager to do it. A 16mm study print of the ballet, with choreography by Roland Petit, was shot in order to raise money for a 35mm color version. Anger approached many producers with Cocteau's letter, but none of them were interested because all of Cocteau's films had lost money.

Although Anger would have been the perfect filmmaker to breathe life into a Cocteau conception, the experience turned into a hard lesson of art versus commerce, leaving him very disillusioned.

Then, suddenly, Anger's family cut off his stipend of $25 per week, trying to force him to return. "I was stuck. I had nothing. I was going to jump in the Seine. I was right on the edge and looked in."

Instead, Anger entered one of the most productive periods of his life, working this feeling of desperation into the idea of *Rabbit's Moon*. He went without sleep, building sets and completing the filming within a month.

Anger used a rich pancultural texture of myth to explain his own psychological condition in *Rabbit's Moon*. The rabbit in the moon is lifted out of Japanese myth, with the moon in Crowleyan terms representing the female principal. The character Pierrot was based on Crowley's tarot card of the Fool, which meant divine inspiration in spiritual or creative matters, but folly, mania, or death in everyday affairs. The highly stylized mime movements of the actors, which was part of early twentieth-century avant-garde theater, recalls both Kabuki and commedia dell'arte, where Columbine emotionally tortures Pierrot with Harlequin's assistance. The set itself resembles the art deco forest of silver trees in *A Midsummer Night's Dream*.

Though Anger was admired at the time for his perceptive portrayal of aggressive male homosexuality in film, he played out in *Rabbit's Moon* a universal sadomasochism inherent in the human condition. Pierrot (André Soubeyran, a Marcel Marceau mime student) tries to woo and romance Columbine (Nadine Valence), an idealized feminine figure considerably different from her commedia dell'arte origins as a bawdy working-class girl. Harlequin (Claude Revenant) is the archetypical sadist, with arched eyebrows, a sinister leer, and vicious laugh. He feeds Pierrot's self-loathing and humiliates him by taking the girl. You suspect he cares nothing for her but is motivated by a sexual sadism toward the clown all along.

Braunberger returned at the end of the month. He was more than annoyed at the carpentry that had been wreaked upon the studio. Anger was given the bum's rush. His first attempt to continue the natural progression to 35mm was tragically halted. About twenty minutes of film had been shot. (Final cuts in 1971 and 1979 would be fourteen and seven minutes, respectively; considering the ratio of film shot to film used, Anger was doing extremely well in terms of cost efficiency.)

Disheartened, Anger stored the rushes with Cinémathèque

Française. Anger had become friendly with Henri Langlois, head of the Cinémathèque. He describes the time spent with Langlois as "a willing bondage." Although instrumental in reviving movies that would influence *nouvelle vague* directors like Truffaut, the Cinémathèque also had a reputation of being disorganized, with a basement filled with uncatalogued prints.

At the Cinémathèque Anger was able to see rare Méliès and Lumière prints. Langlois allowed him to edit mediocre 16mm work prints of Eisenstein's *Que Viva Mexico!*, the film dear to Anger since childhood, even in its bastardized form. "I don't think it's any great revelation. It was just that nobody before me had put the film in the right order—to Eisenstein's written scenario."

Around this time Anger became interested in filming Lautréamont's surrealistic novel, *Les Chants de Maldoror*. Lautréamont was a Uruguyan émigré to Paris who reinvented himself as a count; like another of Anger's heroes, Aubrey Beardsley, he died prematurely. *Les Chants de Maldoror* is a free-form exercise in dream imagery extending into such taboo realms as pedophilia and necrophilia. Anger prepared extensive pre-production sketches. Certain streets in Paris that had remained unchanged since the last century were earmarked as locations.

Curtis Harrington came to visit Anger in Paris. Anger was helpful to him because of the contacts he had made. Anger introduced Harrington to the people at the Cinémathèque, such as Henri Langlois and Mary Merseer. They ran the Cinémathèque, were very friendly with Anger, and became equally friendly with Harrington.

The Cinémathèque was located in the Avenue de Messine. The building consisted of three or four floors, with a screening room on the ground floor. It was a mazelike structure, containing many corridors and passageways. Each day the Cinémathèque showed at least three feature films.

Anger invited Harrington to see a performance of the Stravinsky/Cocteau adaptation of *Oedipus Rex*. They had first performed this work in 1927. Cocteau would read his text, which had been heavily edited by Stravinsky, during orchestral intervals. At the time there was a considerable anti-Cocteau clique because of his behavior during the Nazi occupation. Cocteau knew the audience would be filled with his detractors, so he squeezed the orchestra into the first row of the theater, put loudspeakers under a dozen seats, and blared the music. Stravinsky's son had to get the composer drunk to fly to Paris. He was terrified of riots, which had occurred at the premiere of *The Rite of Spring*, and terrified of audiences. Stravinsky finally arrived clad in sandals and garishly colored slacks. Cocteau wore a fur-lapeled tuxedo jacket over his bare chest, a rose in his navel.

The theater itself was small and tawdry. Cocteau stood on the stage in front of the orchestra and read the text. Above the orchestra was a platform where an audaciously designed dumb show, with masks by Cocteau for Oedipus and his mother and the legend's various other characters, was performed. The actors told the story in pantomime, wearing Cocteau's huge, larger-than-lifesize heads, like carnival heads.

In the middle of this performance, the anti-Cocteau clique began to boo and hiss. Then the people who admired Cocteau began to say, "Ssshhh, ssshhh." Pandemonium was not far away in the auditorium, but the detractors were hissing and booing Cocteau and his dumb show, not Stravinsky. Cocteau maintained incredible poise and dignity through all this. He neither flinched nor moved. Finally, the noise died down. He said, "Mr. Stravinsky and I have created this work with a sense of respect for the public. All we ask in return is that we receive respect when we perform it." Everybody then broke into applause, and the performance continued.

Harrington and Anger had shared an incredible evening. Afterward, Anger introduced Harrington to Cocteau. They all walked out of the theater together. Just outside the theater entrance, a huge truck, obviously used for transporting scenery, was parked. Cocteau pointed at it. "I remember," he said in French, "Sarah Bernhardt used to travel in a caravan this size when she went on tour."

"It was wonderful," recalls Harrington. "I wonder if Kenneth remembers all that about that evening." Harrington found that, while Anger wasn't Cocteau's protégé, "they were certainly friendly. He was someone Cocteau had admired, taken up, and written about. It gave him a lot of cachet to have Cocteau's support behind him."

In 1953 Anger traveled to Rome. He had wanted to make a film about teenage Cardinal d'Este, the youngest son of an aristocratic family who built the Fountains of Tivoli. Anger enjoyed a perverse identification with this sixteenth-century sex magick cultist.

Anger calls d'Este "a sexual pervert. There are very few things I call sexual perversion, but he liked to fuck goats, and that is technically a perversion. Even if you like kiddies, it's still human, but I mean goats—the goats don't seem to mind, they don't squeal in pain, they just sort of continue chewing their cuds. I think he was secretly a devil worshiper. Fucking goats is something associated with Satanism. The goat is like a beast of the devil."

D'Este's other kink was water sports. "He liked being pissed on," Anger says. "By goats, men, women, I don't know—whoever's capable of pissing. So the whole garden is actually a private dirty joke. It has ten thousand fountains and everything is pissing on everything else and it's like inexhaustible piss. There are sphinxes pissing out of their tits, which I think is wonderful. He used to throw orgies in this garden at night, lasting all night, lit by torches."

Eaux d'Artifice was supposed to be the first part of a four-part film which was supposed to become increasingly sexually graphic, but Anger only completed the first part. As Anger says, "The title itself, *Eaux d'Artifice*, is a French pun on "fireworks" (*feux d'artifice*)—and could be translated as "waterworks." It also had the sound, in the usual mispronunciation, of "ode orifice."

The one reel that was completed of *Eaux d'Artifice* was shot in daytime on black and white infrared film through a filter to create the effect of moonlight. The sole cast member, apart from the real star, the Tivoli fountains, has been billed variously as Carmillo or Carmilla Salvatorelli, of indeterminate gender. Anger likes to say Carmillo/Carmilla was a circus dwarf. The film cost only a few hundred dollars and was fun to make. Anger had become acquainted with some well-off Europeans, including a countess who had given him a thousand feet of infrared film. Thad Lovett, an obscure presence in the European art film world, was the camera assistant.

The title *Eaux d'Artifice* appears at the outset of the film in arcane lettering, followed by "Un Film d'Anger." A blue-tinted and white figure appears. A fountain spurts between trees, the beads of water shimmering in close-up. The figure obscures the fountain and is shrouded in enigma under layers of gowns, a mask, and a huge headdress.

The figure descends steps, passing fountains, a stream, water over stone. A devil face spurts water from its mouth. Water cascades, goes down steps, transforms into a waterfall, and erupts in geysers. The devil-face eyes the figure from behind. From this point on, objects blend and melt into each other in blue-gray tones.

Two circular objects appear, separated by a crater. The figure descends a huge, well-lit stairwell. An enormous shower spills over circles surrounded by fountains, ten fountains at once. The devil-face continues to spit water as the figure slowly passes and is enveloped by the fountains.

Water cascades over steps, leading into larger fountains. The figure is seen through a wall of water, fluid against a black background. Water flies into the air, the peak of a fountain.

The figure is at the head of the stairs. Another devil-face is drenched in water. The figure produces a hand-tinted gold fan and spreads it. The leering face spits liquid. The figure descends the stairs, and again the lewd, leering devil-face is seen spewing water.

Another fountain peak. The figure runs past the fountains in daylight, away from the camera, toward the camera, in side view, then from behind again. It runs up stairs. Water spurts from stone as a giant fountain is superimposed. The figure runs past.

The figure fades into an incandescent spray of water beads. There's a shell-like stone. The figure emerges from a cave, walking toward the camera as black water envelopes the images.

"*Fin*" appears in arcane lettering.

In thirteen minutes *Eaux d'Artifice* lulls you into a trance with its calm, blue tint. It has the feeling of an intermission piece in the best sense, as was René Clair's *Entr'acte*. It's one of Anger's most tranquil works; his editing makes it soft, lush, and inviting. *Eaux d'Artifice* remains a secretive romp through a private garden, all for the masked figure's and the viewer-voyeur's pleasure.

Chapter 5

Dancing with One's Own Madness . . . Welcome!

When Anger's mother, Lillian, died in the fall of 1953, he had to return to America to settle her will, which embroiled all the siblings in yet another familial conflict.

Bob Anglemyer said the conflict had nothing to do with the fact that Anger had cashed in his share of the securities his mother had left him. He recalls coming home on leave from the Navy to help settle his mother's estate. Wilbur, their father, had paid for Anger's travel expenses so he could come to the funeral. Bob was there to do the necessary paperwork.

Bob recalls that "my mother left Ken some money, but my sister was the executrix, so she had to handle it. She had to dole out the money to Ken for about ten years; see, my mother didn't trust him, either. A day or two after I left, Ken decided to have a big, wild party at the place. My father practically had to throw him out. It was his lifestyle and the way he treated my father that Ken and I never saw eye to eye on."

Despite his personal turmoil, Anger was, at this point, an established figurehead in the underground. *Fireworks* turned out to be one of Cinema 16's most popular titles. During this time, Anger visited San Francisco and met the young filmmaker Stan Brakhage, who had been inspired by *Fireworks*.

Brakhage was experimenting with films along similar psychosexual lines as *Fireworks*, such as *Desistfilm*, in which teenage libidos get unhinged at a party. Brakhage would develop into a major abstract artist of the twentieth century who used film as his medium. Employing a swirling point of view with a hand-held camera, Brakhage painted his images on the viewer's iris.

Despite the surface dissimilarity in their techniques, there were aesthetic similarities in Anger's and Brakhage's work. Both men were addressing nothing less than the question of life and death and the terrifying inevitabilities in between. Brakhage was as unafraid as Anger in approaching severe and private subject matter—masturbation in *Flesh of Morning* (1957); his wife's childbirth in *Window Water Baby Moving* (1959); their sex life in *Loving* (1957) and *Lovemaking* (1968), which also focuses on animals, a homosexual couple, and the Brakhage children romping nude on a bed; and what happens after death in the autopsy documentary *The Act of Seeing with One's Own Eyes* (1971).

Anger and Brakhage both used subliminal, hypnotic images to evoke pleasure and pain responses from the viewer, utilizing editing to give their films an irresistible, metronomic heartbeat. There have only been a handful of directors capable of such editing since Eisenstein. His tradition was carried on in the underground by artists like Anger, Brakhage, and Harry Smith, and later the underground-influenced Martin Scorsese, the contemporary mainstream exponent of this style.

Anger first met Brakhage when he was visiting the basement apartment of poets Robert Duncan and Jess Collins at 1724 Baker Street in San Francisco. Brakhage heard a voice outside shouting "ROBERT! ROOOOBBBBERRRRT!" Anger had shown up.

He entertained everyone with stories of living in Paris and rolled up a joint which, to Brakhage, was a highly illicit activity. This only heightened the sensory perception of their first contact. The meeting ended with Anger sucking the smoke out of the air.

LSD (not yet illegal), peyote, and other hallucinogenic substances were also floating around. Aldous Huxley's influential "The Doors of Perception" had reached artists who wanted these doors to their psyches opened. Anger would leave his doors propped open wide for decades to come.

Artist Jess Collins had made cutouts from pictures in thousands of muscle magazines. They were components used like a jigsaw puzzle to create the image of a giant man. It was Anger's idea to bring life cinematically to this form. As he had collaborated with Chester Kessler and Curtis Harrington on other projects, Brakhage was the cameraman. Through the lens, heat waves from an ashtray beneath this collage gave it the appearance of movement.

Like Anger's earlier *The Love That Whirls*, the Anger-Brakhage collaboration was confiscated by Kodak. Brakhage states as fact that there was only a one-in-ten chance of getting anything back from the Kodak labs at that time.

Back in Hollywood, there was no one left in Anger's natural family from whom he felt any love. In his mind he was an orphan. The new Crowley philosophies he was embracing helped him deal with this pain and provided him with a new family. About half of his new family were interested in occultism; the others were artists and celebrities on the boho scene: artist Renate Druks and her lover, Paul Mathiesen; Curtis Harrington; Samson De Brier. Anaïs Nin was the most famous of the lot, cultured and well traveled.

Anaïs Nin was a perfect instance of what Anger would refer to as elementals, people who in a Crowleyan sense incarnate the primal spirits of air, fire, water, or earth. They possessed a natural magnetism and power that was not self-conscious. Crowleyites believe that elementals in human form perform occult rituals whether or not they are aware of it.

The wild card in this deck was Marjorie Cameron, a committed follower of Crowley. Druks, Nin, and the other women were intimidated by her, and there was little contact between them. A tall, hawklike woman with a soft voice, her involvement in occult circles was scandalous, and Anger knew her through her late husband.

There was legend behind Cameron. She was the widow of John Whiteside Parsons—Jack to friends—a brilliant scientist who worked at Jet Propulsion Laboratory in Pasadena. Although he hailed from an affluent Pasadena background and was a chemist of impressive repute, ranking as one of the nation's leading experts in explosives, Parsons was dedicated to Crowley's magick. Like Anger, Parsons had become obsessed with Crowley's writings while in high school, which led to a correspondence with Crowley.

Crowley's methodology of using himself as the subject of sexual and consciousness-expanding experiments appealed to the scientific mind of his pupil. Parsons used morphine, cocaine, peyote, and marijuana to reach the recesses of his inner being. In full accord with Crowley, he placed sex at the heart of his magick. Parsons's writings, recently released in a short volume called *Freedom Is a Two-Edged Sword*, focus on such topics as societal repression of the libido, along with such novel concepts as female polygamy. Parsons believed that what conventional religions regarded as the sin of the scarlet woman was actually a sacrament that bestowed life and love. Believing himself to be above jealousy, which he regarded as a base and wrongheaded human emotion, he encouraged his partners to have extracurricular affairs, and felt it was his wont to do the same.

Parsons joined the Agape Lodge of the O.T.O. in the late 1930s. Later, he moved into his mansion, the "Parsonage." Each day the Agape Lodge would celebrate Crowley's Gnostic Mass. A scantily clad woman would arise from a coffin and the subsequent activity would play heavily on the (lapsed) Judeo-Christian guilty pleasures of the constituency.

In the fall of 1945, L. Ron Hubbard, future founder of the religions of Dianetics and Scientology, turned up at the Parsonage. Hubbard had recently been discharged from the Navy and was initiating a series of disability claims against the government. Like Eliphas Levi, he had a career as a freelance writer, a profession known for its erratic cash flow, prior to his theological revelations.

Parsons was impressed with Hubbard, who had an extremely charismatic personality and was equally dashing in looks, and they rapidly became close friends. Parsons broke his oath of secrecy by revealing to Hubbard some of the O.T.O. rituals, thus introducing Hubbard to the Crowley world that had "the aim of religion, the method of science," a world that encompassed hypnosis and the use of words, symbols, and numbers to elicit the desired responses in people.

In early 1946 Parsons and Hubbard embarked on the "Babalon Working." Driven by his own scientific nature and inspired by Crowley's novel *Moonchild*, Parsons attempted to create a homunculus, literally an artificially conceived person occupied by a praeterhuman spirit. Among the oldest of alchemical legends, *Moonchild* suggested that a homunculus could be created when both parents were Crowleyan initiates who performed the requisite sex magick rituals. The embryo created by their congress would act as a "butterfly net" that would capture the appropriate spirit. The resultant child would be human in a commonplace biological sense, but for all pragmatic occult purposes function as a homunculus. This kind of operation has a pop image in films like *Rosemary's Baby*, in which the heroine is impregnated by the devil. The spirit that Parsons was seeking to incarnate, however, was Babalon, the Crowleyan idealization of the scarlet woman.

Parsons needed to summon an elemental to be the mother of Babalon and performed eighth-degree workings of magickal masturbation in order to effect this. On January 18, 1946, the desired elemental appeared in the Parsonage kitchen. Parsons had finally found his scarlet woman: Marjorie Cameron, who, like Hubbard, had recently left the U.S. Navy. She was eager to participate in the sex magick workings he had in mind. Parsons excitedly described Cameron to Crowley as having "red hair and slant green eyes as specified. She is an artist, strong-minded and determined, with strong masculine characteristics and a fanatical independence."

Subsequently, Hubbard acted as scribe, or seer, in devising a reworking of the ninth-degree O.T.O. ritual of heterosexual magick. After the appropriate chants, intonations, and gestures, Parsons and Cameron commenced sex magick congress in the presence of Hubbard, who played the role of describing the activity on the astral plane. The next day the three resumed their activities, this time using a white sheet smeared with menstrual blood as a talisman. The third and final day included the recitation of a poem celebrating the "holy whoredom" of Babalon.

Despite his initial enthusiasm, Parsons was troubled by the thought that conception had not occurred, and he was ultimately correct. Meanwhile, Hubbard's financial situation was not becoming any easier. He and Parsons had formed a corporation, Allied Enterprises. Parsons had put up his life savings of $20,000 and Hubbard contributed $1,200. Hubbard withdrew $10,000 from the account, purchased a schooner, and took off to Miami with Betty, Parsons's last girlfriend, who also was the sister of Parsons's first wife.

Parsons then pursued Hubbard and Betty to Miami. In his hotel room he donned his ceremonial robe, traced a magick circle on the floor, and did a full invocation to Mars, the spirit of war. The schooner was then struck by a terrible storm that Betty later recalled as life-threatening. The following day, a despondent Parsons filed suit against Hubbard and Betty in Dade County Circuit Court.

Subsequently, Hubbard had a brief, stormy marriage with Betty, who would be the second of his three wives. Parsons married Cameron. In 1948 he took the Oath of the Antichrist, in which he regarded himself to be the chief spiritual opponent of Jesus Christ on Earth, and changed his name to "Belarion Armiluss All Dajjal Antichrist."

Tragically, Parsons's union with Cameron, as well as his ground-breaking magickal and scientific careers, would be cut short. On June 20, 1952, Parsons was blown apart by an explosion in his garage. Bloody body parts were visible in the rubble. When informed that her son had died, Parsons's mother committed suicide by swallowing a bottle of sleeping pills while her wheelchair-bound friend watched, powerless to stop her.

Today Parsons is credited with aiding the creation of solid rocket fuel, which is commonly used in space exploration. There is a crater on the moon named after him honoring his achievements in this field. His flame burned briefly but brightly through the O.T.O. For better or worse, much of contemporary American occultism can be traced back to the Agape Lodge.

Anger found the Parsons-Cameron-Hubbard psychodrama nothing less than a living myth enacted by demigods. He was so excited by it that he made his own additions to the legend, his most oft-repeated one being that Howard Hughes had Parsons murdered after Parsons refused to work for him: "I've got all the newspapers. Their headlines on it—here again is the Hughes connivance with Hearst—said 'Black Magic Cult Discovered in Pasadena,' 'Witches in Pasadena,' and 'Wizard Blows Himself to Bits.' They made a complete *Enquirer*-type story about the thing."

Dennis Hopper had arrived in L.A. from Kansas with very little money and a lot of ambition. "I wanted to make films, direct films." He began to meet people and make connections with the bohemian side of the artistic community. It was in this way that he became acquainted with the crowd that would form the cast of Anger's *Inauguration of the Pleasure Dome*.

Hopper met Curtis Harrington, who was working as producer Jerry Wald's assistant at Columbia Pictures. "Curtis seemed to be around a younger group of people. He was an executive to us, a very serious young man who seemed much older than his years. I'm sure that helped. He had some sort of quiet diplomacy. We had coffee houses in those days and galleries that showed movies. Sort of a strong underground scene which Curtis was around."

Marjorie Cameron, Hopper recalls, was a witch. "Out and out witch. She had been married to a scientist. I guess she and her husband had been involved in Aleister Crowley–type animal sacrifices in Pasadena and so on and had large groups of people involved. There was a story that a young man fell down a flight of stairs and broke his neck. Before the ambulance had gotten there, a number of women had fucked him because he had a hard-on from breaking his neck. They were busted for this sort of cult, black magic thing. Then later her husband, who was supposedly trying to make human beings, blew himself up in the garage. I mean, these are all rumors; these are the stories that were told. Whether they were true or not, I believed them. I wanted to believe them."

Samson De Brier was "an oddity" to Hopper.

"His personality was about as interesting as Andy Warhol's. I mean, it wasn't interesting at all, but if you didn't go to Samson's house, you weren't really in Hollywood. It was like a baptismal rite in Hollywood. You were inside if you knew him. Why you were inside I don't know. He'd give you coffee or tea and you'd wander through this sort of labyrinth of materials: drapes, cloth, and things draped over everything. He basically had a lot of old things, old clothes that actresses had worn, pieces of sets, maybe a cup that somebody used in a movie, stuff like that. He had a history at a time when Hollywood had no history that anybody thought about holding on to. It was like going to an antique shop, very cheap, sort of off the wall, very dark, mysterious."

Renate Druks was living with Paul Mathiesen at the time, though the relationship caused her a great deal of pain. Paul, with his blond hair and blue eyes, was truly Pan, imp of the perverse. He wished to seduce everyone but was basically homosexual. Druks could not stand the agony, or "agonia" as she put it with her Viennese accent, of Paul's body being given to another. "A man must have cruelty," Mathiesen asserted. He would have to find it in his secret lives. He certainly couldn't expect it from gentle Renate. Mathiesen told her, "You insisted on entering a world which was locked to you. You crashed through and now what you found hurts you. I had never given anyone else what belongs to you." Anaïs Nin felt sympathy for both, seeing that Druks "could not avert her eyes" to Paul's "multiple lives."

The couple were known for their outrageous parties. They threw a "Come As Your Madness" masquerade ball. Druks greeted the guests at the door decked out in a hat inspired by *The Merry Widow*, a constricting waist cincher, and a black leotard. She carried two death masks on sticks, putting them to her face, whipping one off, then the other. This terminal kink costume was inspired by the sensuality and death obsession of Juan Guadalupe Posada, a popular nineteenth-century Mexican artist known for his portrayal of voluptuous females with skulls for heads. Mathiesen transformed himself into a negative of his being, dying his hair black, painting on a mustache, and cutting a male drag Don Juan figure.

Burning incense wafted through the house, which was bathed in candlelight. Bare rooms became a forest, with branches and Mexican masks hung from the walls. The costumed guests intermingling made it all the more surreal.

Nin wore a daring, sexy feline leotard, leopard fur earrings glued on her nipples, a leopard fur belt, and a jungle scene painted on her back, two-inch eyelashes, and hair dusted with gold powder. Her crowning glory was a birdcage surrounding her head like a fishbowl. Within this were rolls of paper on which she had lines from her books, calling them the "ticker tape of the unconscious."

Curtis Harrington came as the beautifully embalmed corpse, the somnambulist from *The Cabinet of Dr. Caligari*. Walking around in a hypnotized stance, he was a male conception of Sleeping Beauty. De Brier wafted about dressed as an Eastern potentate with a dash of camp Roman, and seemed to have used Nin's makeup kit. Attendees also included an antisocial trio who shared the madness of two attendants and a body on a stretcher. Kate Kadell, a sculptress, came as a curious, jovial Cleopatra.

Anger hid in a bedroom waiting for Druks to give the word for his grand entrance when the party was in full swing. With all the goings on, she forgot about him. Then suddenly, hurrying to retrieve him, she discovered a doleful Anger sulking in the room, his candle half burned down.

But his entrance was worth the wait. Everyone stood in awe. He was Hecate, goddess of the earth's infernal regions and sorcery. In a berserk outburst of drag, he was swathed in an explosion of feathers, beads, cloth, veils, with only one Cyclops eye visible. He looked like a Busby Berkeley girl in a massive headdress and would have gone up like a Christmas tree if the candle he held got too close to his costume. Druks, dancing with him, commented that "it was so tiring to dance with one's own madness."

"Come As Your Own Madness" inspired Anger. He painted a portrait of the party, which he gave to De Brier, who promptly hung it.

De Brier's house would provide the set for *Inauguration of the Pleasure Dome* when shooting commenced in December 1953. Anger's cast members were revelers from the "Madness" party wearing their same or similar costumes. Nin compared Anger's method to Maya Deren's: "trying to capture elusive aspects of our personalities, undirected, spontaneous, accidental."

Anger frantically rearranged De Brier's house. The furniture was carted out of his living room and replaced by Anger's set pieces. Fanatical about cleanliness, he lovingly polished each object in De Brier's bedroom. De Brier's womblike, labyrinthine dwelling became even more so—black walls, gold ceilings, beaded curtains, a gold-painted Venetian backdrop. The colors were intensified by the use of gels on the floodlights. The primary group shots took an entire weekend.

One of the many personality clashes on the set flared up between Anger and De Brier's house guest of the moment, Betty Vaughn, whom he had cast as Hecate. Vaughn placed a candle in the cellar in the event that the lighting and camera caused a power failure. Anger snatched the candle. Vaughn confronted him. It degenerated into a mad screaming match, with the candle flying in the air between them and Vaughn dismissed. With Vaughn out, Anger would now reprise his role as Hecate.

Curtis Harrington said that nobody in the cast knew how they were going to be used in the finished film. "It was entirely in Kenneth Anger's head. It was not like a play where you say, 'What is my motivation?' Your motivation is to do what you're told because we were all nonactors. It certainly had nothing to do with drugs. I mean, somebody might have smoked a joint or something along the way, but, believe me, those people in the film are not high on drugs. You have to have your wits about you when you make a film that's going to hold together. Kenneth was very strong in getting something that he wants to get, which is true of most directors. You can't pussyfoot around."

Anger politely addressed Nin as "Anaïs dear" and "Anaïs darling" in whipped-butter tones. He had originally ingratiated himself by saying, "I want you as Astarte. I want to capture that luminosity which startled everyone at the party. It is an inner light and so difficult to capture," he confided.

But the knowing Crowleyite was setting the stage for a multitiered mental catfight among his female stars. Anger later said that the movie was made "mainly as a showcase for Marjorie, much to the chagrin of Anaïs Nin, who thought she was the star. I had these two female stars and there was an incredible sort of tension and rivalry between them because Anaïs Nin isn't used to playing second fiddle for anybody. And because Marjorie Cameron's personality was more charismatic and came across better on the screen she dominates the film, rather than Anaïs Nin."

Nin had met Crowley with Henry Miller, but Marjorie was her first meeting with a committed disciple. She recalls Harrington and Anger talking of Cameron as being "capable of witchcraft. She was the dark spirit of the group. There is an aura of evil around her."

Cameron and Druks were also at odds with each other. And Mathiesen also "played his little games" (as De Brier put it), but Druks nonetheless did the makeup.

Characters kept metamorphosing, confusing people even further about their roles. The endless personality flare-ups were especially nerve-wracking for Druks and Nin, the submissive females of the group. At one point, Harrington the somnambulist carried a goblet of elixir that was supposed to create ecstasy. Anger wanted Druks's tiny son Peter, who played Ganymede, the beautiful boy of Greek mythology who was seized by Zeus in one of the first daddy-relationship legends, to dip his finger in the goblet and go into a trance. Peter had been costumed as a twin to Anger's *A Midsummer Night's Dream* changeling persona. Druks was horrified and would not allow her child to pretend to be poisoned. Finally, after a lengthy battle, Druks relented. Nin's blood ran cold about the scene.

Beads kept falling off flapper gowns, cutting Nin's feet. She went to sweep them up, but Anger grabbed the broom. Kate Kadell, playing Isis in her Cleopatra garb, was four months pregnant. Druks had constructed foot-long fingernails that were painted shiny red for one of De Brier's many costumes. He would coyly wiggle them at the girls, a mock terrorist trying for a giggle.

The film took three months to complete. *Inauguration of the Pleasure Dome* is Anger's version of a glittering MGM musical. The personalities he used to cast it were a drastic change from the unknowns he had employed in *Fireworks*. The current version of *Pleasure Dome*, the 1966 "Sacred Mushroom Edition," is subtitled "Lord Shiva's Dream." The credits, in the style of Beardsley, swirl up like a cloud of smoke. Auspicious gladiator music, slightly campy and organ heavy, thunders on the soundtrack.

Like something out of J. K. Huysmans's *Against the Grain*, jewels are dragged over a leopard-skin bed and wrapped methodically around a hand. A man plays with them. He reaches for a table containing dozens of rings on black velvet. He puts them on each finger, unravels the strand of jewels, and gathers them.

Samson De Brier, in his Eastern potentate costume, lies down and raises the jewels over his mouth, slowly dropping them in. He takes a pair of scissors, rises, and opens a door to a red room, where he comes across dual mirrors, one showing a pentagram.

Intercut is De Brier as the Great Beast. Druks created this costume to replicate Aleister Crowley's "Dead Souls" painting. De Brier pats his face and walks away.

Marjorie Cameron strikes a dramatically assertive pose, paradoxically masculine, in very short flame-red hair, as the Scarlet Woman presiding over the ensuing spectacle.

The Great Beast communicates with his giant fingernails. The Scarlet Woman, with gargantuan eyelashes, brings her hand slowly to the camera to reveal a figurine of a horned devil. She offers it to the Beast in awe. It bursts into flames as soon as he touches it.

The Scarlet Woman raises a cigar-size joint, as Crowley in his Arabian alchemist costume is superimposed in ghostly blue over the ritual. The tiny horned devil lights the joint of the Scarlet Woman, who inhales deeply.

A voluptuous woman holding an apple walks through flames and comes to an urn. This fetishistic fifties Roman cutie is Druks playing Lilith, the kabbalistic goddess of destruction. Lilith offers an apple to a disinterested De Brier, who, with huge eyelashes, plays Emperor Nero.

Kate Kadell as Isis tries to rouse her husband-brother Osiris. He looks like a lizard and she like a pinup Cleopatra. She is so overly made up that she seems to be in female drag. The Great Beast glances over and Osiris is spasmodically roused.

Lilith flits around among fake butterflies, offering a jewel out of a pentagram-shaped box. De Brier, now as Count Cagliostro, swallows it ecstatically. Calgiostro's status as a hypnotist, enemy of the Catholic Church, and manipulator of people has made him a figure of admiration to occultists. Crowley celebrates him as a saint in the Gnostic Mass, and Eliphas Levi immortalized him in *The History of Magic*. De Brier's characterization of Cagliostro is of a totally fake man. He is played as effeminate, with the mocking quality of an elegantly dressed priest.

Lilith goes into a rapture, drops her gown, a hat falls on her head, and she starts wiggling her bustier like a Paris showgirl. In a multilayered collage, she walks toward the camera with the hermetic symbol of the eye in the triangle superimposed over her.

De Brier looks startled as Pan (Paul Mathiesen) approaches, offering him grapes. He picks the grapes like jewels, taking one particularly plump and juicy one. Suddenly, Pan looks like a sailor from *Fireworks*. A blond woman swallows. Pan looks back at her. Pan's red boots walk over an ornate floor. Isis dances before Osiris. The boots continue walking as Nero and Lilith toast each other. The ritual is proceeding; the boots go faster. A large pendant is presented to Cagliostro. The grapes are half gone as De Brier looks at Mathiesen's crotch. The camera pans up as De Brier rubs the grapes. Pan appears highly masculine in LSD-drenched color. There is also a lady posed like a mermaid.

Anaïs Nin steps out as Astarte, goddess of the moon, an aspect of Crowleyan female principle. She is seen in a painterly setting with a blue-encircled moon superimposed like a halo over her head. Her black fishnet stockinged feet with their painted red toenails step on a fur rug. She wears the cage over her head. Pan looks on in interest at her. She gestures to the skies and sets something free that comes back as a sphere, which grows larger as she makes another circular pass at the sky. She offers the sphere to De Brier as Lord Shiva, the Hindu god of destruction, regeneration, and *bhang* (marijuana). The sphere grows smaller and smaller until Shiva eats it. He grows wings like a fairy and makes silly smiling faces. The movie is filled with reaction shots.

The Scarlet Woman wants a light again from the Great Beast. Harrington appears as the Somnambulist. He is directed by the Great Beast and the Scarlet Woman through a labyrinth to a Boschian painting of an old woman with an inverted pentagram, a sign of evil. Superimposed over the face is a door opening. The Somnambulist passes through the doorway. The symbol of the goat and the pentagram, along with the seal of Thelema, appears over it.

The Somnambulist walks toward Anger, as Hecate, who gives him an urn of liquid containing *yage*, an age-old hallucinogenic brew. The Somnambulist slowly walks away. He looks briefly over his shoulder (recalling James Sibley Watson's and Melville Webber's *Lot in Sodom*) and passes through a black room blazing with candles.

He serves the vintage of Hecate in ornate goblets. De Brier's character's face turns green. He's slightly paranoid and stoned. Lilith drinks from the goblet. Isis pours it down, then laughs. Lord Shiva and Lilith toast and drink up as two black candles burn between them. They begin to laugh and talk. The Scarlet Woman is superimposed between them. Pan looks happy, spilling the elixir in unabashed gusto all over himself.

Dozens of superimpositions follow, heralded by triumphant music. The dresses from *Puce Moment* shake at the camera, super-imposed. Each character takes off a mask and laughs uproariously. After removing two identical masks, Cameron reveals a huge mouth, resembling Crowley's sketch of his wife, Maria Theresa de Miramar, the "High Priestess of Voodoo."

Astarte does a freewheeling shimmy. Hecate comes slowly through the door. Ganymede serves, behind multiple overlays of

Astarte's shimmy and the other girls, who are attacking Pan in the corner.

Red-tinted footage from the silent *Dante's Inferno* represents hellfire, which spurts up as Cameron dangles what Nin later called "a lifeless breast." She's now Lady Kali, goddess of death, presiding over the fires of the devil.

The Somnambulist continues serving the elixir. Everyone is tinted blue and red. Yvonne Marquis from *Puce Moment* is superimposed reclining on her floating bed. Anger/Hecate does a mixture of interpretive surreal steps and an Indian war dance. Like so many snowflakes, none of the superimposed permutations look alike. The Somnambulist is even smiling.

The focus turns to Pan—stripped, scratched, and tormented by the girls as Hecate watches excitedly and gyrates outlandishly. The Somnambulist appears in the throws of orgasm. Lady Kali signals a halt by raising her hand. The Great Beast appears frightened. Anger looks terrified now, costumed very much as he was in *A Midsummer Night's Dream*. He flings the goblet at the revelers, who seem distant.

Things grow increasingly unreal. The party is out of control. Pan's hair is being ripped at. Hecate is having a fit. The multidimensional pentagram appears. The face of the Scarlet Woman seems the motivator of all the activity. The eye in the triangle appears. De Brier contentedly puts his hands together.

"End" appears in Beardsley-style lettering.

In addition to its occult references, *Pleasure Dome* pays homage to the silents Anger loved. De Brier's impersonations recall the masochistic makeup and costume transformations that Lon Chaney, one of Anger's favorite stars, endured. There is also the use of the footage from the silent *Dante's Inferno* and D. W. Griffith touches from *Intolerance* in the handmade costumes. Méliès is reflected in the creation of an elaborate, fantastic universe through the imaginative use of inexpensive materials.

Eisenstein's montage techniques are employed throughout and strongly resemble Eisenstein's *Ivan the Terrible*, a visually beautiful yet airless film, like an opera without song. The movie is also dedicated to the examination of a cultural sensibility: as Russian history was to Eisenstein, Thelemic myth was to Anger. *Inauguration of the Pleasure Dome* was unprecedented in its attempt to visualize the deities and practice of Crowley's theology. For the uninitiated, the film possesses an inertia absent from Anger's other work, but with repeated viewings the film grows on the viewer.

Curtis Harrington is the secret star of *Pleasure Dome*. While De Brier is the ostensible lead, Harrington's Somnambulist has a quiet magnetism. While everyone else grandstands, he is minimalist and severe. Visually, he resembles a Germanic, sexually attractive corpse. Harrington and Anger were always a good team, complementing instead of complicating each other. Their collaborations resulted in nothing less than a very precious piece of American art, very fragile, a joy to behold. The moment when the Somnambulist encounters Hecate in the labyrinth has a powerful emotional undercurrent.

Anger never tired of revising *Pleasure Dome* and it became perhaps his strongest example of the D. W. Griffith principle that no two prints should be the same. Music, scenes, superimpositions, and additional screens would be added, dropped, and reshuffled endlessly. As all of Anger's films were, it was well liked on the Cinema 16 circuit. Parker Tyler ranked it as an archetype of an underground "pad" movie—one that was contained within its maker's self-created environment—as well as a "turned-on camp masquerade." However, the film would reach the summit of its popularity in the trippy sixties, when it would be acclaimed as one of the first "head movies."

Anger had gotten friendly with avant-garde composer Harry Partch, who constructed original instruments out of objects such as glass bottles to make his music. Partch lent Anger some tapes that the filmmaker used for *Pleasure Dome*. Partch was infuriated, telling Nin that he didn't want his music used for film. During a screening, Partch walked out, trailing threats of a lawsuit when Nin's Astarte made her entrance.

When he returned to Europe Anger discovered Janáček's "Galgolitic Mass," which was appropriately exultant yet tempered with horror-movie organ pastiche. He used this composition for the "Sacred Mushroom Edition" of the film. For a short time during the late 1970s and early 1980s Anger put an emotionally vacant but mainstream electro-pop collection of Electric Light Orchestra cuts on the soundtrack.

Because of their literary, artistic, and cinematic associations, the people who starred in *Pleasure Dome* transformed it into an actual slice of history. Insomuch that it is a record of those cast members, *Pleasure Dome* instantly became a sophisticated collector's item. More deeply, it was an adept's homage to Anger's elders. Marjorie Cameron now provided him with a rather formidable maternal figure.

Chapter 6

Gall Wasps

Man delights me not, no, nor woman neither.

ALFRED C. KINSEY

HIGH SCHOOL PHOTO CAPTION

anger met Dr. Alfred C. Kinsey around 1947, when Kinsey approached him to purchase a print of *Fireworks*. Kinsey was then completing his magnum opus, *Sexual Behavior in the Human Male*. In the process he collected such examples of the erotic imagination as underground movies, obscene private publications, and toilet stall writings. *Fireworks* was of great interest to Kinsey in that it was an aesthetically superior illumination of the pornographic sensibility as well as a meditation on the subject that compelled his attention the most—male homosexuality.

Kinsey took down Anger's personal sexual history, since he approached virtually anyone he met for this sort of intimate interview. Kinsey's nonjudgmental technique and genuine interest in Anger's homosexuality left a strong sense of paternal acceptance in the young Anger, a quality completely lacking in his strained relationship with his father. Aleister Crowley was an idealization, but with Kinsey, Anger had finally met a father figure he could both interact with and emulate. Anger would one day say that Kinsey would have made the best American president.

Kinsey's persistent, black-encircled eyes, shock of white hair, and manner that radiated disapproval in every direction all left their mark vividly in the minds of those who encountered him. He was a case unto himself, certainly one of the most bizarre figures ever to write a chapter in the history of psychosexual research.

Kinsey was never formally trained for the work that brought him renown. His father wanted him to become an engineer, but Kinsey hated his father with a passion and studied biology instead. Kinsey initiated his fetish for collecting by accumulating the largest collection of gall wasps in America, traveling throughout the U.S. and Mexico in pursuit of this study. The collecting extended to stamps, records, flowers, and rum recipes, though he was seen seemingly drunk only once. The bread and butter of his obsession, however, would be sexual histories—men, women, teenagers, small children, animals—everything was fair game.

Dr. Kinsey made himself available to every organization where there were children—Boy Scouts, Sunday school, camp counseling, teaching. The sexuality of young boys was constantly under his scrutiny. Where there were kids, there was "Prok," a nickname that evolved from the campers' abbreviation of "Professor K."

Prok always walked stiffly, palms outstretched in messianic pronouncement, and always wore bow ties. Gum chewing, beards, and mustaches made him crazed with loathing. However, among his coterie of male assistants was mustachioed Paul Gebhardt. Though it was the 1950s, Gebhardt curiously resembled a denizen of Greenwich Village's Christopher Street during the out-of-the-closet 1970s. He would remain a militant lifetime supporter of Prok, and the only person to take Kinsey's sexual history.

The third clinician of the group was Dr. Wardell D. Pomeroy, who played Man Friday to Kinsey's voracious sexual adventurer. Pomeroy would later spill the beans on what really happened within the confines of Prok's private empire in his astonishing 1971 book, *Dr. Kinsey and the Institute for Sex Research*.

Kinsey's powers of persuasion were enormous, rivaling any cult leader. Beginning in the 1940s, despite rampant sexual repression and the suppression of pornography in American society, he could persuade straight, middle-class people to speak about their sexual practices and perversions. However, human nature being what it is, who really knew how much was the truth and how much the fantasies of the interviewee?

Armed with financing from both Indiana University and the Rockefeller Foundation, Kinsey's work with sexual outlaws was thorough. Undeterred by dangerous surroundings, he'd reach his subjects by any means necessary. The Times Square hustlers' grapevine would spread the line that a guy in a hotel just wanted to listen, ask a few questions, then you could leave. The street people knew Kinsey wasn't a cop after he had built up a reputation in the area. The hustler would get paid for his time, and the Ratso Rizzo who pimped for the interview would get a little something for his troubles, too.

The three ordinary Midwesterners calling themselves scientists worked in seedy hotel rooms in Times Square (and many other red-light districts in the United States) measuring the exact dimensions of a male hustler's genitals, even if it meant paying him a little extra. This would happen after the loosening-up period, in which the interviewee described in detail his sex life. Not surprisingly, Kinsey was often hassled for this research by law enforcement officials. After he was taken, irate, to the station house, he would call someone at Indiana University who would confirm his position, releasing him from this latest hot water. One Times Square hotel threw Kinsey and his colleagues out for their actions after the management observed the stampede of hustlers and servicemen passing through their lobby to the Kinsey room.

Prok also talked to farmers who had erotic attachments to their livestock and to incest practitioners. Even his staff was not immune from his compulsive curiosity.

Prok's data provided him with a certain power. Pomeroy stated that Kinsey "liked secrets, that their possession gave him a sense of power. . . . [His subjects] included political, social, and business leaders of the first rank, and with his intimate knowledge of their lives [he] could have figuratively blown up the U.S. socially and politically."

The secrecy extended to Prok's personal life. Though he demanded everyone's confessions and was highly opinionated on certain matters, he never told anyone his views on sex or religion. This obsession with privacy engendered his obnoxious attempts to censor articles about him. He always demanded prior approval of journalists' stories.

The most startling revelation of *Sexual Behavior in the Human Male* was that, in 1948, a lot of men had sex with other men, whether as kids, before marriage, behind the wife's back, or as a regular practice. Many repressed American guys suddenly knew they had brethren in closets throughout the United States—mailmen, teachers, auto mechanics. Homosexuality was no longer pigeonholed as being only characteristic of nelly queen faggots. According to Kinsey, half of all American males were heterosexually inclined, with the other half indulging in occasional to frequent homosexuality. Most important, Kinsey spoke out against repressive laws against homosexuality, asserting that almost any man could be entrapped.

In Kinsey's viewpoint, men's sexuality fell along a spectrum ranging from complete homosexuality to complete heterosexuality. There were few absolutes; instead, people had a stronger inclination toward one or the other. He believed that people acted exclusively straight or gay because of societal pressure. Without this interference everyone would be bisexual, open to either sex at any time. He greatly admired sharp, articulate people who behaved in socially taboo ways. He believed that the deepest and strongest taboos were against homosexuality, even stronger than those against such supposedly aberrant acts as bestiality, yet it was the most common taboo behavior practiced.

When a subject proved compelling enough, Prok would preserve the image for posterity in the form of a film loop. The bigger the social taboo, the better. With his faithful cameraman, William Dellenback, behind the whirring box, animals were taken into consideration—rabbits, chimps, hogs, cattle, porcupines—as well as all kinds of human intercourse, including homosexual orgies. Prok eventually got caught fibbing to Indiana University when he said he was taking animal movies while actually photographing humans having sex in an attic. Kinsey would pore through bookstores for hours looking for acquisitions for his Institute. His collection of stag and amateur pornographic films was staggering, which is how he originally met Anger. Since 1947 Anger played up the fact that *Fireworks* had been seen by doctors and psychiatrists.

The professor and the filmmaker were made for each other. Their obsessive fascination with the hidden side of the erotic psyche was equal. In Prok, Anger found an accepting paternal confessor, one with whom he could endlessly discuss his psychosexual complaints. Like Crowley, Kinsey's presence would dominate Anger for the rest of his life, but unfortunately Kinsey's influence on him was not completely positive. Kinsey's unusual rationalization of scientific investigation to get at what sexually interested him taught Anger a contorted form of self-denial.

Anger was overwhelmed by Prok's collection of more than five thousand stag films. "Through the years Kinsey built up contacts," Anger explains. "Let's say a police department in Memphis confiscates a blue film. Instead of throwing out the films, they'd ship them to Prok. He had some that were from 1910. The earlier they were, the better you could see the distance time gives to things. They become more quaint. For instance, in the ones from 1900, the people really looked different. The idea of beauty then was the hourglass figure—women with very heavy thighs, big hips and bosoms. They did funny things, like wearing domino masks, as if this would conceal their identity. In the twenties the guys always kept on their socks and garters and wore pomaded Valentino hair styles. In the forties, there were the girls with beehives and pompadours. Bobby socks would identify those in the Sinatra period, about 1942. Kinsey had no idea when the films were made, so I gave an educated guess.

"It was no particular erotic trip. I assisted in evaluating whether they had any artistic merit (which most didn't), whether they were humorous or serious, and whether they accurately reflected some erotic impulse or were faked. I found a few that were almost like works of art and a few that were conscious works of art. I remember particularly some made in Siam. They were called 'honeymoon films,' with couples who were really going to be married filmed in very idyllic nature spots with a waterfall in the background or a bamboo grove, really beautiful."

Well into the 1980s, Anger remained a faithful Kinsey archivist, identifying himself as "a volunteer working for the Kinsey Institute."

Both Prok and Anger were Tennessee Williams fans. Kinsey attempted to correlate the sexual behavior of the cast members of *A Streetcar Named Desire* with their acting. Marlon Brando as Stanley Kowalski in this performance would give Anger lifelong fodder for his erotic imagination. Prok was also interested in Somerset Maugham; his favorite movie was *Quartet* (1948), from the Somerset Maugham stories. Although generally unemotional, Prok would unabashedly burst into tears while watching it, regardless of the audience surrounding him.

There was one man that passionately united Maugham, Kinsey, and Anger: Aleister Crowley. Kinsey said that Crowley was "the most prominent fraud who ever lived," but he was intensely interested in Crowley's sex magick practices. Kinsey was obsessed with obtaining the Great Beast's day-to-day sex diaries, the rather decorously titled *Rex de Arte Regia* (*King of the Royal Art*). It recorded many of Crowley's New York City dalliances, such as his adventures with hookers: "Viola. Hideous taurine doped prostitute. Helen Marshall. Irish American prostitute. Taurus rising. Beautiful lazy type. Not actually passionate or perverse. A cheerful comfortable girl. Anna Grey, prostitute. Big fat negress, very passionate." Crowley also included his interludes in a bathhouse, like one evening when he blew two tricks and got fucked by a third. There were also comments about his drug use, such as "another nosebleed upon waking" and the effects of heroin and cocaine on sex.

Kinsey's accusation of fraud against Crowley could have simply been the jealous rage of someone needing a respectable front to get what he truly wanted. To obtain grant monies and maintain the support of the university, Kinsey needed the excuse of research to validate his twenty-four-hours-a-day obsession with sex. However, Prok's battle cry of "Do your best and let other people react as they will" seemed a variation on Crowley's "Do what thou wilt" maxim. Kinsey also shared Crowley's arithromaniacal tendencies, with the degrees of Crowley's sex magick orders having their analogue in Prok's "tone scales" of sexuality, in which tendencies are numerically classified. *Sexual Behavior in the Human Male* is filled with statistics and numbers, many of which have no meaning to the average reader. The shorthand code in which Kinsey recorded his subjects' histories is also highly reminiscent of ritual cipher manuscripts found in Crowleyan secret societies.

While he took pains to question Crowley's adventurer status and sexual abilities, Kinsey nevertheless thought Crowley was a brilliant erotic writer. He especially admired two homosexual works: the infamous *White Stains* and *The Scented Garden*.

Prok rewarded Anger's help and enthusiasm by including him on the 1955 pilgrimage to Thelema Abbey. Thelema Abbey was perhaps the grandest misadventure of Crowley's complicated life, an occult abbey in Sicily in which he put into practice his theories about human sexual behavior.

The idea for Thelema Abbey took hold over Crowley in London during the early 1920s, when he met Raoul Loveday and his wife, Betty May. Betty May was a heavy user of morphine, cocaine, and alcohol. Quiet, thin Raoul became one of Crowley's most special friends. They took some astral journeys together with the help of ether, a deliriant anesthetic that temporarily causes loss of motor control.

Far from a paganistic shrine to nirvana, the Abbey was a shabby, filthy house that was little more than a shanty. Betty May and Raoul were joined by Crowley's Scarlet Woman, Leah Hersig, and other Thelemic invitees. Crowley adorned the walls with frescos of demons, goats fucking women, and two men fucking each other with their semen spilling on a woman below them. Crowley also asked his pregnant mistress, Ninette Fraux, to join them.

All the hedonism at the Abbey eventually soured. The sex magick ceremonies became gruesome, involving the sacrifice of animals, attempted couplings with goats as they were having their throats slit, and the drinking of the blood of the sacrificed animals.

Thelema Abbey became fraught with death and disease. Crowley's baby with Leah, Poupee, died. Raoul became ill and died because of the unsanitary conditions. The remnants of the Thelemites were deported from Sicily on May 1, 1923.

Thelema Abbey fascinated Prok, who valued the study of "sex cults." The Abbey proved to be a working model for other extreme love-hate cults that followed in Crowley's wake. When Anger and Prok arrived at Thelema Abbey, it was a shell and a mess. Anger began scrubbing the fascist whitewash off the walls. He cleaned with a rag and a combustible mixture of water and hydrochloric acid, his hands protected by heavy black rubber gloves and a kerosene lantern lighting his way. Under the grime he uncovered a one-eyed demon, an ugly psychedelic Cyclops that resembled Mr. Clean; leering, toothy psychotic faces; a pornographic mural on the back of a door. Other pictures were revealed depicting congress between men, women, children, and goats.

Even as his jeans became encased in soot, Anger's earnestness and excitement of discovery were strong. He also helped remove a cement floor to reveal a magic circle in the Abbey's temple room.

An extraordinary photograph of Kinsey with Anger at Thelema Abbey ran in *Picture Post* magazine, the British equivalent to *Life*. The often-seen photo of a bald, scowling Crowley hangs on a wall, and Prok's arms are outstretched, Christ-like, as he eyes the photo. His shadow falls over it, looking ominously like someone being hanged. Anger hovers submissively before his two fathers, Kinsey and Crowley, impishly holding a lantern, not unlike his favorite character in *Fantasia*—Mickey Mouse acting as magician's apprentice.

Kinsey was apparently thrilled at uncovering Crowley's artwork, though officially he dismissed it as very crude.

Thelema Abbey, a half-hour sound film, was made of this event and shown on British TV, sponsored by *Picture Post*. Anger takes credit for this work in his filmography, though he claims that when he went to *Picture Post* to pick up his print, the magazine had closed and the film was lost forever. Except within the walls of the Kinsey Institute—Prok, supreme collector that he was, was going to have Anger preserve their meeting with the Great Beast for himself.

The beautifully lit stills in *Picture Post* make *Thelema Abbey* look lovely, in a darkly contemplative and slightly menacing manner. It was as if Crowley were to enter his candle-lit temple at any moment and begin his revels again. The Abbey's visual influence would recur later in one of Anger's most popular and enjoyable films, *Lucifer Rising*.

Before they left Italy, Anger got as close as he could to Prok. He took Prok on a tour of European cruising spots. But when Anger expressed the hope that homosexuality might one day become widely accepted, saying "I suppose it would all get better," Prok curtly replied, "Don't count on it."

Like many individuals associated with Thelema Abbey, Prok would die not long after encountering it. In 1956, with his Rockefeller grant money withdrawn to his chagrin, yet still furiously gathering histories, Dr. Alfred C. Kinsey died of a heart attack.

Chapter 7

Single-Room Occupancy

I prefer to fight alone.

MARIA CASARÈS IN *LES DAMES DU BOIS DE BOULOGNE* (1945)

after Prok's death Anger remained in Paris, existing in a five-by-six single room. He was surviving on heavily creamed and sugared coffee. Charles Henri Ford recalled that "we'd have dinner together. Kenneth would be not at all talkative, sometimes too calm. He seemed always perceptive. It wasn't that he was not there, he just seemed to want to listen more than talk. I guess that's part of his voyeurism and that's what you are doing when you're making a movie—you're not doing the talking, you're letting somebody else do it for you."

Anger popped up again in Anaïs Nin's life. He told her that he was making a biography of the Marquis de Sade, filming in de Sade's actual castle. At this point Nin found Anger extremely remote and lonely.

Little is known about Anger's activities during the mid-1950s. By 1958 he still had not been able to complete any films in Paris. He held on to his hope of completing *Maldoror*. His stack of pre-production notes and sketches had grown larger and he had plans to photograph nudes in a graveyard. Several Parisian surrealists threatened to hand Anger's head to him if he shot *Maldoror*. The book's fluid, dreamlike imagery had been one of the trailblazers of surrealism, and his detractors felt that a gauche American with a reputation for pop iconography and bold homosexual statement would debase a sacred text.

The 1958 Brussels World's Fair was presenting an exhibition of avant-garde films. Agnes Varda previewed a new short film; she would later make important cinema verité films. Marie Menken, one of the original underground filmmakers from the days of Creative Film Associates, attended with Stan Brakhage.

Brakhage has always raged that mainstream moviemakers sap underground energy. He found that at the World's Fair, the French *nouvelle vague* directors, as represented by François Truffaut, Jean-Luc Godard, and Alain Resnais, were using techniques developed by experimentalists, but they refused to acknowledge this influence. According to their auteurist critical sensibilities, experimental or underground films did not have a beginning, middle, and end. These directors put a distinction on being a narrative filmmaker and an artist who uses celluloid as a medium.

Through European sources such as the Cinémathèque, Anger

had become familiar with Abel Gance's split-screen techniques in *Napoléon*. Now he prepared a three-screen version of *Inauguration of the Pleasure Dome* for the World's Fair. He desperately needed the prize money if he were to continue working and seeking backers. The audience was amazed at his three-screen *Pleasure Dome*. The central image grew wings as the two other images were projected. However, the projectionists had not executed Anger's instructions with the necessary exactness, and he charged into their booth, screaming inflammatory epithets. The burly German projectionists stared at Anger in disbelief. Anger dragged his head against the stucco wall of the booth until his blood seeped down it.

While Anger won the Prix du Ciné-Club Belge and the Prix de l'Age d'Or, he received no cash prizes. As the other filmmakers well knew, he didn't have a chance to begin with: the Communists had all voted in a block, making the festival's prizes meaningless.

Anger took the three-screen *Pleasure Dome* to the Belgian film festival at Knokke-le-Zoute later that year. At the end of the festival, there was a *grande bouffe*, compliments of a local film company touting their product. The experimental filmmakers had all been invited, along with luminaries like Abel Gance. Throughout the evening, Anger played *enfant terrible*.

Two buses collected the directors and brought them to the film company's factory, which was a Dada vision of the industrialism that the perpetual motion of *Entr'acte* personified. Everyone was made to sit through the company's boring industrial films as well as speeches by its officers. Anger remained with a male companion, laughing and making facetious remarks. Next, on to the banquet, guests were treated to manly cigars. Once the guests were dolefully sucking on their cigars, cigarette girls pranced out with trays of the company's grade-B film stock. All the avant-gardists made wild grabs for the film like junkies grabbing free bags of dope, stuffing their pockets with all the booty they could get.

Anger's reputation in Paris was now on tenuous ground. *Maldoror* was buried. He continued to live penniless in his single room. Desperate for money, he asked *Cahiers du Cinéma* to buy some stories and they suggested that he put them in a book.

Anger commenced writing *Hollywood Babylone*, and found a publisher in Jean Jacques Pauvert, who had continued to publish the Marquis de Sade in France when it was still illegal.

In putting *Hollywood Babylone* together, Anger was influenced by Bob Harrison's scandalous *Confidential* magazine, which flagrantly insulted celebrities and used grotesquely garish layouts. He also wanted to employ Aleister Crowley's writing style, which was more verbally battering, stark, and death-obsessed than, for instance, William Burroughs's writing. Crowley's *The Book of the Law* provided the opening quote for the book, "Every Man and every Woman is a Star." Freudian underpinnings were also at work: Anger had heard the stories as a young child, and they had eroticized his impression of stars.

Finally, there was the simple pleasure of schadenfreude, "That marvelous German word," says Anger, that describes "that particularly Hunnish pleasure in seeing your enemies fall to pieces in front of your eyes. All I've had to do is sit back and wait to see the whole empire of Hollywood Babylon crumble into dust." The sad realization that he would never realize his childhood dream of being a Hollywood movie star had also hit Anger. The "soft voice that never rose above a semi-whisper" that Ed Earle remembered would never work on a conventional soundtrack. Though he might look like Valentino, his voice undermined his chances, as voices had affected so many silent screen stars. Anger had his fifteen minutes of fame in *A Midsummer Night's Dream*. His resentment against Hollywood was further fueled by being a filmmaker without funds.

Hollywood Babylone came out as one of a series of Pauvert coffee table books that also included *Eros in the Cinema* and a stills and script tie-in to *La Dolce Vita*. The *Babylone* cover was red, black, and white. The French edition was slightly smaller and photographically more restrained than subsequent American incarnations. Anger describes it as "a picture book, a page turner with pictures and words working together."

Cast out of star heaven, Anger proved stars to be mortals. In *Hollywood Babylone* the angels fell with a resounding thud. The stars themselves were all unhappy dysfunctionals. The book exposed

hidden libidos such as that of Valentino, who had wielded enormous power over people's fantasies and erotic imaginations but
had a submissive love for dominant women. It also recognized little victims on the fringes, like Peg Entwistle, who threw herself off
the HOLLYWOOD sign and died days later with cactus needles stuck
all over her.

Anger tells stories with mostly terminal overtones. Lupe Velez,
Hollywood's "Mexican Spitfire," had a series of torrid affairs and
wanted to leave a beautiful corpse behind for the photographers.
An unpredictable reaction to a Seconal overdose thwarted her. She
died with her head in the toilet, drowned by her own vomit. Anger
is not ridiculing her toilet end; he identified with her desire to
keep dignity in death and to leave a beautiful corpse.

What Susan Sontag would ultimately acclaim as a pre-camp
manifesto was Kenneth Anger's Big Book of Hollywood Martyrs.

The French *Hollywood Babylone* reached only a limited audience
in the United States. This rare Pauvert edition is now a choice
Anger collectible, valued at over $300 if it can be found.

Cinematically, Anger's next project in France was a 16mm black
and white version of *The Story of O*. Keeping the book's conceit of
a female narrator, Anger emulated another filmmaker, Robert
Bresson, who had made the classic film *Les Dames du Bois de
Boulogne* during the occupation of France.

There were to be no explicit sex scenes or explicit S&M violence in *The Story of O*. "Explicit sex on the screen is like watching
an eye operation or somebody having their stomach cut open,"
states Anger. "There were leather costumes and high heels and
chains and whips but they were just sort of fondled and looked at.
You hear sound effects. They [the leads] close the door and you
hear beyond the door the sound of whips and moans and things
like that. But it's being done in a very discreet style."

Anger's version of *The Story of O* would have been a smash in
Paris. One can imagine what Anger could have done with this classic story of one person's willing subjugation. It would have translated his homosexual sadomasochistic theorem into a popular,
mainstream heterosexual realm.

Due to various problems, Anger was only able to complete

twenty minutes of the film, and stored the footage at the Cinémathèque. One photograph is frequently reproduced in "Sex in the Cinema" histories—a very artfully composed, heterosexual variant on *Firework*'s imagery, much like the work Helmut Newton, the internationally known fashion and S&M photographer, would produce approximately twenty years later. A nude woman sits on a stone staircase, a cape draped over her eyes and spreading out beneath her. She wears a black leather collar with a dungeon chain, held by a man who looks like a more muscular version of Anger. He's wearing leather pants and a leather vest; there's a whip on his lap. Her legs are crossed; the sole of her bare foot faces the camera. The man looks at the woman with love and attentiveness. Other photographs from *The Story of O* have recently surfaced in such high-class European erotic magazines like *Diva's Marquis de Sade*, which made clear that Anger's stills had a stylistic influence on the later, commercial version of the movie.

The Story of O ended Anger's attempts to make films in France. His reputation as a filmmaker there was hampered by a string of incomplete or failed projects. The royalties from *Hollywood Babylone* couldn't sustain his living expenses forever, and he was at his wit's end.

In a Paris café Stan Brakhage shot some close-ups of Anger's face that he later used in his film *The Dead* (1960). Anger's face is at a slight tilt in the film, intercut with tombstones and miserable people trudging to work. Feeling that Anger's situation in Paris was making him as good as dead, Brakhage talked with him about how he could pull himself out of it. A short time later, as the 1960s began, Anger returned to America.

Part II

The Father

Chapter 8

Some don't like sunshine, especially illuminating the bed-room. . . . Scorpio . . . your astrological sign?

CHARLES CHAPLIN IN *MONSIEUR VERDOUX*

To be macho is to be a sadomasochist.

BRUCE BYRON A.K.A. SCORPIO, 1991

the bitter experience in France changed Anger. Adaptations of classics had seemed his most commercial avenue, and these projects had all met with dismal failure. He had recently turned thirty-three and the rupture with his biological family was complete and irreparable. They had persecuted him and attempted to make him feel ridiculous for being an artist. Professor Kinsey and his grandmother, his proxy parent figures, were no longer alive to provide a base of support, nor was his natural mother.

In 1961 Anger stayed with Marjorie Cameron in a run-down part of Los Angeles. Stan Brakhage came by one day to visit; he had not seen Anger since Paris the year before. They were gathered in the kitchen when, much to Anger's dismay, Stanton Kaye showed up uninvited. Kaye, an avant-garde filmmaker, would later cross over into a more commercial realm with his features *Brandy in the Wilderness*, an autobiographical film, and *Georg*, which dealt with bigotry against a man who had been a German soldier in World War II. Although irritated by Kaye, Anger remained gracious. Then Anger began making weird hand gestures over Kaye's head. Kaye passed out in mid-sentence. Brakhage looked on, not knowing what the hell had happened.

The conversation continued for another few hours. Kaye's long nod lifted as Anger again did the hand jive over his head. Kaye awakened and finished the sentence he had started hours earlier. Brakhage was confused, remembered little, and wondered if he himself had been hypnotized into believing it had happened. Perhaps he had been hypnotized. However, this sick/fainting/dead scenario is frequently played out before initiates in a multitude of fraternal organizations and other secret societies. Anger and Cameron plied the confused Brakhage with books by Aleister Crowley, but for Brakhage there was something about Crowley that didn't sit right, and he put the books aside.

With Cameron at his side, Anger was beginning to feel more at home and secure about his place in the world. Throughout his life Anger would make allusions to living for several months with a woman he loved. This was Cameron, a dominant personality, like most of Anger's women friends. Although the time they spent together would be emotionally charged, they would maintain a lifetime bond. Anger readjusted to the United States on his home turf in L.A., living and learning with Cameron. By 1962, bolstered by her confidence, he was ready to try his luck in New York.

Filmmakers Marie Menken and Willard Maas put Anger up at their Brooklyn Heights penthouse on Montague Street. The couple had known him since Cinema 16 and the early days of the avant-garde film movement. Menken had dedicated a film to Anger the year before. *Arabesque for Kenneth Anger* was a stop-motion study of Moorish castles in Spain.

Maas and Menken were, in Anger's view, "two notorious drunks who were the models for *Who's Afraid of Virginia Woolf?* It was fun. I was the referee. Virginia was Marie Menken. Her husband was a gay professor from Wagner College on Staten Island. A monster. She worked at *Time* magazine in the cable room taking communications from overseas, which is a very important job and very difficult. He taught English literature, put the make on all his students, and gave them A's if they dropped their pants.

"I was living with them in sort of a doghouse on the roof. A shack, but it had a wonderful view of Manhattan. Every Friday they would start drinking at five P.M. They finished drinking at nine A.M. on Monday morning. They wouldn't sleep for that period. They'd have these Punch and Judy fights, throwing plates, pushing each other. They'd get out on the terrace of the penthouse and stand on a little wall. It was a fifteen-story drop. They'd push each other and they were both overweight. So I'd want to save her. I thought if I appeared in their fight I'd be the one who'd go over the wall and they'd still be up there. But they were interesting."

Besides Anger, there was yet another mouth to feed at the Menken-Maas household: a young Italian from the Bronx who was a student at Wagner College. Gerard Malanga aspired to a belles lettres milieu, and soon snagged a job assisting Andy Warhol.

Malanga would come into the penthouse and Anger would be working on the dining room table, putting together comic strips he was shooting for a film. "This went on for a couple of months," recalled Malanga. "Even Willard and Marie—I don't think they were fully aware of what this footage led up to be."

As if on a citywide safari, Anger was aggressively filming bike boys. He bagged a lot of exotic creatures on these adventures. "I spent the first part of the summer of 1962 at Coney Island on the beach under the boardwalk." Boardwalks, especially this one, were notorious cruising areas and trick spots. Anger spied a bunch of Brooklyn Italian guys tinkering with their motorbikes. He found it all "strange as darkest Africa." So crass. So American. So sexual.

Scorpio Rising.

To fill this film out, Anger needed professionals as well as the Brooklyn amateurs. A foray through Times Square put him on the infamous Tenderloin corner of the Deuce—Forty-second Street and Eighth Avenue—a spot rife with midnight cowboys. It was here, in November 1962, that he made the acquaintance of a non-descript blond Irish guy named Richard MacAulay, a.k.a. Richard Byron, a.k.a. Bruce Byron, a.k.a. Scorpio.

Byron had arrived in New York "in '54 with my denim jacket, denim trousers, and motorcycle boots." He claims, as many others have, that he was the first in Times Square to wear a cowboy hat and Levi's. "Times Square was nice in the fifties. It was beautiful. I had a lot of friends there. You never went hungry. You always had a friend to buy you a cup of coffee, a sandwich. Go to the movie house for twenty-five cents in the morning, thirty-five cents in the evening. You could put your feet up and go to sleep all day in the movie house. There were no problems like today.

"I was raised on a farm in New Hampshire. My mother deserted me when I was about eight years old. She said, 'Get out of the car. Walk up the road. There's a house on the hill. When you get there, there's a white-haired, big-boned woman. She'll ask you your name. You say Richard and that's where you're going to live.'

"This old lady was very Victorian. I was never allowed to read funny books in her house. One time she caught me washing myself with soap. I was washing my dick, or *whatever it is.* She thought I was playing with myself. She came in and pulled me out of the water and beat the living shit out of me.

"When I was in the Sea Scouts in Connecticut, they showed us the death house. They said, 'Does anyone want to volunteer to sit in the electric chair? We want to show you what we do to bad guys.' I was the only volunteer. They strapped me in the electric chair. I was like thirteen, fourteen years old. I never forgot it."

Byron forgets few of his S&M experiences. He believes that "all ideas arise out of the libido. All things are caused by sexual frustration. All bombs, pistols, guns, clubs are made in the form of phallic symbolism. Because man can't get himself together sexually, all his sexual energy goes into destructive things. To be macho is to be a sadomasochist."

Byron says he joined the Marines during the Korean War. Instead of being sent overseas, a lot of his time was spent in the brig being assaulted in a variety of ways. "My commanding officer said I threatened to kill him. They threw me in a Quiet Room. I was naked. My hands were covering my privates. They beat me up, called me a Communist." He mentions having several homosexual experiences in the service with other "manly" men.

Byron's personality traits would provide the centrifugal force for Anger's film fragments. In his new incarnation as Scorpio, the lead in *Scorpio Rising*, Byron would embody everything negative about sexuality: narcissism, fake masculinity, sadomasochism arising out of impotence, sexual frustration seeking release in violence, delusions of grandeur masking self-loathing. Worst of all, the existence of a sloppy emulator of a male idealization who's forever damned to inadequacy. Death would prove the only acceptable sexual climax.

Byron remembers being on Forty-second Street and Eighth Avenue when "a guy comes running up with a little Kodak camera on his arm. He said, 'I want to make a film about bike guys.' So I gave him my name and address and said, 'Give me a call and come over.' He came over, but he didn't have a script or anything.

"We got along all right. We both got stoned a little on speed. Ken was a very thin guy. He always seemed to be in some kind of hurry. In a way, very effeminate acting." Byron turns demure and red-faced when asked if there was any sexual activity between them. "Kenneth and I didn't have any kind of relationship, any kind of physical contact," he insists, over and over.

For his star, Anger had picked a winner, the right guy to personify Scorpio. "We went to a store on Fifty-fifth Street and Seventh Avenue. Little motorcycle toys, like cops on motorcycles, a button saying BORN TO RAISE HELL, a T-shirt with MAFIA on it because Brando didn't have anything on the T-shirt in *Streetcar*. I set my room up. Pictures on the wall, the James Dean pictures. We did a couple of scenes at my apartment, like me with the Siamese cats."

The next scene they'd work on would be a party scene. "I had the death mask on in the party scene. I went out there with my wife, Rosemary. A small neighborhood bike club out by Coney Island Avenue, three, four guys. Ken knew 'em. The party scene was his idea. We were just kidding around, goofing. It wasn't homosexual, per se."

The culmination of their filming together was their desecration of a church. "We snuck in the church. The church was already broken into, in Brooklyn Heights. It was being renovated. Anyone could just walk off the street in there." Anger had him perform an array of blasphemous acts, from kicking Bibles to urinating atop the altar.

"Basically, the scenes I'm in are what I was about. Here I was, an ex-Marine with three years in the Marine Corps. I wasn't some kid. I was a man, twenty-nine years old at the time." Anger was thirty-five.

A burst of rockabilly guitar opens *Scorpio Rising* as Ricky Nelson sings "Fools Rush In." In a garage, the camera spies a bike covered by a white blanket. The bike's taillights lie on the floor. Its owner is on his knees, rubbing the phallic front fender with two fingers extended, polishing it hard.

A leather-capped man models the back of his ornate leather jacket that spells out in studs SCORPIO RISING. —KENNETH ANGER, which is also spelled out in studs on the jacket's belt. The guy turns and reveals an extremely pale abdominal area, which contrasts sharply to his black leather jacket. He walks toward the camera as an image of a scorpion flashes.

"Wind-Up Doll" by the Ran-Dells, another obsure one-hit wonder, heralds a shot of a very red bike. Starting with the leather cap hanging on the clutch end of the handlebars, the camera pans down the rest of the bike.

A little boy (Johnny Dodds), his tiny leather cap obscuring his face, a BORN TO RAISE HELL button pinned on the lapel of his miniature motorcycle jacket, is hunched on the ground playing with a toy of a man on a motorcycle. He smiles as the toy goes around in a circle.

A big boy, the mechanic, tightens some nuts on his bike in tune to the girl group's chorus. The guy's face is revealed: a perfect fifties greaser, a real doo-wop-era dinosaur—a cigarette dangling from his mouth, oil practically dripping off the curls of his hair.

The toy comes at the camera and the man on the motorcycle is a little cop. Three little cop toys jiggle. A broken mirror leans against a door in the background. The talisman of a triangle and circle meeting is formed by measuring tools. Inside the triangle is a motorcycle manual.

A black-cloaked skull fills the screen as the Angels' "My Boyfriend's Back" introduces another greaser with an equally impressive pompadour and just one dramatic curl. He's in a smaller but cleaner area with chains on the wall. This character is dressed in black, a sadist smoothie. He poses with his arms folded over his knee, savoring the hard job he's completed, seeing in his perfect bike his own utter perfection. The skeleton looms over his shoulder as he surveys his work.

Torn jeans over legs introduce the song "Blue Velvet." We're moving away from the greasers and entering a new domain, that of the emulator—the macho caricature of the fake serviceman or biker. Pinstripe (John Palone) is a mere slip of a bleached blond with nifty leather fringes. He's intercut with another greaser putting on his jacket, which is studded but not quite as perfect and unused. The greaser puts on his leather cap, which has a white visor like Brando's in *The Wild One*. Pinstripe puts a slave chain that looks like a dog leash around his waist. Tattoos decorate his arms, along with an elaborate leather wristband.

Cut to the Back (Bill Dorfman) lying on a single bed, white jeans with black leather sewn onto the inner thighs. A cap is over his nose, as if he's taking a snooze in the back of a garage. He looks like a Mapplethorpe concept of marbleized beauty; a leather-capped model resembling him is the centerpiece of Mapplethorpe's *Scorpio Rising* homage in the book of his "Early Works" exhibition.

Bill Dorfman's smiling face assaults the camera as he does a sudden, armless sit-up toward the lens. There's a long shot of him from down a hallway. He obligingly walks toward the camera, still smiling, another friendly narcissist, feeling the warmth of being enjoyed and appreciated, like the sailor who entertained Anger with hand walking and muscle gyrations in *Fireworks*.

Cut to the greaser, who's moving his bike out. A fast chord progression in Elvis Presley's "Devil in Disguise" almost stumbles over itself. An image from the Sunday funnies appears subliminally. A blond chicken has his open mouth poised next to an unmistakably phallic tailpipe. "For twenty-five dollars I think I made a good investment. That ought to do," the kid exclaims.

Scorpio, Bruce Byron, the toughest of the greaser emulators, is reading an episode of "Dondi" while lying in a single bed in an infantile, messy room the size of a jail cell. Dondi says to a shadowy, sinister older gentleman, "Queenie sleeps in my bed. The others are empty."

"Are you offering to share your room with *me*?!!!" the older man excitedly responds.

We see the next panel, Dondi's house.

"I'm grateful your parents permitted me to share your quarters, Dondi. I'll be a good roommate. I won't even snore."

"I'm the grateful one," Dondi cagily replies.

His bureau is strewn with trinkets. Brando's Johnny swaggers on the television set. A photo of James Dean on a motorcycle hangs above it. Bruce's heroes surround him. The images of what he'd like to be give him the strength to keep up his homosexual, worshipful emulation of them.

A now frantic Elvis screams in an amphetamine frenzy on the soundtrack. The camera pores over the pennant for the James Dean Memorial Foundation, which is crudely taped to the wall with the ends of Band-Aids. A Marine Corps discharge on the wall proves what a badass Scorpio is, although the Dean photos are everywhere, like the unrequited crush of a teenage girl. Over one Dean photo, which is above another BORN TO RAISE HELL button, is the image of a stern, Betty Page-esque woman glowering.

At first it looks as if a Band-Aid is tucked under Byron's black sunglasses, but it's another Lucky Strike. On TV, Brando is giving someone the once-over in *The Wild One*. Byron whips the cig out from behind the glasses, sighs nervously, and tries to light a wooden match on his teeth. The match doesn't light the first time, but the second time it goes off, visibly burns him, and he bellows some sort of crudity. He lights the Lucky. Brando lights up, too. Scorpio seems to have known that moment was coming: the movie on TV has enabled him to interact with an icon.

Scorpio returns to the funnies. "Dick Tracy" is a landscape of skulls. In "Peanuts" Lucy whacks somebody over the head with a WOP! A "Li'l Abner" episode is called "The Sons Also Rise." Scorpio sits in his tiny kingdom as two boys, blond and dark-haired, walk with arms around each other, practically kissing.

'Yo' Skunk Hollowers hain't no different from us Dogpatchers—'cept maybe dirtier, 's all," says one.

Anger is cannily using cartoons to convey the concept of sexual slumming. To parents who think their son or daughter is of a higher class than others, sexual slumming virtually represents the murder of the family. The prohibition against it, of course, only makes the slummer long for the person from the wrong side of the tracks even more.

After the sons rise in "Li'l Abner," Scorpio puts his bare feet into leather boots. His Siamese cats hover by a blood-red wall. Intercut are Brooklyn guys hanging out by the Cyclone roller coaster in Coney Island. This is shot like a home movie, grainy, spontaneous, which adds to the voyeuristic aspect of the film.

Scorpio's Siamese yawns and scratches as his owner puts on more biker drag to "Hit the Road, Jack." A close-up shows Scorpio's leather wristband, large enough to hide track marks and good for producing blood-engorged veins.

The Raylettes taunt Ray Charles, and Brando and his wild ones take off. A slow pan of Scorpio's table reveals a newspaper clipping about two visiting brothers killed in Times Square by an out-of-control motorbike. A spice rack bottle marked SAFFRON contains white powder; there's a red sticker saying POISON over it.

Scorpio grabs the saffron bottle, dips a finger in, and scoops out some of the crystal meth. As he snorts it off his index finger, a hangman's noose hangs parallel to his head. The screen goes red and the painted wind-up doll that introduced the movie reappears. With the help of the meth Scorpio *is* Brando or Dean. Before cutting back to Johnny, there's a shot of someone strongly resembling Gerard Malanga in the darkness at the edge of the screen. Barely visible to the eye, the image is extremely Warholian in its sparseness.

Scorpio lays his look on thick with a flamboyant belt around his longish leather jacket. His pirate flag waves in the breeze as he ties a scarf around his neck. To top it all off, he adds a pair of leather gloves.

Western icon Wyatt Earp appears for a second in front of a menorah, a faded paternal figure presiding over the paternalism of Judaism, as Scorpio pretends to shoot the menorah with a fake rifle. Then he takes aim at an elaborate cross. He shoots again at a Calvary cross on TV.

Scorpio blows imagined smoke off the barrel of the gun. He looks at his scorpion paperweight trapped in glass and kisses it. The final touch in Scorpio's getup is his cop hat, which he straps to his head, making himself look like one of the toys that opened the film. As he takes his flashlight off the funnies, there's a quick crotch shot.

To the Phil Spector hit of the Crystals' "He's a Rebel," Bruce's bike boots trudge through a filthy linoleum tenement hallway. The boots are garishly overlit with a spotlight. One boot has toilet paper haphazardly stuck on it. At this point, it's hard not to take Scorpio as the humorous embodiment of the movie's theme: too much of everything superficially and not enough of what he needs internally. Scorpio has become a friend you've visited at his house. You've shared some amphetamine with him and now you're going to meet some of his friends, who are going to get high, too, and freak out together. Scorpio is the rising erection that is leading to a messy climax at a party.

An appallingly cheap and wooden movie about Jesus Christ, Family Films' *The Road to Jerusalem*, is now intercut with Scorpio in action. As Scorpio walks down Tenth Avenue gutters, Christ leads the disciples. As Scorpio kicks tires, Christ cures the blind man. As Christ touches the blind man's eyes, Scorpio pesters those who can see all too well right through him, placing fake tickets on motorcycles for nonexistent violations. As Jesus cures the blind man, there's a nearly subliminal shot of a very real all-male orgy. Genitals aren't visible, but the scene is Dionysian, with a weird mingling of naked legs and disjointed bodies. The blind man falls to his knees before Christ. Intercut is a stiff dick popping out of jeans.

The party kicks off with one-hit wonder Claudine Clark's "Party Lights." Carnival lights are reflected in windows. A tacked-up fifties photo of what looks like a female stripper is seen as Jesus' disciples enter a tent.

Except for Byron, the actors in this Halloween party scene are different from the greasers who appeared earlier and are not as masculine. One enters with a Dracula cape, fake horns, and a button saying I HATE SEX. He's naked save for a big pair of white Fruit of the Loom boxer shorts under the cape. There is a quick cut of a guy getting head from another guy and pulling away coyly. Another is poking his dick through a skeleton. Another is beating a huge bongo drum, held between his legs. A reveler sticks his head up the dress of a startled fag hag. A guy shows his ass as another guy jumps him, hard cock in hand.

Scorpio walks by a sign that says GREASED. The party is turning into an orgy. A guy tries to press his dick into a woman's crinoline dress as they dance. Everyone looks drunk. Scorpio stays against a wall, peering at everything through his orange-tinted sunglasses, acting as the superior voyeur.

A guy is held down for the purposes of sucking a cock, his head moving away. Kris Jensen's "Torture" plays on the soundtrack. The party takes an evil turn with the appearance of a bespectacled nerd. His pants are pulled down by a group of guys. Mustard is spilled on his stomach and genitals. Pig noises, growls, and screams of "Gonna get him!" are mixed in with the tune "Torture."

A merchant offers Jesus two bags of gold. He turns away in disgust. The nerd is being swung back and forth by his wrists and ankles while the mustard drips off him. Scorpio walks into an empty church, illuminating it with his flashlight.

Gene McDaniels sings "Point of No Return" as Scorpio

unleashes his tremendous pent-up hostility at the patriarchal church. His infantilism is in full swing as he rages and stomps. A wave of his pirate flag triggers the motorcycle race that is intercut. Christ rides the burro. "Point of No Return" wafts as a grainy photo of Hitler appears. Pirate flag in one hand, gun in the other, Scorpio threatens no one in particular and everyone at once, challenging something no one can see but him.

Little Peggy March's "I Will Follow Him" is heard as the symbol of the scorpion appears over the pirate emblem. The two boys from "Li'l Abner" flash on again, arm in arm, illuminated by a moon. Mickey Rooney as Puck from *A Midsummer Night's Dream* roars and hugs himself, like a miniature Tarzan.

Scorpio goes wild on the altar. A TV commercial for dog food is intercut with him urinating in his helmet and holding it up as an offering to some unseen icon. Stills of Nazi soldiers appear. Scorpio is suddenly wearing a leather mask as he offers his piss. Everything is turning ugly and severe, as it can with speed use.

After a shot from behind of the group of motorcycle racers, Scorpio raises his gun. Images of skulls. He kicks Bibles. Nazi emblems. The bikers start to leave Coney Island, implying that they're splitting from the party.

As "I Will Follow Him" fades into the joker's laugh of the Surfaris' "Wipe Out," the famous *Life* cover of "America's Youth Today" appears: a skeleton head marked YOUTH in a woman's wig, smoking a cigarette. Superimposed over the black eye sockets is a bathetic picture of Jesus with his hand on a young boy's shoulder, pointing him toward the right-hand path.

Scorpio Rising closes with rapid-fire cuts rhythmically set to the manic surf guitar of "Wipe Out." Scorpio ranting. Nazi flags. A checkerboard with swastika checkers. Assorted shots of bikers in Coney Island. The Back posing. A guy spilling out in the motorcycle race. A skull. Three guys yelling "Hooray!" Ambulance arriving. A dead helmeted face seen under a red strobe.

END written in studs on a leather belt whacks across the screen.

Anger the alchemist has offered some yarns about the synchronicity of events surrounding the shooting and assembling of

Scorpio Rising. About the Jesus footage, he says, "The postman left a package on my porch. It turned out it was a Sunday school film, which was delivered to me by mistake. Because I was in the middle of cutting *Scorpio Rising* I saw parallels with what I was doing and a kind of theme of leaders and followers. It fit right in." Byron says he suggested that Anger use the Hollywood Christ movie *King of Kings*, with Jeffrey Hunter as a pensive Jesus and several graphic torture and death scenes. However, Anger preferred the grade-Z Jesus film, which more probably was purchased in a camera store than found on his doorstep.

Anger also supplied a story about his casting method for *Scorpio Rising* that resembled the story about casting sailors for *Fireworks*. Partly as his own wish fulfillment, partly as a satire on Hollywood's use of homosexual men as heterosexual icons, Anger manufactured a myth of a working-class biker, some Fonzie with a girl and a regular job, with "a quarter of one percent," as he coyly puts it, that would be receptive to homosexual attention. "I was able to approach them through photographing their bikes. And they accepted me as kind of a camera nut. I worked completely alone, without any crew. So I was able to go into their garages, and, finally, into their house. They were *real* bikers. Quite a gentle group. Not anything like Hell's Angels.

"They had an exhibitionistic streak. They look very queer on the screen, but those guys were not gay, not queer, not homosexual. They all had girlfriends. Their girlfriends were present during nearly all of the filming, but, because of an Italian macho type of weirdness, they didn't want their girlfriends in the picture. There are only a couple of scenes—when they're coming into the party. They said, 'You sit on the side' at the Halloween party. 'Sit there and watch.' They were gossiping and laughing and the girlfriends thought it was a big riot. Everybody was heavily stoned and drunk on beer, so everyone had a good time.

"They were perfect actors for me because they lived in a state of wonderful innocence. They were big innocent lummoxes; they would do things and wouldn't say, 'I shouldn't do this because maybe I'm gonna get married two years from now and there's going to be this picture of daddy getting fucked in the ass.' They wouldn't say that because they just did it because that's the way they were. They weren't even into a dress-up trip. They had a few leather jackets and chains. They were totally innocent about these having any sexual overtones at all. They just liked to wear them. If you told them, 'Hey, you must be kinky wearing those chains and leather jackets and tight Levi's and engineer's boots they would have knocked your block off. I admire that. They're genuine people."

Byron wasn't the first choice for Scorpio. Fueling the film's death worship, Anger speaks of selecting a man named Jim Powers to play Scorpio. "The lead actor died after the film started. He crashed into a wall at eighty miles per hour."

After one visit to the editing room, Byron "never saw Anger. We didn't have a falling out. He just disappeared." The seven days he spent with Anger incarnating the role of Scorpio would provide the myopic focal point for the rest of Byron's life.

Scorpio Rising came out in 1963 and initially went undiscovered by the general public because its sexual content relegated it to the underground circuit. However, it distinguished itself immediately from the other major underground films of the year, many of which dealt with homosexuality in one form or another. It did not depict sex acts in any pornographic detail, as did Andy Warhol's *Couch*. It didn't get hooted off the screen for mythological pretentiousness like Gregory Markopoulos's *Twice a Man*. It was not a depressive's bacchanal like Jack Smith's *Flaming Creatures*, nor a bunch of heads talking about a married man's night in the baths like Andy Milligan's *Vapors*.

Anger has called *Scorpio Rising* "a death mirror held up to American culture . . . Thanatos in chrome, black leather, and bursting jeans." He uses *Scorpio Rising* to form a perfectly symmetrical geometric pattern in which the centrifugal force is death. Emanating from this terminal core and moving out toward the farther reaches of the circle are various types of males. There are the homosexuals who meet in a private club. There are occasional visitors to such a club who emulate the biker lifestyle, pristine and obvious in their worship. At the outer border of the circle are the grease-monkey narcissists being emulated, who nonetheless crave that other men find them masculine, thus dispelling any sexual insecurity they may have. Females are relegated to being ornaments, party guests. The phallic symbol of the motorcycle, the harbinger of death, unites all the men.

Anger uses the character of Scorpio to explode the "Leather Boy" myth of the macho homosexual by attacking its inherent latent passivity. As played by Bruce Byron, Scorpio personifies relentless cock-anal sexuality. If you imagine this person with a partner, he would be totally passive in the sexual sense: he would get fucked or get blown. This sort of person doesn't do anything; he is not the aggressor that his hypermasculine appearance promises, but a mannequin.

Scorpio Rising shows the powerful influence of Aleister Crowley on Anger's aesthetic. Anger utilized the theories of the "cult of the dying father" in sexually forthright terms, using the private world of the Leather Boy to the commercial conception of Jesus Christ as exponents. Pop culture iconography and songs supporting the central theme are juggled and thrust at the viewer like Crowley's hermetic symbols, evoking strong emotional responses. Anger's mastery of Eisenstein's montage technique pulls all the disparate elements together, making the film irresistibly intense to the visual and aural senses. In the years to come it would prove to be one of Anger's most popular, accessible, and influential films.

Chapter 9

Kustomized

by 1963 the distribution and exhibition outlets for underground film were in a state of flux. Cinema 16, which received no grant or foundation money, was forced to close because of financial difficulties. Grove Press, headed by Barney Rossett, was interested in avant-garde cinema. Vogel wrote a letter to the filmmakers stating that although Cinema 16 could not continue, distribution through Grove Press was an option. The Cinema 16 filmmakers who wanted to go with Grove would include Anger. But right before Cinema 16 folded, Anger came pounding on Vogel's door.

"Ken came to me one day and said that he was in a bad way and he needed a loan of several hundred dollars," Vogel says. "I said I would love to be able to help him, but I couldn't. I didn't have it, which is why we ultimately closed up—we didn't have any money. Now, this is the cause of the breakup between Kenneth Anger and me. He was livid. It was the end. I think personally he was looking for some excuse to break up, because I've heard it from any number of people that there's inevitably a breakup somewhere with him. . . . I mean, he didn't want to talk to me, didn't want to do anything."

Anger was developing a reputation for exiting a combative encounter making threats in the form of Crowleyan curses, but, as far as Vogel was aware, there were no hexes thrown his way. "Maybe Ken realized it wouldn't have worked. I would've said, 'Go ahead.'"

As financial problems crushed Cinema 16, Jonas Mekas began his ascent in the world of underground film. Mekas and his brother, Adolfas, arrived in New York City in 1949 as displaced persons.

In 1955 Mekas published the first issue of his magazine, *Film Culture*. He attacked avant-garde films, calling them technically crude, thematically limited, uninspired, adolescent, and united by a "conspiracy of homosexuality," of which Anger was the ringleader. The old guard of undergrounders was furious. Maya Deren and Willard Maas held an emergency meeting in which a lawsuit was discussed.

Actually, by arousing their unified ire, Mekas obtained a clear picture of a disenfranchised group of filmmakers. He had gained their notice through provocation, and then provided them with a forum, his magazine. Half of *Film Culture* was then devoted to the avant-garde, including articles by the filmmakers themselves.

Along with Shirley Clarke, known for her cinema verité classic about a black homosexual, *Portrait of Jason* (1967), and Emile De Antonio, Mekas formed the New American Cinema Group as a distribution outlet. Conflicts among the membership arose immediately. Some filmmakers aspired to have their work widely distributed, while Mekas took a staunch archivist stance, treating the films like museum pieces for a limited audience. Unlike Vogel's imaginative salad bowl of film programming, Mekas had a decidedly restrictive concept of what was avant-garde. Any film that had inclinations toward the commercial was out, no matter how subversive, and if he liked the filmmaker, he'd uncritically accept their work. Mekas held open screenings at the Charles Theater, located on the ghastly slum corner of Twelfth Street and Avenue B and, in the process, became a celebrity.

Although supposedly involved in film out of love for the art form, Mekas was preoccupied with money: begging for it or revealing the shaky finances of the avant-garde filmmakers. For Mekas, lack of cash was a requisite for sainthood. Almost every issue of *Film Culture* contained humiliating correspondence from a filmmaker about being broke.

Mekas also had a hand in creating the Film-Makers' Cooperative, another distribution outlet, and the Film-Makers' Cinémathèque on Forty-first Street, which held screenings. Mekas started dabbling in filmmaking himself, making *Guns of the Trees*, which dealt with young people on the Lower East Side. His brother Adolfas made the post-Beat *Hallelujah the Hills*, which actually played some commercial venues.

Anger's movies had not yet been handled by Mekas, and some of *Scorpio Rising*'s early screenings took place in curious venues. In his book *City of Night* John Rechy recalls roaming into a Hollywood homosexual bar with murals of motorcyclists and seeing movies about leather guys. Anger has mentioned that there was an illicit black and white dupe of *Scorpio Rising* floating around the West

Coast at this time. Fred Halsted, who hung out at private leather clubs in the early sixties, would find the film a particular inspiration when he later made his own unique films.

In art circles, *Scorpio Rising* was regarded as an impressive piece of craftsmanship. The Ford Foundation was experimenting with giving avant-garde filmmakers grants of $10,000 and Anger had caught their attention with *Scorpio Rising*. To secure the grant, Anger presented a proposal for a film to be called *Kustom Kar Kommandos*. This proposal was one of his most brilliant pieces of writing, a perfect balance of the intellectual, topical, visual, and technical. *Scorpio Rising's* broad narrative framework of short vignettes wedded to pop songs provided the format for *Kustom Kar Kommandos*, but Aleister Crowley's concepts of occult initiatory rituals provided its governing internal logic.

Anger was awarded the $10,000 Ford Foundation grant to produce *Kustom Kar Kommandos*. Parker Tyler commented that Anger had always protested the meager funding available to independent filmmakers, and that this sum would finally be enough to make a film. Anger shot some footage of hot-rodders who had caught his erotic eye, but he used most of the grant money for living expenses and improvements on his prior films. *Scorpio Rising* was tightened and polished, with some effects and shots spruced up; early prints were withdrawn. He also began tinkering with the complex superimpositions that would be utilized in the 1966 "Sacred Mushroom Edition" of *Inauguration of the Pleasure Dome*. Although immensely popular at Cinema 16 showings, *Puce Moment* was removed from circulation, to be subsumed in the revised version of *Pleasure Dome*.

Anger moved into a small apartment above The Movie, an art house located at 1032½ Kearny Street in the North Beach section of San Francisco. He adorned his new surroundings with occult paraphernalia, homosexual and heterosexual pornography, tarot cards, and a blood-red decor.

"Next time I heard of him," Bruce Byron said, "he was in the theater in North Beach. I sent him a telegram saying he did a good job on the editing [of *Scorpio*] and bringing out the ideas. Good luck and everything." Ignored by Anger, Byron was aware that

Anger had made some money and felt that he deserved both cash payment and recognition for his efforts. Unlike other underground performers who came from well-off backgrounds and were slumming it by appearing in films, Byron was the genuine article of aggression who demanded payment. Byron maintains Anger paid him in "tea with lemon," which brewed a lifetime of Byron's personal inferno.

Anger enjoyed casting types like Byron who could never have been movie stars on their own. Byron's life had always occupied the gray area of Times Square, drugs, all-night jobs, hustles, weekly hotels, and mornings spent waking up in all-night movie houses dressed like a cowboy. The act of getting through each day was an exhaustive struggle of survival.

In effect, Anger told Byron that he was nothing before him and would be even less without him. Anger ripped the pedestal from beneath this insecure narcissist's feet, leaving Byron shattered.

Scorpio Rising played The Movie in early 1964. It had been made prior to the biker boom, which Hunter S. Thompson was in the process of documenting for his landmark book, *Hell's Angels*. The Angels were making good newspaper copy and Anger was savvy enough to reap the reward of their notoriety. What initially attracted the Angels to The Movie was the clippings about them that Anger had plastered on the sidewalk under the marquee. They weren't so much mad but pissed that some fag was using their name to hawk his movie.

Thompson's book includes the comments on *Scorpio Rising* made by Frenchy, a main Angel. "Hell, I liked the film, but it didn't have anything to do with us. But we all enjoyed it." Still, the trip was a bum kick. The Angels felt they were being conned. To throw further salt upon Frenchy's wounds, he was plagued by the idea that people would suspect bikers were queers on the basis of the film. He complained, "Shit, did you see the way those punks were dressed? And those silly, goddamn junkwagon bikes?"

Both Anger and the Angels fed into each other, each obtaining a boost in visibility. With *Scorpio Rising*, Anger gave them the push into myth that the Angels sorely needed. It made them seem more lyrical after all the media reports on the gang rapes, chain whipping, and stomping they were doing. And it made Anger's "actor" emulators seem more masculine.

Scorpio Rising was blurring the line between art and pornography. It made the strongest crossover into the newly burgeoning sexploitation market of any underground film of the time. For example, it was booked at the Plaza Art burlesque house in Chicago. The theater offered it as the headliner in a "Something for Everyone" package. Supporting films included *Fireworks* and one of Radley Metzger's soft-core imports from France for straights, *The Fast Set*. A bunch of strippers, the Plaza Playmates, supplied the live entertainment.

A wave of residual fifties' puritanism was lashing out at artists like Henry Miller and Lenny Bruce. *Scorpio Rising*, with its outfront homosexuality and considerable reputation on both underground and sexploitation circuits, was also an inevitable target. The heavy hand of the American justice system came down on the film in Los Angeles on March 7, 1964. *Scorpio Rising* was playing at the Cinema Theater on 1122 North Western Avenue in Hollywood. The theater manager, twenty-five-year-old Michael Getz, was charged with lewd exhibition.

Getz had been involved with setting up underground screenings on the West Coast through his uncle, Lou Sher, owner of the Cinema Theater. Sher would become an instrumental figure in expanding screen freedom. His company, Sherpix, distributed sexually explicit films in which the pornographic and avant-garde underground overlapped. After much FBI attention, Sher closed shop and put his prints in storage, but at this point he was ready to battle the charges against his nephew in court.

An industrial photographer filed the original complaint against *Scorpio Rising*. Prosecutor Warren I. Wolfe's witnesses included a Hollywood vice cop, an LAPD photographer, a Boy Scout leader, and a shrink.

The Anger defense camp was strong, led by attorney Stanley Fleischman, who had previously gotten *Fireworks* out of legal wrangles. The numerous witnesses on *Scorpio Rising*'s behalf included Hollywood director Martin Ritt, *Hollywood Reporter* film critic Jim Powers, Mel Sloane of *Saturday Review*, film editor

Verna Fields, two anthropology professors, a Unitarian minister, a rabbi, and Ruth Hirschman, program director for KPFK radio.

Prosecutor Wolfe refused to show the film in its entirety to the all-female jury; instead, jurors were presented with twenty-five blown-up stills of the objectionable footage. These stills were culled from three shots that totaled eighteen and two-thirds seconds of the thirty-one-minute movie. Naturally, what Wolfe felt was the offending matter occurred in the party scene: one reveler flapping his dick through the skeleton; a guy mooning; another guy, stiff cock in hand, jumping toward the fella mooning.

Witness Warren Day, the Boy Scout leader, spent an entire day testifying about why he found the film obscene. Prosecutor Wolfe warned the jury that if *Scorpio Rising* was let off the hook, this type of "filth" would soon be flooding their homes on TV. To hammer the point home, he read what he considered a blue passage from *Tropic of Cancer*.

The jury returned a verdict of guilty. The *L.A. Free Press* declared PURITANISM SCORES VICTORY—ALL-WOMAN JURY FINDS KEN ANGER'S ANTI-FASCIST FILM "OBSCENE." Theater manager Getz issued a statement after the trial saying that he was "frightened that the Vice Squad functions as a censor board."

It was during this time of *Scorpio Rising*'s legal hassles that it became an inspiration to a young NYU student and aspiring film-maker, Martin Scorsese. He recalls that "Vernon Zimmerman, who later made *Unholy Rollers* and *Fade to Black*, had a loft in the Village where he showed *Scorpio Rising*. It had been banned, but the shocking thing about it wasn't the Hell's Angels stuff, it was the use of music. This was music I knew, and we had always been told by our professors at NYU that we couldn't use it in student films because of copyright. Now here was Kenneth Anger's film in and out of the courts on obscenity charges, but no one seemed to be complaining that he'd used all those incredible tracks by Elvis Presley and Ricky Nelson. That gave me the idea to use whatever music I really needed."

The *Scorpio Rising* obscenity verdict was appealed to the California State Supreme Court, which overturned the verdict. *Scorpio* was, once again, ready to roar, and immediately resumed playing at adult houses, even being considered a date movie.

Back in New York City, Andy Warhol had just made a splash by making eight-hour movies of the Empire State Building and poet John Giorno sleeping. Warhol was surrounded by wealthy patrons and foundation officials, and Mekas presented Warhol with *Film Culture*'s 1964 annual award. Veteran avant-gardists like Gregory Markopoulos and Stan Brakhage were enraged. Brakhage even resigned in protest from the Film-Makers' Cooperative.

Mekas was aware of the publicity that an obscenity bust could generate; after all, Warhol had quipped that this was the easiest way to infamy. At approximately the same time of *Scorpio Rising*'s legal troubles, Mekas was screening Jack Smith's *Flaming Creatures*. New York City District Attorney Frank Hogan, who was hounding Lenny Bruce to death, sent two peace officers to seize the movie. Mekas followed up with a showing of Jean Genet's short film, *Un Chant d'Amour*, and got busted again. Mekas had cannily planned the filmmakers' battle for free speech—he knew that Genet's name had recognized literary value, thus making the two movies a sticky situation for obscenity prosecutors.

Not a particularly stable individual to begin with, Smith could not bear the strain of being poster boy for the First Amendment. Stan Brakhage recalled being present at a Mattachine Society (the sixties gay liberation organization) screening in which Mekas was attempting to solicit funds for Smith's legal defense. Smith was cowering in the kitchen behind a refrigerator like a mouse.

Eventually, prints of *Flaming Creatures* filtered down to Washington, where it became a government workers' stag party favorite. Ultimately, Smith ceased showing the film.

In the meantime, Anger's Ford Foundation money was running low and he had to do something for a quick buck. This situation led him to become acquainted with the infamous Mephistopheles, publisher Marvin Miller.

Miller had a ghastly childhood straight out of Dickens. His cabbie father had died before he was born, leaving a troubled, mentally ill mother to care for him. After getting arrested for stealing a loaf of bread at age six, he was placed in a series of foster homes by Jewish welfare agencies. Miller spent his early manhood assisting businesses in trouble and bringing them out of debt. Some of these involvements would end with fingers being pointed at Miller for embezzlement or arson.

Miller's business eventually became publishing: men's mags, a cheesecake newsmagazine, and various one-shots that still haunt the earth in dust-ridden out-of-print bookstores, available for people who still hold that kink. Like a true entrepreneur, Miller carefully considered what people would privately appreciate, how he could obtain the item, and how he could sell it. Miller purchased books of a sexual nature overseas, hotfooted it back to the United States, and quickly printed up knock-offs. His Greenleaf Classics imitated the format of Olympia Press's green-jacketed Traveller's Companion series. Not coincidentally, much of Olympia's (and Pauvert's) painstakingly assembled catalog was shamelessly bootlegged by Miller. He was taking all the cream of the controversy to become a millionaire many times over.

Miller approached Anger about doing an American version of *Hollywood Babylone*. On spec, Anger presented him with two-thirds of the book translated from French. If a contract was signed, it was a meaningless piece of paper to Miller. Miller was not artistically inclined but knew he could make money off the *aesthetique du schlock*. Anger was an artist but was in perpetual need of cash to propel his work. If ever there were two people destined to oppose each other, it was these two. Formidable foes, each committed to the ends justifying the means.

The Miller *Hollywood Babylon* came out in 1964 as a paperback replete with the cover photo of Jayne Mansfield's breasts spilling out of her low-cut dress, the same one used in the legitimate edition. Its vague copyright is credited to Professional Services, Inc., located at a Phoenix post office box address. Sold in a plain brown wrapper, the whole affair was extremely tabloid, a pinnacle of sleaze, the photos contained in the book crude reproductions.

Anger insists that Miller took it upon himself to write the last third of the book, much of which was not in the French edition. He also claims that he would never stoop to use the vulgarisms sprinkled throughout. However, those juicy bons mots, which are absent from the later Straight Arrow Press edition, seem curiously similar to Anger's written style. Humphrey Bogart had "the biggest jing-jang in Hollywood." James Dean liked "sex spiced with know-ing cigarette burns." Charles Laughton enjoyed "kicks in the fanny from young men." Tyrone Power was a "shit fancier."

Hollywood Babylon was a swift seller. Estimates are that it sold two million copies during the sixties. Kable News Network, its distributor, discovering a chapter asserting that William Randolph Hearst shot his mistress Marion Davies's boyfriend, Tom Ince, was fearful that the Hearst family would sue. Kable went to yank the copies and found that 70 percent of the initial two hundred thou-sand they had put in circulation had already been sold.

Rumors of multiple versions of the bootleg *Hollywood Babylon* exist. Like all gossip, it built on itself over the years, and some individuals claim to have read parts that others cannot recall.

The book developed a strong underground reputation. A then obscure, sleaze-obsessed Baltimorean, John Waters, was so smitten by the Miller paperback that he would later use it as a prop in his early film, *Mondo Trasho*. He was also using Anger's *Eaux d'Artifice* to drum up business for his own local showings, billing it as a fea-ture from "Kenneth 'Scorpio Rising' Anger," the rental for *Scorpio Rising* being beyond his budget.

Anger is also credited as translator of *History of Eroticism*, another Pauvert book that was knocked off by Miller at this time. A small paperback with an odd rectangular shape, it's a miniatur-ization of a coffee table book. A Venus de Milo image adorns its pink and white cover. The author is Lo Duca, the author of many histories of sex in comic strips. Besides the inevitable Kama Sutra illustrations, *History of Eroticism* includes a heavily sadomasochistic, necrophiliac bent. The most memorable photograph is a still of Brigitte Bardot with her heart ripped out of her chest à la Herschell Gordon Lewis's *Blood Feast* from *Love Is My Profession*. *History of Eroticism* is not well known in the Anger oeuvre. During the seven-ties it would turn up for as little as a dollar at Tenderloin book-stores in San Franciso; it's now virtually impossible to find. The Miller version of *Hollywood Babylon* is an equally obscure catch today. A copy can fetch up to $100.

With *Hollywood Babylon* Anger had entered a commercial arena and did not get paid his due. What caused him further angst was the lack of control he felt. In the real world of business transactions, there are far stronger magicians than Anger. He wanted to do something legally to Miller, but it was too difficult to penetrate the wall of P.O. boxes. To attempt a lawsuit would take money he didn't have, and his nerves couldn't stand the aggravation.

It is not surprising that Anger subsequently started fashioning a more extreme image for himself. In early 1965 a journalist from *Aspen City News* interviewed him at his abode above The Movie and observed the large amount of occult bric-a-brac. Anger declared, "I am a warlock. I follow the beliefs of Aleister Crowley." The journalist noted "in his dark eyes, a certain power that one finds in both geniuses and madmen."

Anger presented a bloody T-shirt, a personal magickal talisman that supposedly belonged to a *Kustom Kar Kommandos* kid who had died in a car wreck. He reinforced his ominous image with the story of Jack Parsons's shocking death, which was reduced here to "someone got careless with the nitroglycerin." Anger snickered that "I don't think the Ford people are going to be very pleased with what I did with their money." He planned a benefit to raise more funds for *Kustom*, claiming "it was an expensive film to make. Not because the actors were paid. Cost was mainly color film, beer and free dinners."

Anger had been filming a sadist doctor working guys over. This doctor was rumored to be the model for Neil, the leatherman character in *City of Night*. He had a nice suburban home complete with a soundproof basement torture chamber stocked with whips, chains, and an iron maiden. Inexplicably, Anger dropped off the footage for development at a local drugstore. The masochist who was photographed looked so battered that the police thought it was a possible snuff movie and arrested the doctor. Anger was interrogated and loved every second of it.

"The Italian sergeant who questioned me," Anger crowed, "asked me some extraordinary questions. 'Do you believe in a higher being? Were you baptized? What church do you belong to?' It was the first time outside fascist Spain that I have been questioned by a policeman who kept a crucifix right on top of his desk!" To add more fire to this smoldering satanic brew, Anger told the

Aspen City News that *The Love That Whirls* had been destroyed by the lab because of its very "realistic" human sacrifice.

No charges were filed against Anger for the sadist doctor footage. The Kinsey Institute shielded him, classifying him as a freelance gatherer of sex films. However, Anger was told to remain in California as the state's witness. Anger nonetheless took off for Colorado to do a film program with Stan Brakhage. While he was in Brakhage's kitchen, the town sheriff drove up. Brakhage had always enjoyed a pleasant rapport with the sheriff; it was one of the genial things he liked about life in the sticks. He assumed it was a social call and bemusedly told Anger that he was about to meet a real western sheriff.

The sheriff knocked at Brakhage's door apologetically, because he had in tow an assistant D.A. from San Jose County, California. The D.A. had a warrant for a federal fugitive named Kenneth Anger and asked if Brakhage was harboring him. Brakhage was shocked and didn't know what to do. He didn't want the excitable Anger to jump out his back window, leaving him holding the bag. Stalling for time, he excused himself and went back in the house.

Anger was collared in the kitchen. Unfortunately for Brakhage, his friendly relations with the sheriff ended that day, and the sheriff henceforth kept a file on him. Brakhage could never fathom why Anger could have dropped off film with such contents at a drugstore, where it was sure to attract notice. None of this legal attention deterred Anger from continuing to make his "private little movies."

More than a year had elapsed since he had received the $10,000 grant to make *Kustom Kar Kommandos*. In April 1965, he told the small art magazine *Spider* that "right now it's [*Kustom Kar Kommandos*] hung up because I've run out of money. When I got the Ford Foundation grant, I was completely breadless, and I conscientiously paid off lab bills and things like that. So by the time I'd taken care of my debts there was a piece missing of the $10,000, and then I got a used station wagon, and some extra equipment I needed. And so a friend and I set off across the country from here to New York to film.

"The material I'm filming is teenagers in relationship to machines. And so my film is ostensibly about teenagers and drag racing and kustom cars.

"The cars, particularly the drag races—what they call the rail jobs—not only are obviously power symbols, terribly phallic and all this, but they're also an involvement in a controlled ordeal, in a controlled death-tempting ritual. The kids I'm interested in are the ones who create the cars themselves, not the ones who have the money to hire one of these super-duper kustomizers to make their dreamboat project."

Anger was studying his subjects carefully, since research had always been the hallmark of his success. "They're terribly touched by anyone that shows any interest in the thing they dig. I've had to do quite a bit of homework, memorizing things that are really quite foreign to me, so that I could talk on their level enough to be accepted."

Anger was holding on to a hope that this *Death in Venice* obsession with youth could be channeled into a mainstream movie. "I think I could make a good teenage film, that would still be for them, and that wouldn't get the parents upset about their kiddies seeing it. Maybe I'm fooling myself, but I think I could get away with it."

In 1965 the final result of Anger's Ford Foundation grant differed greatly from the written proposal he had submitted to secure the funds the previous year. But the film is still a glittering, three-minute gem.

Like an auto emblem, the title *Kustom Kar Kommandos* appears against a pink backdrop in gold letters. Two boys are seen checking out a perfect engine, highlighted by stunning orange and pink pastel colors. The darker, Italian-looking boy is in black. The other boy (Sandy Trent) is wearing a white tank top and jeans.

An engine roars. The Paris Sisters' version of "Dream Lover" purrs as the camera observes the hot rod's red vinyl seats with white piping. Sandy's muscular body rises between twin dual cam-heads. He gets up slowly, with his tremendous basket next to the silver engine. His hands are on his hips. The camera closes in on his crotch.

A huge pink powder puff methodically massages the candy-apple red car over its silver machinery. The camera lingers over the phallic engine. There's a shot of Sandy's statue-perfect ass. He looks at himself in the shine of the car's paint job. The camera pans down to the California license plate, KBL 852. A gust of wind gently flutters the powder puff as it rises up out of frame. Cut to the seats. The door opens and Sandy gets in with his legs slightly raised. Shoeless, his sky-blue socks pump the pedals; he starts the engine, loosens the clutch, and shifts the gears.

Seen mostly in profile, Sandy is a remnant of the Dick Dale surf era, with his neat, oiled pompadour. He accomplishes the act of looking pristine without being prissy, a rare accomplishment for a grease monkey. He is also freshly bathed.

The work has been done. He's ready to ride his baby. A human could never compete with the dead, impassive perfection of the car. He fiddles with the controls. Sandy looks like a regular guy bemusedly embarrassed by Anger/the camera's attention, a peacock who doesn't know how captivating his feathers are. He smirks a little and blinks a lot.

Fade to overhead shot of the car taking off, its hot-rod engine roaring as "Dream Lover" ends. ANGER '65 is seen in yellow as someone politely polishes a hood ornament.

Kustom Kar Kommandos is a deeply romantic manifesto. Like Anger, the hot-rodder is creating his own reality. One can see the little boy inside, making a Tinkertoy, which turns into a big, powerful machine.

The movie is very yin and yang. Rudolph Valentino's pink powder puff gently caresses a powerful love machine, with the soft fibers caressing hard metal. Even though he's holding the puff, Sandy Trent nevertheless looks quite masculine. Remove the hot-rod documentary trappings, add a tab of acid to Anger's creative mind, and Sandy Trent turns into his vision of any suburbanite guy polishing his Thunderbird or Impala on a Saturday afternoon.

Kustom Kar Kommandos is realized in intense and sensual colors. Anger achieved these resonant pastels with his camera assistant, Arnold Baskin, who also shot *The Farmer's Other Daughter*, a hillbilly epic directed by low-budget whiz Paul Leder.

Although it is the perfect peeper's length at three minutes, *Kustom Kar Kommandos* left many Anger aficionados wanting more. Playing on their expectations, Anger began presenting the film as if it were a product reel, a work in progress with more to come.

How Anger met Sandy Trent and his anonymous, dark-haired costar remains an enigma. Enhancing the terminal kink mythology, Anger said that the "star" of the film, one Jerry Main, had died. This tale was analogous to the bloody T-shirt souvenir that Anger would occasionally flash for shock effect.

The Ford Foundation was displeased with the fact that Anger had spent $10,000 on a three-minute fragment that was not even one of the vignettes described in his written proposal, not to mention being irked about his flippant remarks to the press about his other uses of the grant money. The Ford Foundation awards to filmmakers were subsequently discontinued.

As 1965 progressed, Anger's mood grew more wigged and unnerved. In a story he told reporters about the Cyclops child, he began practicing a scary mantra that he'd repeat for at least a decade:

"I know of the existence of a beautiful Mexican child who is being held captive by scientists in Los Angeles. The child is now two years old. It is very intelligent. It has one beautiful perfect eye in the middle of its forehead and that is all. And the scientists—the doctors—they've got this child in an isolated clinic room and there are no mirrors and it has never seen another child. And the mother, of course, when she learned she had some kind of freak, looked at it for maybe a split second and screamed for the saints. They took the baby away and she's never seen it since. It's like the child has just about been born out of a seashell. The Cyclops child could lead the world."

For additional ominous mythos, Anger also mentioned that the American Nazi Party had tried to sue him for desecrating the swastika in *Scorpio Rising*.

By April 1965 Anger's sour grapes had grown heavy. He complained of being beat up on stage at the Cinema Theater as Jack Smith and Gregory Markopoulos laughed and jeered. Anger claimed a print of *Pleasure Dome* was stolen during this melee, saying that Stanton Kaye had pinpointed the culprit as John Fles. A most unlikely suspect, Fles had actually written a poem in *Film Culture* inspired by *Scorpio Rising* about looking tough in a leather jacket.

Anger furiously declared, "I'm just about ready for mayhem right now."

Chapter 10

Beautiful Son

Ken is really—I mean, he puts this thing out like he's off
into these circles of hard-core guys and in reality he's not.
He's very paranoid and afraid of them—intimidated by the
real thing. I picked that up and learned that pretty early.

BOBBY BEAUSOLEIL

My first Lucifer proved to be a bit too demonic. He's a
remarkable person who made an unfortunate mistake.

KENNETH ANGER

In early 1966 LSD came mostly in the form of sugar cubes and had yet to become illegal. Ken Kesey's "acid test" gatherings were in full swing. *Inauguration of the Pleasure Dome* enjoyed a psychedelic revival at The Movie as "The Acid Test Program" with ads exhorting patrons to "drop your acid and see 'the movie.'" About two months later LSD was illegal and Anger's *Pleasure Dome* had lines around the block. "Unfortunately," Anger recalls, "[the theater] also had people vomiting in the aisles—some people didn't know how to handle their acid." Psychedelic influences were also having their way with Anger's mind. In February of 1966 he claims to have had one of the most significant events of his life: the sighting of a flying saucer, the best one he'd had to date, in England.

At this time, Anger's films were becoming prominent influences on exploitation movies. Ironically, the first person to assimilate *Scorpio Rising* into his own work was Willard Maas's old signal corps pal, Russ Meyer. Russ had made his own mark on screen freedom in 1959 with *The Immoral Mr. Teas*, which brought the nudie-cutie feature into full-length narrative format, complete with the filmmaker's real name in the credits. Meyer produced and distributed his films with his wife, Eve, herself a Meyer bust model, under the banner of Eve Productions.

By 1966 the nudie-cuties had run their course. The times, they were a-changin', and Meyer had to keep up. Roughies, the new genre pivoting on violence and sadism, could play both drive-ins and adult theaters. Meyer entered this field with *Motor Psycho*, about three hunks on hogs. Blockheads sporting baskets, led by Stephen Oliver, terrorize a gentle veterinarian, played by Alex Rocco. Meyer was famed for doing all his own ad campaigns and *Motor Psycho*'s artwork was similar to *Scorpio Rising*'s "Something for Everyone" ad. Meyer then blasted off from the *Kustom Kar Kommandos* motif with one of his best-known hits, *Faster Pussycat! Kill! Kill!*, a melodrama about three lesbians in dragsters.

Exploitation mogul Roger Corman glommed on to the commercial possibilities in the *Scorpio Rising* axis after Russ Meyer's roughies proved so successful. In 1966 he released the first of the Hollywood bike pictures, *The Wild Angels*, starring such unthreatening presences as Peter Fonda and Nancy Sinatra. It was a rather typical American International Pictures affair, spiced up with a few real-life biker extras way in the background. The big shock scene was an orgy in a church during a biker funeral, a mishmash of Hunter S. Thompson's description of such an event in *Hell's Angels* and Scorpio's climactic rage against institutionalized religion. Through Corman's lens this was regurgitated as wacky frugging and go-go dancing on the altar, safely eschewing nudity.

Anger was a San Francisco resident, but in March 1966 he returned to New York City, strong-willed, feisty, and filled with pride. The purpose of his visit was to present the "Magick Lantern Cycle"—the title he gave the collection of his work he deemed suitable for public screening—at the Film-Makers' Cinémathèque at 125 West Forty-first Street. For this special celebration of Spring Equinox 1966, Anger designed a witty, visually tasty playbill booklet, printed by Graphics Press, to accompany the event. It is one of the most joyous, good-natured encapsulations of his work. The cover urged the viewer to "follow me into the flower called nowhere" next to a French cartoon of a pictograph billowing steam, pointing through a hole at the *Scorpio Rising* title jacket.

The program commenced with the Anger Aquarian Arcadum. This prelude involved Anger showing slides of occult symbols associated with Aleister Crowley. They were images of things he held dear, that motivated him, encaptivated him, such as Eliphas Levi's portrait of the goat-god Baphomet and the seal of the Knights Templar.

Next was the preview of *Kustom Kar Kommandos '65–'66*, which was still called a work in progress. The cast was referred to as "The All-Chrome Ruby Plush Dream Buggy, and the Maker," instead of simply Sandy Trent. The program notes also say that Anger spent $20,000 on this film and interested investors were, as always, urged to contact him.

Third up on this psychedelic placard was *Fireworks*. In the program credits for *Fireworks*, Anger gives the characters names like the Dreamer, the Show-Off, and the Bodybuilding Sailor and proclaims that "this flick is all I have to say about being seventeen, the United States Navy, American Christmas, and the Fourth of July."

Fireworks was now dedicated to Denham Fouts, who Anger says "first turned me on." Denham Fouts was the ultimate beautiful and glamorous kept boy, a legend in thirties' and forties' homosexual circles. Like Anger, Fouts invented his own past, giving a slew of wildly differing stories about his background depending on the listener. Fouts was actually from an intolerant, well-off family in Jacksonville, Florida, that he made it his ambition to outrage at every turn. His daddy tried shipping him up north to an uncle who worked for Safeway stores to set him straight. Fouts was adamant about not wanting a job and wanting to be kept, so at the age of eighteen, in 1933, he embarked on his life's work as a prostitute.

Fouts was taught proper upper-echelon hustler etiquette, the M.O. being to pursue an artistic endeavor, making the john feel like a patron or benefactor instead of a flat-out mark. A German baron who whisked him to Europe was his first conquest. Fouts promptly scored higher and higher fees off individuals with bigger and bigger titles. Recognized as an erotic icon, Fouts achieved a sad sort of immortality as a fictional character in the work of Gore Vidal, Truman Capote, and Christopher Isherwood. Underneath the successful hustler cynicism was the reality of Denny the opium addict. Eventually he became a somnambulist, sleeping all day and leaving his high-priced Paris apartment only at night. The drugs eventually destroyed his libido, thus ruining his chosen career. At age thirty-five he died, living in Rome on a pension, being cared for by a younger admirer. Fouts was buried in Rome's Protestant cemetery.

Anger's meeting with Fouts had occurred on the beach at Santa Monica during the forties. He was extremely impressed with Fouts's lot in life and brought his friend Curtis Harrington to meet him. Harrington was vastly less impressed and found Fouts not anyone to emulate, much less spend time with.

Coming down from the emotional peaks of *Fireworks* on the "Magick Lantern" program was the settling *Eaux d'Artifice*. Anger now dedicated the film to Pavel Tchelitchew, a close friend of poet-filmmaker Charles Henri Ford. Tchelitchew had created homoerotic watercolors to adorn the Ford–Parker Tyler novel *The Young and the Evil*. The sole character of *Eaux d'Artifice* is described as "The Water Witch." The film was made with the auspicious-sounding "special permission of the Italian Department of Antiquities, on Ferrania Infra-Red. Printed on Ektachrome through a Cyan Filter." Anger himself had hand-tinted the Witch's "fan of exorcism" frame by frame. He would repair this fan like a jeweler crafting an etched diamond in the years to come.

There now came a brief intermission. The program instructs that "psychedelic researchers desirous to Turn On for Pleasure Dome should absorb their sugar cubes at this point." If this expert advice was heeded, you would then blast off to *Scorpio Rising*, the product of Autumn Equinox in the occult calendar of 1964. Anger had essentially finished the movie in late 1962, but he was rightfully proud to show off its subsequent sweetening and added flourishes. Explicitly acknowledging Crowley as an influence, Anger quotes him as "The Master Therion" on his use of music: corresponding seven planets to seven instruments to the seven stops of Pan, an orgiastic magickal experience will ensue.

The program description of *Scorpio Rising* is broken into sections of male types, like the infamous pornographer Toby Ross's boy movies. "Part I: Boys and Bolts" in the film has the scene of teeny tyke Johnny Dodds wearing a BORN TO RAISE HELL button and a leatherman cap. If you were feeling the acid, you'd be in the perfect mood for Part II, which depicts the masochistic slavery of central figure Scorpio to his love objects. The isolation, loneliness, and antisocial patterns of an idol worshiper are explored. Part III grooves on with the Walpurgis Night party. Scorpio's voyeur gets down to business. Devil on one shoulder, Christ on the other, Scorpio is rendered motionless and impotent. For his nonparticipation he is tormented by seeing a nerd, much less manly than himself, receiving all the attention. The sexual frustration of Scorpio leads to Part IV, his explosion in the church. It's the metaphorical source of his angst and he unleashes his own fury his own way with his own hand by his own rules.

Scorpio Rising was dedicated to "Jack Parsons, Victor Childe, Jim Powers, James Dean, T. E. Lawrence, Hart Crane, Kurt Mann, the Society of Spartans, the Hell's Angels and all overgrown boys who will ever follow the whistle of Love's Brother." All production credits in the program went solely to Anger. He lists the characters as Scorpio, Taurus, Leo, Pinstripe, The Life of the Party, Pledge, the Sissy Cyclist, and the Fallen Cyclist (the late Jim Powers). The epitaph of Brick Shithouse was bestowed upon Bill Dorfman, whose character is usually called Back.

Again, the Master allows a brief intermission. He gives the clinical advice that "psychedelic researchers preparing for *Pleasure Dome* should remain seated during this intermission. The following film should, under ideal circumstances, be experienced in the Holy Trance called High." Anger knew better than to unleash heads who were peaking on acid on those not in the same mental space. They could disrupt the showing and be ejected.

Anger finally showed the "Sacred Mushroom Edition," Spring Equinox '66, of *Inauguration of the Pleasure Dome*, subtitled *Lord Shiva's Dream*. At this stage the ebb and flow of your subconscious from the psychedelic trance of the tripping audience members now receives the messages from the Great Beat. It is a celebration of Aleister Crowley, a clarion cry to the Crowned and Conquering Child, who is heralding the new Age of Aquarius.

Two close friends of Anger's are not listed in the program: Paul Mathiesen as Pan, the erotic icon of the party, and Curtis Harrington, as the scene-stealing somnambulist. Harrington quietly dominates the film at the times he appears, although he quickly responds "Heresy! That was Samson's movie!" Anger had petulantly and mockingly referred to Harrington as "The Slave" in earlier cast listings. There had since been a falling out between the men that neither would elaborate on. A painful shared experience, both felt it was better left unsaid then and now.

Under the program's description of *Pleasure Dome* is a pretty Aleister Crowley poem of hope, "One Star in Sight," emphasizing the principle that "every man and every woman is a star."

The program also notes that film prints for private collectors were available at Robert Frazier's Indica Gallery. Located at 69 Duke Street, London W1, the mod gallery had been named after the particularly potent and ever popular hash-tasting marijuana. The film connoisseur could obtain photo packs and frame enlargements—what present-day collectors call "still sets"—from *KKK*, *Fireworks*, *Scorpio*, and *Pleasure Dome*.

The program booklet included beautiful stills and Anger's collage, *The Golden Grope of Marilyn Monroe*, which is certainly in the French surrealist tradition. A nude Marilyn Monroe, taken from the infamous *Playboy* calendar shot, lies prone on her back in a receptive position, hand extended to cover the genitals of a statuette of Apollo. A tree is present, perhaps symbolizing the Tree of Life of the Kabbalah. A woman's legs are descending the tree as a blood-lusting gorilla is about to wreak havoc on it all.

Finally, the program included a statement from the creator next to a superb photo of him. It's the best picture ever taken of Anger, lensed by Chester Kessler, who shot *Fireworks*. Looking like pure sex, dressed entirely in leather, Anger is shown in this photo as someone might want to look all his life, even only for that one posed moment.

Above the photo was a highly entertaining Anger-Crowleyan slambook column. This was followed by a nifty thumbnail "auto-hagiography" by Anger himself. Under the figure of Aquarius, he paraphrases Crowley's yellow press moniker of "The Wickedest Man in the World" by calling himself "The Most Monstrous Moviemaker in the Underground." The program confirms that legends about Anger abound—warlock, satanist, drug addict, sex maniac, murderer, madman. Anger claims to be the man with the answers to the age-old queries of "Magick, mysticism, psychology, philosophy, the world, God and man (*and* Woman!)."

The essay ends by challenging the viewer: "Is there manhood in you yet? Then watch these films, if you will, and meet the most monstrous moviemaker in the underground. Meet Kenneth Anger."

Anger continued his travels, showing *Scorpio Rising* in Paris, where the combination of leather and Nazi paraphernalia caused a stir. Photographer-filmmaker William Klein, an American expatriate, remembered that *Scorpio Rising* became "the film that everybody was talking about. America, homosexuality, heavy metal, Nazi insignias—all that sort of thing was very, very new and scandalous. That was *unthinkable* in France—these tough guys with bikes and chains and all that shit and tattoos and stuff. It gave people goose pimples to know that this sort of thing existed. They relished it. French intellectuals didn't deal with these kind of people."

In West Germany Anger met the legendary Nazi film propagandist, Leni Riefenstahl, creator of *Triumph of the Will* and *Olympiad*. The meeting was apparently a letdown for Anger since she refused to be as scandalous as he had hoped. "I've come to the conclusion," he stated, "that she has lost touch with reality. She's told a story about her innocence of involvement with the Nazis so many times that I think she believes it now herself."

Anger also claims to have made a trip into East Germany at this time. The purpose of his mission was viewing Nazi propaganda films for research. By Anger's description, the films demonstrated how "the children were seduced, first with hiking trips, bands, torchlight parades in Tyrolean costumes and were given, as rewards, first a badge, then a knife, a dagger, and finally a gun." These flourishes of Germanic style would provide entertaining interview fodder for Anger throughout 1966 and 1967.

While Anger was doing his international wild thing, *Scorpio Rising* was playing with Jonas Mekas's *The Brig* in May 1966 at Greenwich Village's Bleecker Street Cinema, a smash engagement engineered by Mekas. At this point *Scorpio Rising* was among the first films to elevate itself out of the underground/sexploitation axis, in part due to much favorable mainstream press. *The New Yorker* called it the most beautiful movie of the underground; *Variety* felt it was the most professional film of its kind; and the daily tabloid the *New York Post* found it fascinating.

However, the glare of all this publicity was causing Bruce Byron to crack. He remained grounded in the awful reality of New York City's Hell's Kitchen, the slum area adjacent to Times Square. He was driving a cab. He didn't feel he was getting his due. To Byron, the double bill was a double slap in the face—no credit for *Scorpio Rising* and none for *The Brig*, which he insists the Living Theater ripped off from a play he sent them about his Marine brig experiences.

Byron wasn't even receiving the meager crumbs that fell to the Warhol "superstars," such as swinging with Hollywood stars like Jane Fonda, being invited to nightclubs to spice up the atmosphere, or free dinners on fans' tabs. If anything, desolate Byron was the equivalent of a porno star, an oddity. The biggest invitation he received was from two "policemen," who took a photo of him posed with a skeleton. Unlike Warhol, who pressed his super-stars to make contacts and fend for themselves as well as they were capable of, Anger wanted his performers to be seen and not heard. All the publicity was for Anger alone. This left performers like Byron, who wanted to be recognized for something, in a limbo land of appearing in a film and getting nothing out of it except personal anguish and mental uncertainty. Like Joe Buck in *Midnight Cowboy*, when he poses in front of the poster of Paul Newman as *Hud* and admires himself in the mirror, Byron had no awareness of the whys and wherefores of what was going on. Every night it was the same thing for him. Put on the outfit: sleeveless leather vest with SCORPIO RISING glittering in studs on the back; studded wristband; macho leatherman cap; fingers festooned with cheap silver rings. Then pull up cab outside theater. Stare at peo-ple in the line. Go in lobby. Look at picture of self. No one knows . . . no one knows . . . no one knows. . . .

It didn't take long before the pot boiled over. Byron stood in front of the Bleecker Street Cinema when the crowd was letting out, hoping he'd be recognized. After being ignored, he went across the street to the Figaro coffee house in his full SCORPIO RIS-ING drag, raving once again that he was the creator and star of the film. Not that anyone wanted to listen; this was Greenwich Village, home of the dissatisfied ranter. Byron sporting a Star of David within an iron cross also grated on nerves.

Enough was enough. The manager wanted him out.

"I'll leave on my own two feet," Byron purred in his best Brandoese.

The manager swung at Byron.

It was almost as good as being Johnny, beaten up and thrown out of a greasy spoon, for just being . . . *himself.* No one under-stood. How could they? He was a loner, a rebel.

All witnesses noticed that Byron got knocked on the floor, laid there, and didn't fight back. The rumble rolled into night court, where Byron literally wigged out, clutching a wig stand that he called his inspiration before the judge. The judge was so confused the case was postponed until a later date. They all wobbled out of court at dawn, and nothing ever came of it.

A few weeks later, the authorities found Byron kicking out the jambs in Hoboken, New Jersey. Someone had called the police because Byron's leather drag, whips, and phony weapons were provoking suspicion. Residents were alarmed by a guy in a leather getup marching around a decrepit, abandoned synagogue. Nobody knew he was attempting to shoot an 8mm film, nor did they care. Get this freak outta here!

Like Byron's Figaro fisticuffs, this melee made the "Scenes" column of the *Village Voice*. The photo by Fred McDarrah accompanying the piece showed a manic Byron returned to his brunette origins, looking very fried and extremely older than in *Scorpio Rising*.

Back in San Francisco, Anger was striking while the iron was hot. He was actively seeking investors. *Kustom Kar Kommandos* remained a viable project, a vision to be expanded upon if a financier so desired. Another proposal was a commercial narrative feature about how various individuals' lives were changed after seeing a flying saucer. Most important, there would be a film about the dawning of the Age of Aquarius, Anger's fallen angel manifesto. Its working title was *Lucifer Rising*.

Lucifer Rising was to document the so-called hippie scene emerging in California. Anger was pushing forty, and the hippie credo of "Never trust anyone over thirty"—all espoused by men over thirty themselves—was becoming an oft-repeated cliché. The *Death in Venice* meat hooks were ripping at Anger's flesh more intensely than ever before.

As opposed to the cynical, world-weary beatniks, who were his contemporaries, Anger wanted to join the latest young set on what he called their "love trip." He wanted to capture on film "today's new tribes of teenagers, turned-on children—teeny-boppers and adolescent hippies."

With hippies and the love generation came what author, sexual theorist, and pioneer libertine Marco Vassi classified as "metasex." The macho/sissy act of *Fireworks* was on the way out. In metasexual terms, whatever caused an orgasm became a justifiable end in itself. One could use a member of the opposite sex, the same sex, oneself, a device, or, even in an extreme case, an animal. Anything sensual and consensual was okay. Everything should be explored; nothing should be shunted. Drugs aided this mind-set.

The metasex types became prey for the old-line Crowleyans and their extreme splinter spin-off groups. Guilty pleasures, reacting against puritanical upbringings, and mystical rationalizations for offbeat sexual behavior were still the motivation for much of this crowd. These sex magicians felt that the metasex individuals had great natural power, practicing Crowleyan methodologies without acknowledging a unifying philosophy. They were thus an elemental force to be harnessed.

Blasting off from Crowley's doctrine of Lucifer as the light-bearing god, Lucifer became Anger's metaphor for the ultimate bad little boy who could corrupt you without coercion.

With the help of lots of LSD, Anger's id was flying high. He was transferring his psychosexual needs to occult legends and wanted to personify them himself and with someone he deemed appropriate. Anger believed he was following in the Great Beast's footsteps and took inspiration from Crowley's poem "Hymn to Lucifer," in which Lucifer is cast out of heaven by an angry God, a paternal deity jealous of his progeny's beauty. The central line in Crowley's poem was "the key to joy is disobedience." So why be good? Anger also felt that he was in perfect accordance with the principles of *The Book of the Law*, in which the "Crowned and Conquering Child," the id within, dominated and ultimately cast off the old, killjoy paternal superego.

Anger's first choice for the "Crowned and Conquering Child" was the free-soul wunderkind Godot, offspring of a sexually swinging L.A. duo, Vito and Szou. He described Godot as "a beautiful child with platinum blond hair, which his parents never cut, since he was born, so it was shoulder length."

Anger was impressed that Godot had gotten rid of two cops who had arrived to bust a pot party—if not also one of Vito's omnipresent reveries, which eventually caused Vito to flee the country. "He answered the door on his own initiative, stared at the policemen in the boots, and simply said 'FUCK OFF, cops.' They just backed off and split. It was the most astonishing thing I've ever seen in my life."

Godot died at age five from injuries suffered from falling through a skylight during a photo session.

By mid-1966 Anger had moved his operation into the grandly titled Russian Embassy, located at 1198 Fulton Street in the Haight, an enormous Victorian house that he rented for a song. It had once been the Russian consulate, which had escaped the turn-of-the-century San Francisco earthquake.

The house was a crumbling old affair and, as virtually every house was in the Haight at the time, was a shared living situation. Filmmaker Richard Patton resided on the top floor with Madeline Uribe, another tenant was in the basement, and Anger occupied most of the ground floor. Anger kept a small refracting telescope in a turret room. The roof leaked terribly, and repairs were a matter of terrifying improvisation out on the steeply pitched shaky roof.

Patton started helping Anger during the early phases of *Lucifer Rising* as a lighting and camera assistant, while Uribe aided with props and costumes. Patton quickly came to respect Anger as a careful, patient, and generally professional director from whom there was a great deal to be learned. Uribe, of all the Embassy's tenants, came the closest to being friends with Anger. Her nature and background were such that Anger presented no threat to her and aroused no unrealistic expectations. She welcomed him as an interesting human being whose foibles could be taken for granted, and Anger responded by relaxing a bit.

Mike Mideke, a filmmaker who spent considerable time at the Embassy, found Anger reserved to the point of formality. On one of Mideke's visits, Anger relentlessly detailed the technical gaffes in a pentagram that a previous tenant had painted on the floor. One woman who frequently visited the Embassy recalled bikers involved with magick and drugs hanging out. She found the place a "crystal palace," that is, a speed freak's heaven.

After Anger took up residence at the Embassy, the regal title of "Lucifer" was bestowed on any young man who could bear to remain with him more than a few nights. Anger ran a perpetual audition of life actors. Some of the Lucifers arrived complete with a mascot: in one memorable case a rather large and menacing

Great Dane. The Great Dane served as a doorbell, its enormous woofs and growls echoing throughout the building, alerting the residents to visitors. Very few unwanted guests made it past the ground floor.

By the close of 1966 Bobby Beausoleil a.k.a. Cupid a.k.a. Bummer Bob a.k.a. Tophat a.k.a. Bobby Snofox had moved in with Anger and was life-acting the role of Lucifer. Beausoleil wasn't hard on the eyes—a medium build, slender but imposing, with shiny brown locks well past his shoulders and piercing blue eyes. Beausoleil didn't walk, he strutted like a peacock. His look contrasted greatly with the bedraggled, dirty, beaded and tie-dyed population of the Haight. Soft buckskin leather pants, moccasins, and a black top hat capped off his look. Beausoleil cut a striking appearance with Snofox, a beautiful, pretty-eyed white dog that he called the best friend a man ever had.

Beausoleil grew up in Santa Barbara, California, mostly living with his grandmother. After numerous childhood run-ins with authority, he was deemed a juvenile delinquent and was sent off to live within the system. "I went to Juvenile Hall. I got put into sort of a reform school for being out of control of my parents. Then I got sent back to Santa Barbara. Eventually I left there and went to Hollywood and that's where I started out in the music business. I was about seventeen and got turned on for the first time. In order to be able to play clubs I doctored my [driver's] learner's permit so it would look like I was eighteen. I wound up playing in a band. Eventually that worked into a position with Love."

Love is considered a watershed L.A. psychedelic-era band. Prior to Jimi Hendrix, there was Love bandleader Arthur Lee. In the white-dominated, newly emerging acid rock scene he was the only black musician to stand out. When Beausoleil joined Love, the band was fairly new and had no established following. The first time he played with Love was at their regular gig at The Brave New World on Melrose Place, a homosexual private membership club located in a converted warehouse. Beausoleil recalls that "we were just rehearsing because there were only maybe four or five gay couples in the crowd and that was it. That wasn't very satisfying as far as playing.

"The first set break I took off and went to Sunset Boulevard and I put the word out. I was gone for about twenty minutes, but I had told the right people. In about an hour and a half the place was packed with all the kids from the Boulevard. From that point on the place was packed every night." Love had a revolving-door personnel membership and, ultimately, Beausoleil never recorded with them.

Beausoleil subsequently got an acting job, appearing as Cupid addressing his bow in *Mondo Hollywood*, an exploitation film. The moniker of Cupid seemed to fit Beausoleil well enough and it stuck. Also called *Image* or *Hippie Hollywood: The Acid Blasting Freaks*, this was a *Mondo* movie, utilizing a variety of bizarre film clips, including the parents of Godot, Vito and Szou.

Quite odd in *Mondo Hollywood* is the presence of two other individuals: Jack Gerard, who made his living hiring young hippies (including several of the Manson women) via his "theatrical agency" for porno movies and topless dancing, and hairstylist to the stars Jay Sebring, shown presiding over his tony salon.

After Los Angeles, Beausoleil headed for San Francisco, where things seemed to be happening. In late 1965 he began putting a band together called the Orkustra, which was heavily influenced by Sun Ra's free jazz ensemble, the Arkestra. The Orkustra evolved into a five-member group for violin, stand-up bass, percussion, and oboe, and Beausoleil played guitar, bouzouki, and sitar. "We had a fairly full sound—a unique sound, for sure. We played the Winterland, Fillmore, Avalon Ballroom, Carousel Ballroom, plus a lot of club gigs."

It's not known how Beausoleil and Anger first met. The explanation Beausoleil adheres to is the most flattering and mythologically rich. It was during an arranged orgy at a cathedral in which Beausoleil was jamming on his guitar and licking the sweat off a girl's breasts while jamming on his guitar as Anger peeped on him. Anger then approached him after the show for the part of Lucifer.

Yet, casual conversations with Beausoleil yield stories of experiences with Anger that happened several months to two years prior to this "official" meeting. The earliest account indicates that Beausoleil knew Anger while still a juvenile runaway with a doctored learner's permit. This would change their initial contact from early 1969 in San Francisco to the sleazy *City of Night*–era L.A. of 1965, when Beausoleil was playing in the homosexual after-hours club The Brave New World and Anger was involved in making private films like his "doctor" movie.

Both Anger and Beausoleil are mythologists by nature; they enjoy creating a good legend. Perhaps their first meeting was not so mythical.

Upon arriving at the Russian Embassy for his first visit, Beausoleil came upon the Lucifer he was about to replace. In the scuzzy Haight-Ashbury of 1966, a young man in Beausoleil's position had the option of crashing with a bunch of dirty hippies in a communal atmosphere or he could accept the vastly more interesting proposition of living with a well-respected underground filmmaker in a relatively palatial setting. Beausoleil harbored serious aspirations for a life in music and film and felt that this would be a large step in the right direction.

"My space had real high ceilings, angel frescos on the ceilings. I loved the funkiness of the place," recalls Beausoleil. "Kenneth lived in the back of the building. I lived in the front, which was originally the ballroom. Kenneth's room was the only one that was decorated. He had painted his place purple, the walls were purple and the ceiling—there were window alcoves with faces of women in the corners. These round knobs were all around the ceiling; he had painted the strips black and painted the knobs silver so that it looked like studded leather. In the center of the room he put one of those mirrored disco balls on a string, on a thread, and trained some of his studio spotlights on the thing. He had painted the ceiling black, so the little silver balls would reflect the light from the mirrored balls and the room and ceiling would sparkle.

"Before we really got into a discussion of what *Lucifer Rising* was to be about Kenneth showed me his films. I had heard of *Scorpio Rising*, but I hadn't seen any of his films. We went up to the viewing area on the top floor of the Russian Embassy. . . . I thought *Eaux d'Artifice* was lovely. I never did see *Pleasure Dome*, but I saw *Scorpio*, of course, and it was dynamic. *Kustom Kar Kommandos* was cute. I liked his style and his colors, which are just wonderful. All his films are somewhat self-portrait in nature, at least in my interpretation.

"The idea for *Lucifer* was to be the antithesis of *Scorpio*, which was kind of a death-image type of thing." Beausoleil demonstrated to Anger an instinctive grasp of and inclination toward Thelemic theology. "The concept was that I would be representing the coming of the new age," says Beausoleil. "In a mythological sense, we have come through matriarchy, we have come through the mother goddess. We have come to patriarchy where the goddess is male. And the Aquarian Age is supposed to represent the age of the child. This was the character I was supposed to play.

"In the course of our discussions I suggested the idea of doing the film soundtrack. After joining with Kenneth I had to put another band together, so I put together the Magick Powerhouse of Oz. I rehearsed them in the ballroom. They were mainly jazz musicians, a very free style.

"Kenneth provided my basic needs and that was the agreement. I never got a lot of money or anything. From the very beginning of our relationship we had one snag. That is . . . that I am heterosexual in every sense of the word. I'm naturally heterosexual. I couldn't pretend to be anything else. And, of course, Kenneth is gay, so that created some difficulty. He kind of resented my girlfriends which I had over, but I wouldn't let anything stop me—I was young.

"He's strictly gay. He didn't try to disguise the fact. I have always understood that he was a masochist. I imagine slave/master things appeal to him. I surmised that from what I know of him and different little things I picked up when I was around him. . . .

"I began going through Kenneth's library and I began becoming familiar with mythology, which was fascinating for me. He had a lot of books, a lot of them rare. I became fascinated with children's books and children's book illustrations, starting with the Oz books. Their original illustrations have a lot of subliminal sexual symbolism. They're instruction manuals for kids for learning about their own sexuality. They are! Of course, he had Aleister Crowley's collection. He had a picture of Crowley over his bed. Crowley's his guru; he sort of worships the guy. I've seen pictures of Crowley in his book where he was younger, wearing his pointed magician's hat, a magician's outfit. There were some interesting things about the guy when he wasn't being the wizard/professor."

Beausoleil denies accepting Thelema as his personal theology, but he believes the Crowleyan principle that no absolute good or absolute evil exists.

"Kenneth opened up the world of mythology, which fascinates me. I learned it mainly from his library. I'd ask him things, or about a God, and he'd tell me who that was. It was a turning point of sorts for me, as in the months following our initial meeting I was to become acutely aware of ways of looking at the world and at looking at myself in relation to the world that were previously dark shadows to me. I've studied mythology a lot since then. You'll find that as you get into it you learn you're aware of things—unconsciously aware of things. You draw connections. It's almost like a *racial* memory."

One of Beausoleil's least mythological duties was as the master magickian's chauffeur. "I did all the driving. He was terrified. He was afraid to *ride*. When I drove he had one hand on the seat and one hand on the dashboard to brace himself.

"He just had a real hard time with technology. His only stereo in the Russian Embassy was an old electric phonograph player. He doesn't have that one now, but, no doubt, he has the same kind. He burned that one out by putting a mirrored ball on it to spin around."

On January 14, 1967, Beausoleil and Anger attended the massive Human Be-In in Golden Gate Park. "Ken thought it was pretty wild. When it came to the counterculture scene that was going on then, he was more of an observer than a participant. His interpretation of everything was to underscore his own beliefs as far as the coming of the Aquarian Age and all that.

"Ken would fluctuate between treating me like a god and treating me like a friend. It was kind of strange at times, because I was playing a role that he wanted to play himself. He would turn competitive because he would want to fill that role himself. It was just kinda odd."

Anger commenced shooting in his typical fragmentary style.

Christmas 1928: Jean, Kenneth, and Robert Anglemyer. *Courtesy Robert Anglemyer.*

Kenneth in his only Hollywood role as the Changeling Prince in *A Midsummer Night's Dream*, 1935.

Ed Earle, 1940s. He was too close to the schoolroom. *Courtesy Ed Earle.*

Aleister Crowley, age thirty-five, in magickal garb. He would become Anger's lifetime icon.

Dr. Kinsey with his wife in Italy, 1955. He had just visited Crowley's Thelema Abbey in Sicily and would soon die.

Post–*Hollywood Babylon*: Anger begins to unleash his combative streak. *(After Dark* magazine, *1977)/Courtesy New York Public Library.*

Anger as author Landis met him in 1980.
Copyright by Sylvia Plachy.

Anger and Alan French, his escort for the *Lucifer Rising* premiere, at Anger's Manhattan apartment.
Copyright by Sylvia Plachy.

Beausoleil was used as the centerpiece of what Anger referred to as *Lucifer Rising* but would later be known as *Invocation of My Demon Brother*. Beausoleil recalls that "the rolls of film were eight to ten minutes and there weren't that many of them. There were maybe five. Based on the fact I was there on all the shoots, there definitely was not hours of film.

"He doesn't direct the same way that other people do. He'd set up a situation and then he'd film it and want you to make different kinds of moves. For example, he set up a thing where he brought a big roll of black velvet and he did a thing with the Great Northwestern Light Show Company projecting. I was standing on a box on a little foot ladder or something that was covered in black velvet, so it was suspended in space to the point of view of the camera. Some filming was real spontaneous, like when I was smoking the skull pipe. Ken just got the camera out and shot it.

"I was continually pestering him, saying, 'Hey, when are we going to do it? When are we going to do the filming?' Every time he put me in front of a camera he called it a test. I've never seen *Invocation*, so I'm not sure all the stuff was used."

Unfortunately, Beausoleil's persistence in wanting to shoot all the time was driving Anger crazy. He told Beausoleil, "We can't go so fast. I don't have the money. I can't buy another twenty rolls of film to shoot this weekend at fifteen dollars a pop." Anger commented that "Bobby was fine except he wanted to dominate. He wanted to direct the film. He was always making too many suggestions."

In order to attract investors, Anger designed promotional items for the film. Beausoleil recalls that "the original *Lucifer Rising* poster was done by Rick Griffin, a famous San Francisco poster artist. It uses a Gustave Doré illustration of a figure of an eagle lifting a human. I don't know if the person is dead, passed out, or whatever, but the person is wrapped in a cloth and is being carried up into the sky by this eagle. It's like this angel character with sort of a legion of angels behind him. The art is all Egyptian—pillars on the side, stone columns, ancient Babylonian.

"Ken had put together a little package of pictures of me, the poster and some clips from some of the stuff that we shot. He put it in a gold box and put it in this little package to get some backing. Apparently it was successful, because he did have money all of a sudden again. He did have some German people—primarily that's what I was aware of—who were supplying funding for the project."

Underground film had become a new pop sensation—it was immediate, hip, and arty. On February 13, 1967, *Newsweek* published a who's who gallery of filmmakers and scene-makers called "Up From the Underground." Its author, Jack Kroll, had been sympathetic to the movement and offbeat films in particular. Stan Brakhage emerged as a mixture of Rasputin and Buster Brown, Kroll noting his "rock-hard integrity." Gregory Markopoulos was seen as a painter obsessed with narcissism. Peter Emmanuel Goldman's *Echoes of Silence* was lauded as an honest depiction of the emotional emptiness of casual sex in the New York City scene. The Kuchar brothers, George and Mike, were considered remarkable for the amazing number of no-budget, raunchy kitchen-sink comedies they turned out.

The *Newsweek* piece was not the first to pit Anger against Warhol as the leading underground filmmaker. Their movies were not abstractions like Brakhage's or Markopoulos's, making them more accessible to audiences and commercially viable. *Chelsea Girls* was grossing between $10,000 and $15,000 per week at the uptown Regency Theatre, located just a stone's throw from Lincoln Center. *Scorpio Rising* continued to be widely shown, with its run with *The Brig* at the Bleecker Street Cinema very successful.

Warhol and Anger, constantly linked in the press, had some things in common. Both men came from working-class backgrounds, making them feel socially inferior to the rich bourgeoisie who financed their projects. Their frank approach to taboo subject matter had broken new ground for screen freedom. Each man needed central male figures to inspire their work. Anger had his "sailors," "bikers," and "Lucifers." Warhol focused on hot/cold personalities such as Paul America of *My Hustler* and Joe Dallesandro of *Flesh* and *Trash*.

Warhol's task was an easy one. He was a sadistic voyeur, with director Paul Morrissey at his side, casting an unblinking cinema verité eye at the exhibitionistic masochists that formed his coterie.

Screaming Mimis like Viva, poseurs like Ultra Violet, goofs like Ingrid Superstar, and amphetamine sages like Ondine were theatrical neurotics for the camera. A parade of thankless assistants, including Chuck Wein and Ronald Tavel, did the scripting and directing while Warhol loaded the camera and took the applause.

For an underground filmmaker, Warhol had unlimited resources. The Factory, his studio, was a self-propelling publicity machine. Wealthy art collectors who admired his silkscreens literally threw money at him, affording yards of film. Factory superstars like Edie Sedgwick, Brigid Polk, and Viva emerged from the same social strata as his patrons: they were rich kids, slumming. Like the celebrity portraits he made a career doing, Warhol expressed his loathing for the rich by ridiculing them without their realizing it.

Although some may make a case for *Empire* and *Sleep* being minimalist art, at best these films are Dada jokes played on the audience. That audience antagonism also fueled Warhol's story films, even when they were at their most entertaining. Real-time boredom remained an earmark, whether it was in a *Chelsea Girls* sequence or the interminable toilet conversation that concluded *My Hustler*. Poor sound, random camera angles, out-of-focus shots—all stylistic aspects of underground film about which viewers had been forewarned—could be found in any Warhol production.

Anger, instead, romanced the audience. His movies were visually enticing, fast-moving, tight, coherent. Depending on one's frame of mind, they could be interpreted as love stories, erotica, documentaries, psychodramas, mini-spectacles, or mini-musicals. Anger was as resourceful as his hero Georges Méliès in creating total cinematic worlds that appeared far more expensive than their meager budgets allowed. Apart from using an occasional collaborator, Anger conceived, directed, photographed, edited, selected the music, and sometimes appeared in his own films. No harsh New York accents broke the mood. Anger was of the West Coast silent film school in which actors should be seen and not heard, like Valentino. He had to coax the performances out of his painstakingly selected cast members, not the opposite.

When Warhol's productions became more professionally executed, with scripts and direction by Paul Morrissey, movies like *Flesh* concerned themselves with imagining the daily life of a street hustler. Anger's films instead demonstrated why and how certain men were fantasy figures to voyeurs.

In the harsh light of reality, Andy Warhol lived to be famous. Anger remained the true staunch individualist who lived to carve his own legend out of his films.

No former Factory members today can recall a meeting between Warhol and Anger. Paul Morrissey feels that the animosity between them was a matter of professional jealousy on Anger's part. However, the enmity between Warhol and Anger would never cease. As Warhol ascended in social circles and his fame increased, Anger's bitter loathing of him grew proportionately.

Six days after the *Newsweek* piece Anger was interviewed by Elenore Lester in the prestigious Arts and Leisure section of the Sunday *New York Times*. He was singled out as an outstanding yet businesslike underground filmmaker. The popularity of leather jackets and biker accoutrements as a fashion statement was credited to *Scorpio Rising*. Anger said that he was "active in a small sect called Thelema," which had been founded by Aleister Crowley. Anger also expounded on the potential of LSD as a color intensifier, claiming to have experimented with it "under highly controlled conditions in Switzerland several years ago." At this time Anger was a member of a so-called Himalayan Academy with Timothy Leary. The piece ended by stating that Anger was a "magus filmmaker" who had ways of "hexing enemies." Again, it mentioned Warhol as responsible for the big underground commercial breakthrough with *Chelsea Girls*, although *Scorpio Rising* had been made five years prior to it.

Second- and third-generation exploitation film Xeroxes of *Scorpio Rising* via *The Wild Angels* appeared throughout the United States. These included such routine bike flicks as *The Wild Rebels*, *Outlaw Motorcycles*, *The Glory Stompers*, *Devil's Angels*, and *Hell's Angels on Wheels*.

At the Bleecker Street Cinema, site of *Scorpio Rising*'s triumphant run, *Fireworks* enjoyed a revival as a supporting featurette to *Deathwatch*, an obscure adaptation of the Jean Genet play about the sexual magnetism of men on death row. *Deathwatch* was made by a curious contingent of the Hollywood establishment: Vic Morrow directed, Leonard Nimoy played a petty thief, and Paul Mazursky portrayed a flaming queen behind bars.

A special evening was planned in response to the mindless hippie worship of acid-blasting Timothy Leary at the Human Be-In, by the Diggers, along with the Artists' Liberation Front, a radical contingent of Bay Area artists. It was to occur February 24, 1967, at the Glide Memorial Church, situated in the Tenderloin area of San Francisco. The Glide congregation consisted of the area's indigenous population: wandering speed freaks coming in for a bit of peace, hustlers and hookers of all sexes and persuasions, transvestites, and a very large homosexual contingent. Digger Emmett Grogan states in *Ringolevio* that the Glide Church was "maintaining a foundation which studied their [parishioners'] sexual habits and did statistical research in conjunction with the Kinsey Institute."

The event was dubbed the Invisible Circus and announced by a thousand tricolor handbills of a circus wagon promising "a 72-hour environmental community happening sponsored by the Diggers, Artists' Liberation Front, and Glide Church." Otherwise, it was a strictly free, word-of-mouth deal, with no moneymaking promoters involved. The Invisible Circus was intended to be a liberating event structured around permissiveness. Poets Lenore Kandel, Richard Brautigan, ComCo (the counterculture printing company), all the Diggers and all their women were involved. Each mini-group was assigned a church space in which to stage separate happenings within the overall theme.

The Orkustra would play (one of their last gigs). And one of the Kinsey Institute's volunteers in the field, Anger, was sure to be there.

One room was filled with shredded cellophane. Others were "lovemaking salons," draped with Indian carpets. An obscenity conference for community leaders turned into a Digger prank when Slim Minault flashed his family jewels behind the speakers through a crack in the door and poised them on a shelf. The exhibitionism grew more extreme when a couple commenced performing a live sex show, putting an abrupt end to the obscenity discussion. Topless belly dancers danced around them.

Boschian activity spread throughout the church. A blockheaded, narcissistic muscleman whacked off as couples balled on the altar. The Hell's Angels socked it to a woman dressed as a Carmelite nun. Hookers dragged johns in and did them in the pews. Drag queens did their wild thing in confessionals. ComCo's "John Dillinger Service" reports of what was happening in various rooms and on the streets were continually issued, even covering a melee in a nearby bar.

After about eight hours of this wild action, the church started to get damaged in a serious way. The freaks were dripping candle wax all over. A statue of Jesus was somehow bloodied. As it approached its ninth hour, the Glide Church officials felt enough was enough, and the Invisible Circus got its tent folded, its participants stumbling home at sunrise.

A month later, Anger appeared in the April 1967 issue of *Playboy*. Arthur Knight's excellent "Sex in the Cinema" series had focused on underground films. The visuals included a still of Anaïs Nin from *Pleasure Dome*, one of a bloodied Anger from *Fireworks*, and one of Bruce Byron lying on his cot in *Scorpio Rising*. Beausoleil was impressed, while Byron was furious. He was in *Playboy* and his name hadn't even been used under the photo. This made Byron convinced that people would think that the man in *Scorpio* was Anger, not him. Byron now felt that Anger had stolen not only his great performance, but also his very identity.

Anger continued to make films for private collectors. Beausoleil recalls that "every once in a while he'd do a little thing that wouldn't be for distribution. Like one time, he found a couple of boys. He dressed them up not in togas, but little blue loincloths. He did a film of them wrestling. He had this really nice bed in his room. He put the bed in an alcove and he used some blue cloth on the windows and blue cloth on the bed and it made kind of a stage effect, the way the light shone past the curtain, through the window. It was just really well done. He does have some style and some taste. That's about the only thing I've seen other than his regular films. I only saw it one time when he got the film back."

While Beausoleil enjoyed marijuana, he found that "Kenneth wasn't much into pot. Kenneth, when he was doing drugs, was into cocaine. Cocaine and LSD, an occasional LSD thing. I wouldn't see him for days at a time. He'd be gone. And I wasn't too aware of what was going on with him. This led to some of the difficulties which occurred later. We did take some LSD together a few times.

"He used to enjoy entertaining every so often with the help of LSD. He would drag out his memorabilia, like the bloody T-shirt that the teenage kid had died in in the car wreck. Stuff that would blow someone's mind who was under the influence of that particular drug. He was really good at that. In fact, I got pissed off one time because there was this real nice lady that he introduced me to, one of the Hollywood set, and he terrified this woman."

A noted female occultist had come up from L.A. with her daughter to visit Anger. "It started off really nice," recalls Beausoleil. "One of the things she said when all the lights came on and Ken's room started sparkling was, 'Up, just like Kenneth. Ringling Brothers and Barnum and Bailey. Oh, Kenneth's little production.' It gradually evolved into kind of a nasty scene. She was loaded on LSD. He dragged out his death memorabilia and went on this thing about Leni Riefenstahl. There was some secret thing that she and he knew that I was not privy to—but, so were a lot of the things that were going on at the time. He was standing there in this bloody T-shirt. He's wearing that thing.

"I just got fed up with it because you don't drag someone all through San Francisco to do a psychological terrorizing. I didn't want to support it, so I left the room. I let him know I was real disgusted with him over it, and she really appreciated that. She came and told me later that it was okay. I didn't appreciate it. I didn't think it was cool."

Anger continued filming, photographing the Magick Powerhouse of Oz walking downstairs. Beausoleil says, "That was more at my instigation. I was getting impatient. I was sayin', 'When are we gonna do some filming, Ken?' So he set this thing up with the band. He gave us a bunch of costumes and said, 'Walk down the stairs.' He had these little things that you would never know where he was coming from. He had this little genie, a little doll, maybe two and a half feet tall. It was just one of his little artifacts that he had in the house. He put this smelly smoke stuff all over it and came down the stairs, moving it down stop motion."

In *Invocation of My Demon Brother* Anger appears as if he's rolling down the steps on a wheelchair. Beausoleil explains that "he was just holding the doll while taking a step down. You can't see that from the smoke, like some smoky character, but you know it was dramatic things. It was just one of those things that happened as a by-product of whatever he was doing.

"I was there while we were shooting Anton LaVey opening a door. He does have that look, the bald thing, the cap with the plastic horns on it—that's why I call him the plastic devil.

"Kenneth introduced me to LaVey with 'Here's LUCIFER.' There's such a contrast between him and me because I'm not putting out any of this devil shit to begin with. I always knew I was a presence. What comes naturally to me was like plastic horns to him and it's like, Jesus!"

A bald man in a black leather jacket and turtleneck, Anton LaVey, born Howard Levey, was as adept as Anger in re-creating himself. He had formerly been a carny man, calliope player (with his toes, yet), and a police shutterbug. LaVey's love of trashy histrionics, enjoyment of exploitation movies, and reverence for figures like Cagliostro and Rasputin as master con artists fed his new persona.

Devil worship at this point in the sixties was an excuse for exhibitionistic behavior and kinky sex. LaVey transformed his black Victorian house on 1161 California Street into a safe haven for an *All the Loving Couples*–era psychodrama. His denunciations of drugs, antihippie rants, and pro-police yammerings were reassuring to his middle-class constituency. LaVey's Church of Satan ground out a for-the-masses distillation of centuries of mystical thought. He used concepts from such committed albeit troubled occultists as Eliphas Levi, J. K. Huysmans, and Aleister Crowley, reducing their philosophies to advice for the lovelorn.

Despite their major philosophical differences on Aleister Crowley and drugs, Anger and LaVey hooked up through the occult network. Beausoleil comments, "I think they liked the idea of having each other in their lives as sort of a symbol or representative of something, like, 'Hey, I know this weird guy.' But I didn't get the impression they were really that close."

Anger joined LaVey's Magick Circle, an offbeat coffee klatch that would meet to discuss black theosophy. Another early member was their mutual pal, fanzine publisher Forrest J. Ackerman, whom they affectionately referred to as 4E, a clipped form of the nickname "Forry." Curiously, 4E had been L. Ron Hubbard's literary agent when Hubbard was a known but struggling sci-fi writer and had even been one of the first Dianetics auditing guinea pigs. Together, these mismatched characters could feed their trash culture fetishes and enhance one another's myths. Besides being a mutual admiration society, the Magick Circle was a good meeting place to swap tricks of the trade.

Both Anger and LaVey existed in a fringe sexploitation area. Anger's films had become adult house fare. LaVey was familiar with fifties-style Betty Page dominance/submission mentality, and he appeared in nudie spreads for second-string men's mags. Nude "witches" were presented on altars before him as he attempted to turn his portly frame into a badass daddy sex symbol, his bald dome capped by plastic horns. While he regarded LSD as a mind rotter, hippies certainly got naked easily enough for LaVey's purposes. One stripper witch who emerged nude from a coffin was Susan Atkins, a major participant in the Manson murders.

Beausoleil remains steadfast in his feelings toward Anton: "I thought he was a fuckin' jerk, with his black church, with his black house in San Francisco. That's my sentiment."

On September 21, 1967, Beausoleil and Anger presented an Equinox of the Gods event to celebrate the pagan holiday of Autumn Equinox. For a fee one could see the Magick Powerhouse of Oz play and witness Anger going through wild, magickal gyrations.

Beausoleil states that "Kenneth came into the project at the last minute, like two or three days before we were going to do this. All of a sudden he gets involved and wants to help out.

"He brought a few props, had some things made with the symbol of Oz, which was the symbol for the band, like false things covered with ribbons in the shape of Oz, the Z in the center of the

O. He was going to do an Equinox presentation, sort of, ushering in the Aquarian Age, and do a ritual. That was his plan.

"The night that we were doing it—the night of the celebration, performance, whatever you want to call it—Kenneth takes acid. Here we are, in the middle of our thing, and the band comes out. After the band was playing, Kenneth put on his own presentation. It was all cued to a tape he had put together that day, a reading of stuff from his books. He had the tape slowed down or recorded at a speed so that he wouldn't sound quite so effeminate. I guess he didn't like his own voice.

"He was doing dance motions in one of these robes. He had a gold lamé robe he'd actually made for me in the film. He had his eyes done up in the style of the Egyptians, the eyes of Ra. He was doing this sort of pantomime dance movement to the tape he had made. He was loaded on acid.

"The audiotape broke. He went berserk. He was freaking out. I mean, he just—POOF! His whole plan kind of just went out the window and just turned into a fiasco. There was a walking stick I always used. It was a cane I had found in a junk store, but Kenneth had it as a prop for this thing, using it as a wand or something. Flailing it around, he broke it in half. So he picks up both pieces and he throws them into the audience screaming, 'I LOVE YOU!' Ben Van Meter got hit in the forehead with one of those pieces. A quartz or one of his studio lights was trained on the scrim, it fell over and shattered into clouds of smoke.

"It was a disaster. The band went on again, we did a few more things with the gong and tried to smooth things out, but Kenneth was berserk and there really wasn't much to do to save it. Here we are at the end of this thing. Kenneth was coming down. He wants to put a Band-Aid on everything. He wants to smooth it over. He writes these huge checks to the Straight Theater. I don't know if they were ever cashed or not. Everybody, of course, was kind of embarrassed for him, including myself, of course.

"Naturally, I got the blame in Kenneth's viewpoint. He started coming up with these reasons why I was not suitable for the film. It just got ridiculous. The next step was our falling out.

"The next day after the Equinox event, I went back to the Russian

Embassy to get my stuff. Either to talk to Kenneth or to get things straightened out or to leave. He was gone. I didn't know where the hell he'd gone. But he had come back long enough to do this little ritual. He put sheets all over everything. I didn't know what it was. Obviously some sort of purging thing, considering the white.

"I had this incredibly odd vehicle. It was a Studebaker cut in half with like a log cabin built on the back. It looked like half a spaceship and half outhouse. The purchase of the vehicle was not very much, about $400 or something. That was my payment from Kenneth. The vehicle was in my name. I went to pick it up. He had stripped the thing. He's got it all in the ballroom where I lived and it's all locked up. I could see through the window, like it was some sort of purging, like he's purging himself of me. He had my vehicle's battery up on an altar.

"My response to that was—you know, the lock on the door wasn't very substantial—so I broke through the double door into the room. I went in and got my battery from the vehicle so I could make it run. I got my instruments. I loaded it up and then I split."

Anger commenced his "I was robbed" mantra. He complained to the underground newspaper the *Berkeley Barb* that there had been a rip-off at the Straight Theater and that original *Lucifer Rising* footage, along with props and tapes for the film, were gone. Anger believed the thief was seeking "dirty" footage because of the nudity in the film. A handmade twelve-string guitar and a flute used by Straight Theater musicians were also supposedly missing. Anger went on to say that the Russian Embassy had been burgled two days later. His $1,200 Kodak Cine Special camera had vanished. He believed it to be a personal vendetta. Beausoleil's name, however, was not yet mentioned.

Like in the Old West, Anger posted a list of rewards in the *Berkeley Barb*:

$100 for the return of the film
$50 for the return of the tapes
$25 for the return of the props

Anger offered a no-questions-asked situation. If these materials were dropped off at the paper's office at 2886 Telegraph Avenue in

Berkeley, he vowed to leave the reward money there the following day.

It was a nice bit of publicity for Anger, but then things got vindictive. Attempting to reduce Beausoleil to a common hustler, Anger began bellowing that Beausoleil had stolen the *Lucifer Rising* footage and robbed him. Beausoleil maintains that it "never happened. Never happened! What had happened was that Kenneth had spent all the money that was invested in *Lucifer Rising*. He told his creditors that I had stolen the movie.

"I came to find out later he swore out a burglary warrant on me. He did one other thing that did cause me some trouble later on. I hadn't ever signed up for the draft, but I never suspected that he would turn me into the FBI, which is what he did."

In October 1967 Anger participated in the massive March on the Pentagon. Other participants included various Diggers, Yippies led by Abbie Hoffman, and author/tough guy Norman Mailer. These groups intended to make the Pentagon levitate in protest of the Vietnam War. Well, Anger might have, but the others subscribed to the Theater of the Absurd. Anger and Mailer had a shouting match during it.

The night of the march, Anger stood on the Diggers' flatbed truck, screamed "OUT DEMONS OUT," set a pentagram aflame, and hissed and waved magic rings at reporters. A fresh tattoo of LUCIFER flamboyantly scrolled from nipple to nipple was proudly flashed for photographers.

The next time Anger turned up publicly he was dead. A full-page ad appeared in the October 26, 1967, issue of the *Village Voice*:

IN MEMORIUM
KENNETH ANGER
FILMMAKER 1947–1967

Announcements of Anger's death had been sent to various individuals. According to Parker Tyler, Anger admitted to certain acquaintances that it was a publicity stunt to protest the limited financing available to independent filmmakers; after all, the years listed in the ad simply covered his work as a public artist. It was also a jape in the style of Aleister Crowley, who faked his own death to drum up interest in his first painting exhibition.

To further his publicity streak, Anger arrived at the New York City office of the Film-Makers' Cooperative at 175 Lexington Avenue. He burned dozens of films, claiming they were early works like *Ferdinand the Bull*, which had never reached the eyes of the general public.

Anger returned to San Francisco for a final spectacle, which was arranged by Anton LaVey. LaVey was conducting the first public satanic funeral for a sailor parishioner. Anger was more than happy to once again mock the United States Navy.

The photo of the event shows an appropriately somber group. LaVey is the goateed priest standing next to the widow, reading from a book. The open casket has an American flag draped over it. Choir-robed participants stand at attention. Anger, clad in a black robe draped over a white shirt and dark tie, is the "warlock" billed at the center of the photo. Anger appears convincingly stern and formal.

Anger had been hanging tough in the Bay Area for almost four years now. He had been a spectacular scenemaker on several levels—prominent occultist, LSD proselytizer, sexual libertine, vanguard filmmaker. But now he was becoming unglued. His days in San Francisco were growing numbered, and he felt it. Anger turned to Stan Brakhage for help. Even though he was younger than Anger, Brakhage always offered his friend an oasis of compassion, stability, and maturity. Anger didn't feel he had to keep up a big front with Brakhage. He could return to being Kenneth Anglemyer and try to understand himself again. When spending time with Brakhage, he was the epitome of gentleness, a man who'd help an insect cross a road, yet he espoused a bitter pessimism about the human animal.

Brakhage hadn't heard from Anger for some time. He eventually found Anger in the hospital, receiving treatment for exhaustion. Anger seemed desperate to flee San Francisco and begged Brakhage to permit him to visit him again in Colorado. Brakhage was understandably a little nervous in light of the police visit over Anger's "doctor" film the last time Anger visited.

This particular stay would become, in Brakhage's view, an even more terrifying time than the last. Before Anger was about to show up, Brakhage checked his post office box, as was his routine. Greeting him at the post office was what Brakhage described as a big, scary, leather-clad biker. The biker directed Brakhage to bring Anger to the post office immediately after he arrived. Brakhage replied that he wasn't Anger's keeper, but if Anger wanted to see him, he'd bring him. Brakhage asked who the biker was. "You bring him here, because we know where your house is" was the response. Anger was eventually brought to meet this terrifying biker and nothing came of it. Brakhage personally felt strongly that it all had to do with the missing *Lucifer* footage, and that the biker was an emissary from Beausoleil.

It was unlikely, however, that Beausoleil knew Anger's whereabouts, much less cared. He had moved on to new friends, a new lifestyle, and new activities, none of which included Anger. Beausoleil had moved to Topanga Canyon.

Chapter 11

The Mad Hatter

You see what gloomy thoughts a fellow can have, even when he's Fortune's pet.

ALEISTER CROWLEY
DIARY OF A DRUG FIEND

by 1968 San Francisco had deteriorated from the not so idyllic Summer of Love into a speed-freak nightmare. With Beausoleil out of the house and the hate-filled vibes seeping all over the city, Anger had to leave town. He made a pilgrimage to England, Crowley's homeland. It was as much a business trip as a spiritual adventure. Like his idol, Anger was about to take up the obscure occupation of fixing heads.

The mod London of 1968 held a plethora of potential investors for Anger who were in desperate need of having their heads fixed. Wealthy, troubled, addicted rock stars and jaded billionaire socialites with their heads into hard drugs and mysticism wielded a huge influence over their peers, but their personal problems, fueled by intense lives consumed by work, left them vulnerable to a higher power.

This London crowd was into Crowley and Anger could offer astounding knowledge that would stun any interested party. His association with notables such as Marjorie Cameron and Jack Parsons added to his myth. Why, he had even made the pilgrimage to Thelema Abbey with Dr. Kinsey himself!

Anger had used mind-altering chemicals long before they were illegal, having gone the introspective route like astral pioneers Aldous Huxley and Crowley. Being a well-schooled student of human nature, Anger was an expert in the effects of certain drugs on different personalities. Anger himself came off as an acid man, with a splash of coke for intensity. Junkies, in the security of their nod, could block out virtually anything. Acid fanciers, especially with the extra lift-off of a stimulant, could get easily spooked. Both acid and cocaine (and/or speed) are central nervous system stimulants, and combining them is like throwing gasoline on the user's mental bonfire. LSD magnifies the paranoia inherent in the stimulant, while the stimulant exacerbates the acid hallucinations. On the other hand, an experienced tripper who enjoys such a ride is a unique, unstoppable force with which to be reckoned.

In a San Francisco speedball—a mixture of heroin, cocaine, and LSD—the user's id runs rampant, violently excited by the acid and the stimulants, which add a multidimensional level to the free association provided by the heroin. Acid will always win out over heroin in the user's pupils, which remain enlarged instead of pinned. The heroin will also smooth the inevitable crash and eventually will lull the tripper into a nod, followed by exhausted sleep.

There has always been speculation about Anger's use of heroin. He did say that Denham Fouts, a known opium addict, "first turned me on." Crowley, his lifetime icon, had been perpetually addicted to various opiates. However, no one has ever claimed to have witnessed Anger using heroin.

Whatever the particulars were of his intake, Anger possessed a tremendous understanding of the myriad ways heroin, speed, cocaine, and hallucinogens, and the various combinations thereof, can connect with various individuals. London was a head's paradise, fertile ground for an alchemist. In this extreme universe, Anger's Mad Hatter was about to escort their Satanic Majesties to a tea party they would never forget.

Mick Jagger and Keith Richards of the Rolling Stones formed the Glimmer Twins—the Pucks of rock. They had been busted repeatedly for drugs. Both men were involved with decadent women, Marianne Faithfull and Anita Pallenberg.

As he had done as a young man in Hollywood, Anger played social butterfly through the art gallery scene. He hooked into a seriously moneyed, exclusive, cocaine- and heroin-addicted social circle through Robert Frazier and his Indica Gallery in the fashionable Mayfair district. Frazier himself was a drug imbiber and hapless gambler, but epitomized mod cool. (He would later die of AIDS.)

Spinning around the Frazier orbit, Anger met such individuals as J. Paul Getty, Jr., who would become one of the biggest jewels in his magician's crown. Getty's life was shocking. A documented dope addict and lover of excess, his second wife, Talitha Pol, O.D.'d on smack while trying to extricate herself from this scene. Like Anger, Getty had experienced heartbreaking estrangement from a cold father his entire life, the kind no amount of money could numb. However, Getty shared with his father an interest in the arts and the money to patronize them. Although a physical and mental wreck, J. Paul Getty, Jr., was renown for his largesse. He was a contact that would enrich Anger's life evermore.

The Rolling Stones were also in this social circle. It was at Frazier's apartment that Anger would become acquainted with the head Stone. With *Performance* and *Ned Kelly* on the horizon, Jagger was seriously branching into movies, and he was very impressed with Anger's reputation as an avant-garde master of film. Jagger found Anger a rapturous storyteller and cultured about literature, mythology, and the occult, especially Crowley. Ever the shrewd businessman, Jagger knew occultism would be a big marketing technique at the decade's apocalyptic end. With the Vietnam War and the world in the lopsided situation it was, Christianity offered little comfort. Jagger, especially with the aid of cocaine, could play omnipotent devil's advocate for the disenfranchised and the young. Anger asserts that the song "Sympathy for the Devil" arose out of discussions he had with Jagger about Lucifer.

To build his mystique in London, Anger pulled some flashy tricks, playing on everyone's acid paranoia and coke nerves. Frazier had a party for John and Yoko's "white exhibition" at the Indica Gallery. Everyone dressed in white and the guests partook of a hallucinatory white punch. Spaced-out celebrities tried to reach out and touch Anger. He'd drift farther and farther away. Later, he'd just laugh, claiming to have been on a business trip in Germany and not present at the party at all.

Anger later sent Frazier a razor blade in a letter that stated it was the cure for Frazier's stuttering problem. It seemed the most sadistic of practical jokes, but it also represented Anger's unique if cynically expressed pragmatism—is the stuttering really worth killing yourself over? There was also the Crowleyan aspect of attempting to initiate Frazier into Crowley's warped, ego-shattering behavior modification exercise in which cutting one's arm each time an undesirable word or phrase is uttered might cure the ill.

Anger loved the attention. It was clear to him that these people wanted to believe he was capable of magick.

Surrounded by this whirlwind of money, names, and high-intensity action, Anger was itching to resume production on *Lucifer Rising*. The movie was no longer to depict the California love scene but was to be his first intercontinental spectacular.

Although he was dealing with a much more sophisticated crowd,

Anger was using the same casting technique he had employed to find Bruce Byron and Bobby Beausoleil, blatantly appealing to narcissism. He provided the opportunity to live out their god/goddess power trip fantasies. Anger convinced the rock stars that only they had the special *elemental* quality to incarnate the occult deities they would portray.

Anger was attempting to seduce Jagger into playing the role of Lucifer. It was an image Jagger was leaning heavily toward already—he thought it could be utilized well for the stage. Anger also became quite friendly with Jagger's girlfriend Marianne Faithfull, who was still in the honeymoon period of her opiate addiction.

Jagger was both intrigued by Anger as well as a little paranoid about him. Anger was aware, as he put it, that "Mick is a terrific skeptic, but one percent of him is superstitious."

In late 1968 America, Anger's movies were creating a phenomenon and having a sexual impact which caused the kind of attention that he neither welcomed nor wanted. Homosexual pornographic cinema was beginning to crawl. Pat Rocco, a gentle Hollywood resident and showbiz veteran, had been making relatively low-key movies of nude young men. Rocco stated that "I tended to take a very positive point of view in the story line in that everything was OK. It just had to be done honestly." Rocco's shorts were packaged together and presented at the Park Theater in Los Angeles, which was the first to put "gay films" on the marquee. His films also had suggestive advertising calling attention to their specific appeal. All this would not have been possible without *Scorpio Rising*'s legal triumph in establishing a precedent in showing male nudity and homosexual behavior in public theaters.

In New York City, Murray Offen a.k.a. Murray Offer a.k.a. Maury Maura a.k.a. Mr. Murray (depending on who was doing the asking) had success booking Andy Warhol's homosexual-themed *My Hustler* in July 1967 at his Hudson Theater in Times Square. Seeing that the more explicit underground fare could be palatable to the sexploitation crowd, and buoyed by Pat Rocco's example in L.A., Murray opened the Park-Miller Theater on Forty-third Street between Sixth Avenue and Broadway. This three-balcony ancient theatrical palace became the first and most venerable of Manhattan's all-male theaters.

Warhol didn't mind this type of attention. To him, it was both a giggle and an opportunity for his films to play in a commercial venue, thus overstepping the penniless underground quagmire controlled by Mekas. It added to his sensationalism without hurting his legitimacy. He was so well established that he had no fear of having the revered title of artist revoked.

Anger was far from being in the same financial league as Warhol, and he was actively wooing mainstream patrons. He didn't want to play up the pornographic aspects of his work. Anger did not want to be designated as a pornographer with these new, open theatrical venues who wouldn't have a problem playing his films. He was fearful that it would rock the boat when he was at such a major turning point.

Anger successfully continued his mind-play with the Stones. He claimed that "the occult unit within the Stones was Keith and Anita and Brian. I believe that Anita is, for want of a better word, a witch." Richards told *Rolling Stone* magazine that "Kenneth Anger told me I was his right-hand man," echoing sentiments that Dennis Wilson expressed at the same time about Charles Manson, whom he called "the wizard." Richards said, "There are people who think we are acting as unknown agents of Lucifer and others who think we are Lucifer. Everybody's Lucifer."

Richards was saddled with his paranoiac drug addict girlfriend, Anita Pallenberg. Anger played on her uncertain place in the Stones contingent and her coke-induced phobias. Pallenberg could be pretty dominant but could also be on the next plane out at any minute, just a bad memory of excess herself. She needed Anger and his help. This culminated in her traipsing about with garlic to stop enemies whom Anger had warned her might send vampires to attack her.

Anger's Cagliostro status among the Stones is reinforced by Tony Sanchez, author of *Up and Down with the Rolling Stones*. Sanchez was Richards's drug supplier and confidant, and no one knows you better than your dealer. Sanchez saw through Anger's magick tricks and was banished from Anger's presence. The hostility rose to the point that when Anger would arrive at the Richards estate, Redlands, Sanchez would get lost, Richards would nod out, and Pallenberg would rapturously host him, in total awe of his magickal prowess. For a short time Anger actually installed himself at Redlands. His main activity seemed to be swathing himself in psychedelic scarfs and doing funky dances by moonlight.

Anger could really roar in a Merry Pranksters manner. He went to a coffee house with Sanchez and Frazier, deliberately standing next to Sanchez, knowing just how uneasy he made him. Anger graciously ordered everyone's coffees, then, in a blink of an eye, vanished.

The last big trick that Anger pulled on Richards involved the gold door. Pallenberg talked with Anger about her desire to marry Richards. Anger suggested a *real* pagan wedding. He explained the formalities: "The door of the house where the marriage ceremony is to be held must be painted with gold with a magical paint containing special herbs, which represent the sun." Pallenberg was all for it; Richards, the typical junkie, was noncommittal.

Anger left for the evening. The Richards household fell out for another night's doped doze.

The next morning, the heavy wooden door was painted gold on the interior side, awaiting the ceremony. How was it unlocked to be painted? It must have been taken off the hinges. Pallenberg feigned hysterical amazement. "It must be another of Kenneth's powers! It means he can fly into the house anytime he wants to."

But the plan backfired. Richards wasn't about to be pushed into any marriage, and responded in smackhead stubbornness, "I don't want to go through with any black magic wedding. This thing has gone far enough." He seemed most annoyed that while he was passed out someone had penetrated the security system he'd paid so much for.

Pallenberg continued to follow Anger's bizarre beliefs. Sanchez came upon a trunk that he assumed held her drug stash; instead he was horrified and revolted to discover dead animal parts and wrinkled skin.

On July 2, 1969, Brian Jones died. Three days later, perhaps to assuage their guilty consciences over humiliating Jones so badly at the end of his life, Jagger held a free Stones concert in London's Hyde Park. In a peculiar attempt at a eulogy, Jagger recited Shelley. Sanchez's opinion of Jagger's poetry reading was "clumsy, heartless, and awkward."

The finale involved the opening of cardboard boxes packed with white butterflies, which because of the summer heat were mostly dead. Instead of soaring to the heavens in a symbolic representation of Jones's soul, the dead insects showered on tearful fans. To make matters worse, the English Hell's Angels were stomping the enormous crowd.

Anger was at the event filming. Glimpses of it would be seen in his next work, *Invocation of My Demon Brother*.

Chapter 12

Invocations

Enough has now been said to show that the bloody sacrifice has from time immemorial been the most considered part of Magick. The ethics of the thing appear to have concerned no one; nor, to tell the truth, need they do so.

ALEISTER CROWLEY
"OF THE BLOODY SACRIFICE: AND MATTERS COGNATE,"
MAGICK IN THEORY AND PRACTICE

When the police discovered the body of Gary Hinman, it had been rotting for days.

While Anger had been acquainting himself with the Stones, the heavy dragon tail end of the sixties had snapped at Beausoleil. After the break with Anger, the only movie work he could find had been in *Ramrodder*, a soft-core sexploitation western. He began drifting around with members of the sex and drug trade. Unfortunately, he also associated with a confused ex-con with a messianic bent, Charlie Manson.

Beausoleil would be accused of a sadist's crime. He demanded money from the victim, Gary Hinman. When Hinman refused to turn over the bread, a torture slaying ensued with other Manson organization members present. Hinman writhed in pain for days and was finally stabbed to death. Psychobabble written in the victim's blood on the wall meant, according to Beausoleil, "absolutely nothing."

Several days after the murder occurred, Beausoleil was found nodded out in Hinman's Fiat. Police officers woke him and Beausoleil presented them with an ID stating his name as Jason Lee Daniels, a stolen credit card, and a business card from his pregnant teenage girlfriend's parents' ranch. The police found the incriminating bowie knife in the tire well. Beausoleil's life on the outside ended on August 5, 1969.

In London, Anger was shocked to hear the news, but Beausoleil's arrest bolstered the myth that Anger possessed certain paranormal abilities. According to Tony Sanchez, the general consensus was that somehow Anger drove Beausoleil to do it, which served to make Anger more perversely fascinating to the Stones.

Jagger had previously agreed to help Anger execute *Lucifer Rising*. He composed music for the film, an eleven-minute improvisation on his newly acquired Moog synthesizer. At the center of a professional and personal maelstrom, Jagger was doing some of his best work, such as the *Let It Bleed* album, and Anger had tapped him at the right moment. Anger remarked that "he was great. He did it for me in one night; we just climbed on the same wavelength."

Instead of being used for the proposed *Lucifer Rising*, the music provided the soundtrack for *Invocation of My Demon Brother*. Anger rapidly assembled this film out of his San Francisco fragments, most of which pivoted on Beausoleil. *Invocation of My Demon Brother* is a terroristic mosaic. The amount and degree of superimpositions are so highly developed that the images hammer at the viewer's subconscious with machine-gun rapidity. Jagger's score draws the viewer into the hypnosis of the visuals, letting the viewer know that the sonic patterns will stay constant for the entire ride. The film opens with the geometric pattern of three circles forming a pyramid, like such:

O

O   O

Images are credited to Kenneth Anger, the sound to Mick Jagger.

A blue-black painting of Horus, the Crowned and Conquering Child of the New Aeon, appears. An albino, his eyes darting back and forth with the rapidity of a peak LSD experience, is shown in front of two stars. A nude male, his face and genitals obscured by shadows, raises a knife.

The albino's head turns. What he sees, through montage, is one of Anger's loops, a pan of three naked boys. The albino's head turns the opposite way and the camera now pans over the nude boys in the reverse direction. One boy touches another whose penis is visible; he leans back and shakes his head.

There is a flash of an occult tattoo. The albino raises a clear wand. Somebody is being hanged, his jeans and biker boots visible against a blood-red background. An overwashed, reddish shot of soldiers getting off a helicopter to invade Vietnam appears; Anger claims that this footage is looped throughout the entire film and is visible through infrared glasses.

Anger's forearm tattoo of the Seal of Solomon, an occult symbol associated with Crowley and Eliphas Levi, is superimposed over the albino and the eye of Ra. Close-up of the albino's eyes. A nude Bobby Beausoleil holds a statue of Horus in one hand and a knife in the other. His arms are folded as Osiris risen, like the photo of Crowley in his Golden Dawn days.

Beausoleil is then seen smoking a joint through a skull pipe with marble eyes, the joint heating to red. He's wearing his top hat, sports a sparse upper-lip mustache, and has some large rings on and filthy fingernails. Beausoleil passes the pipe to Lenore Kandel, author of the banned sadomasochistic ode, "Poem for Perverts." She passes it to a strong-profiled, Valentinoesque man. The scene harks back to *Inauguration of the Pleasure Dome*, in which a sacrament is being shared. However, while that film was a novice's homage to his elders, Anger is now depicting the initiation of a younger generation into the occult scene.

A Siamese cat reaches for a candle on a small altar where tiny idols sit. Bobby's dog Snofox lies before the altar. Anger suddenly appears as the Magus, dressed in ritualistic red robes and standing against a black background with a psychedelic light show swirling all over him. Anger runs around a magic circle before an audience. This particular footage was shot by Ben Van Meter and is slightly speeded up. Anger's eyes are painted to emulate the eye of Ra, his arms are outstretched, he looks back and forth, points a wand at the audience, and generally appears hyper. Suddenly, he charges into the audience and grabs a little boy.

Cut to a white cat in close-up, possibly a stuffed animal, followed by a still of Anger sitting thronelike surrounded by a few of his primary influences: a ten-cent comic book called *Black*, Aleister Crowley's novel *Moonchild*, and a small, ornate black and gold box. Pan up Anger's bare feet with red flair pants, his open shirt revealing his bare chest. He looks as if he's casting a spell or attempting to receive an astral message.

Another cat is glimpsed for a second. Fast motion whirs as Anger paces a magic circle. A tattoo of a spider leads into the multiple superimpositions that are the unique, distinctive aspect of the film. Beausoleil is visualized as an arachnoid, with his top and bottom mirror images merging into one being.

A man peeks through vegetation again, with a mustachioed, glitter-faced man then appearing. A tarot card of an executioner follows. Anger goes about his magic circle. Saturn is projected on Beausoleil's bare chest.

Anger appears to be freaking out, clutching an Egyptian totem. A kaleidoscope shot of Beausoleil reveals his face, smiling, with glowing eyes. A door is opened to reveal the plastic devil, Anton LaVey, who proceeds with some theatrics. He parts his cape à la Bela Lugosi, holds it up to look threatening, with a skull at crotch level. Cut back to the Beausoleil kaleidoscope. Superimposed over LaVey are British Hell's Angels from the Stones' Hyde Park concert. The composition centers the bike boys on a skull, as if LaVey is presiding.

Anger looks even more hyper in fast motion, showing a piece of paper he burns. A dead cat then bursts into flames. Swirls are overlaid within swirls, with fire predominating. Superimposed over the fire is the back of a kid's jacket with the logo HELL'S ANGELS. Anger's eye of Ra is on the right with a glassy-eyed longhaired guy on the left; the shot lingers. A sex magick ritual featuring some nude supporting cast members is then seen.

Anger is in mid-scream. There's a close-up of a bearded, horned satyr malevolently grinning. Anger ritualistically drapes a swastika flag during a ritual. A light show appears on Beausoleil's chest centering on a large psychedelic swastika. Superimposed over eyes are body parts: a face, a cock, an asshole. A sea of people all with Beausoleil's face is then kaleidoscopically overlaid, followed by the recurrent footage of soldiers getting off the helicopter. The eye in the triangle, a Jungian and Crowley symbol, appears. The soldiers continue invading. Anger flails a swastika flag as a longhaired human does a counterstep. The eye in the triangle presides.

The two boys from the opening scene are now plainly naked. On Anger's arm two tattoos are glimpsed, the Seal of Solomon and Crowley's sigil of solar-phallic power—three concentric circles forming a penile figure with 666 at its center. The albino appears, upside down, peering through Anger's arms. The nude boys wrestle in multiple superimposition, metamorphosing into a tangle of legs.

Under colored gel slides, Beausoleil is wearing his top hat. Angel wings attached to him vaguely flutter; he turns and smiles. The Magick Powerhouse of Oz, hooded, comes down the Russian Embassy stairs. Kandel holds a fishbowl. A playing card of a top hat is intercut before Beausoleil, who's playing a trumpet, clad in a white outfit with cream white leather pants, sporting a huge basket.

Jagger appears pointing to various fans at the Stones' Hyde Park concert. Beausoleil walks down the Russian Embassy stairs, as the image of a nude man and woman engaged in sex magick is superimposed. Beausoleil is before the eye of Ra. Superimpositions of him with closed and open eyes follow, leading into a circular kaleidoscope of Beausoleils. The Beausoleils get closer and smile malevolently.

Anger continues his ritual. Beausoleil is then shown in strutting hustler poses: side view, front view, with light patterns playing on his face. Fade into Jagger holding a child with Beausoleil's eyes a lingering superimposition. Cut to Beausoleil. Beausoleil superimposed over Keith Richards. Beausoleil. Anita Pallenberg. A pentagram.

Anger rolls down a flight of stairs in a puff of smoke to reveal a voodoo doll holding a sign, ZAP YOU'RE PREGNANT—THAT'S WITCHCRAFT. The ever-presiding eye in the triangle appears over a pentagram.

Beausoleil appears with his arms in the air surrounded by black with swirls of light. He brings his arms together and then releases them, like Mickey Rooney's Puck in *A Midsummer Night's Dream*.

The geometric pattern of the three circles forming a pyramid is inverted on red, as such:

The film ends. Everything has come full circle.

Invocation of My Demon Brother is a far cry from the rollercoaster pop satire of *Scorpio Rising*, with its carefully constructed macho fakes. Masculine aggression is the leitmotif in *Invocation*, as manifested by its recurrent images of soldiers, Hell's Angels, intent occultists, Beausoleil, and the film's manic creator.

The film could virtually be subtitled in Crowley's style "The San Francisco Working," for it offers a startlingly upfront look at

Anger's attempt to put Thelemic theory into practice during his stay at the Russian Embassy. In eleven concise minutes it encapsulates Anger's association with the Stones, Beausoleil, and Crowley, while also providing a concentrated summation of the climax of a tumultuous decade. Out of all of Anger's films, *Invocation of My Demon Brother* builds to the most red-hot intensity.

In August 1969 *Invocation* was enthusiastically received on the underground film circuit in the United States. Since his death as a filmmaker announcement had appeared in the *Village Voice* almost two years prior, everyone was eager to see a new Anger film. The movie delivered his promise, reaffirming Anger as one of the underground talents who truly mattered.

The Elgin Theater, located on Eighteenth Street and Eighth Avenue in the Chelsea section of New York, ran *Invocation* as a midnight movie in September 1969 with George Kuchar's *Encyclopedia of the Blessed* and George Landow's *Institutional Quality*. The Elgin's midnight showings, initiated with underground films like these and growing to encompass unusual old classics like *Freaks*, would jump-start the phenomenon of cult movies. Two years later Alejandro Jodorowsky's *El Topo* would have a marathon midnight run at the Elgin.

The biker genre that had its origins in *Scorpio Rising* got its biggest mainstream boost in respectability from Dennis Hopper's *Easy Rider*, widely regarded as a counterculture statement. Anger was quick to point out that Hopper had imitated his lead and the cinematic techniques of *Scorpio Rising*. However, he was being slightly egotistical. Hopper states that "I've never been influenced by him. I'm not saying this is better, I'm just saying I'm much more stylized and much more normalized in my use of camera. I'm pretty old-fashioned in the way I shoot my films, with the exception of the editing. Ken uses a lot of superimpositions. I don't use any. I direct-cut everything."

Hopper was not denying underground influences, having spent time with Bruce Conner, who was a master at swirling found footage around a central thematic thrust, as exemplified by his classic *Cosmic Ray*. "I was much more influenced by Bruce Conner. When I got toward the end of the film, I started back cutting, like in

Conner's film about the Kennedy assassination; when she's going to open the door, but it's back cutting, so Jackie Kennedy's getting farther away from the hands of the door that she's reaching for. I used that kind of editing when I was doing the ride toward the end of the movie. When we were going across the bridge, we were actually getting farther and farther in getting to the other end than when we were progressing."

Martin Scorsese, on the other hand, openly embraced the influence of Anger in his first feature film, *Who's That Knocking at My Door?* The film utilized editing methodology developed in *Scorpio Rising*, as well as the use of pop songs as a running commentary on the action. Much the way Anger studied Bruce Byron's antisocial patterns in *Scorpio Rising*, Scorsese's film examined the religious and sexual hangups and aimless lifestyle of a young man from New York's Little Italy (Harvey Keitel). As was often the case with independent films seeking commercial release, Scorsese had to heat up the film with a few graphic fantasy sex sequences, at distributor Joe Brenner's request.

By October 1969 it had become commonplace for underground films to play the porn circuit. Andy Warhol's *Lonesome Cowboys*, his western parody, was being distributed by Sherpix and was enjoying a marathon run at New York's 55th Street Playhouse. This theater, once an art house specializing in Japanese movies, would become one of Manhattan's major showcases for homosexual porn.

The Park-Miller Theater, thriving as a heavy-duty cruise joint for individuals of all sexual persuasions, showed Anger's films. The Park-Miller's *Village Voice* listing was found on a page festooned with similar ads for adult movie houses (including Frisco split-beaver loops—an early pre-hardcore form of straight porn showing an open pussy—and nude dancers) and was right next to the gay-lib Mattachine Society's film schedule. *Fireworks*, *Scorpio Rising*, and *Inauguration of the Pleasure Dome* (erroneously billed as the "1st New York showing" of *Pleasure Dome*) were packaged under the banner of "The Fabulous Anger Trilogy." Chester Kessler's famous head shot of Anger adorned this "Get-you, Mary"–era ad, albeit in a mutated form. Anger's head had been cut out of the original photo like a paper doll's. The slipshod clip job snipped Anger's collar off and gave him a haircut. The inclusion of *Pleasure Dome* in the ad was typical of exploitation distributors and exhibitors that used flashy titles promising a hotter content than was necessarily there to sell tickets. To make sure the Park-Miller crowd got its money's worth, the bill included the provocatively titled loops *Baskets* and *The Trick*.

The Anger trilogy began to make its way across the American adult theater circuit, although it was sometimes spared the giddy "fabulous" prefix. In London, his films were being more auspiciously shown at cinema clubs, which avoided the oppressive one-man British censor board with a private membership situation. *Scorpio Rising* played the New Cinema Club at 122 Wardour Street as part of a revolving bill, which also included other underground fare and Roger Corman's underground-influenced *The Wild Angels* and *The Trip*.

The Stones were employing all they had managed to learn from their association with Anger. On tour, the top hat was snatched from the legend of Beausoleil. The Crowleyan personal power tripping was filtered through a mishmash of pop iconography and massive amounts of cocaine to fuel Jagger's attempt at incarnating Lucifer.

What the Stones got for their machinations was the concert on December 6, 1969, at Altamont, a more disastrous freebie than Hyde Park, an apocalyptic end to the sixties with a bad time had by all. The unfortunate Jefferson Airplane, opening the concert, was given a hostile reception by the Hell's Angels—guitarist Marty Balin was knocked unconscious. By the time the Stones went on, the audience was being wailed on with leaded pool cues by the Angels, in a frenzy of speed-freak bloodlust. Jagger made a feeble attempt to quell the violence. Finally, an audience member was murdered.

As is so often the case with black magic workings, Jagger had sought to covet the devil's power and was used as a pawn to do his work. Altamont generated much negative press and feelings. There was an overriding suspicion that Jagger had prompted the whole horrendous situation and had gotten what he had asked for. The vibe was so bad that the Hell's Angels even wanted to see him dead.

When Jagger arrived back in London, Anger kept his headaches pounding. Anger sought bigger and bigger pieces of him. Time. Money. Attention. Anger was becoming a control freak pest. Since he was such a control freak himself, Jagger never let things go as far as Anger wanted. He started politely backing away, but Anger kept his talons aimed at Richards and Pallenberg.

The *Lucifer* debacle continued. Anger hooked up with an East Indian barrister, Jimmy Vaughn, who distributed underground movies and sold them to German TV out of his Carnaby Street office. The films were supplied through American Lionel Rogosin's Impact Films. Shortly after their meeting, Anger was living in the basement of Vaughn's Hempstead flat. Anger's magic circle was immediately painted on the floor.

Many projects were brewing in the cauldron of Anger's brain, with an Aleister Crowley biopic ranking high. It was a man's job and Anger was certainly the fellow to tackle it. He was among the eminent authorities on Crowley's life.

Anger made several proposals to various investors. One misguided approach was an interpretive psychedelic collage. He stated it would "intersperse Crowley's spiritual life with contemporary events, such as the sinking of the *Titanic*." Another attempt was a straightforward narrative feature that would focus on Thelema Abbey. Anger said, "I've actually written a script for a life of Aleister Crowley which is concentrating on one particular episode in his life but which really encompasses his whole life. That would require, since it's a dialogue film and everything, a lot of things I don't have."

Universal Pictures had expressed an interest in the Crowley project, and Anger offered them a relatively conventional biopic. The possibility this project could be realized would remain open for the next several years. Unfortunately it never came to fruition.

With Beausoleil out of the picture, Anger had to talent-scout again for a new Lucifer. He found a photogenic piece of British rough trade named Leslie Huggins, who hailed from, according to various interviews with Anger, Middlesborough, Tyneside, or

Yorkshire. Anger was licking his chops because, to his delight, Huggins was prone to violence; he looked as if he'd break a bottle of Guinness over your head. Anger loved to say that he had to strike some sort of deal to keep Huggins out of jail. Huggins was a firecracker waiting to go off. However, unlike Beausoleil, Huggins was not into the artistic process. He was nothing but a hired hand, one that Anger could not keep occupied or mystified for very long.

By April 1970 Anger was fresh out of *Lucifer* funds and Huggins had vanished. Nonetheless, Anger continued to wax hopeful about his new star. "He's an elusive Lucifer. But he is a natural star and absolutely perfect for the part." Anger wanted to believe that Huggins would return. "I hope it's third-time luck."

At age forty-three, Anger was having an obvious problem keeping Lucifers within his orbit. "There's a marvelous old photographer named Edward Steichen who has said that he intends to spend the rest of his life photographing a single tree. He has photographed it growing up, in the summer, and in the fall. He has photographed it in every light combination, and each time, he says, it's completely different. I wish I could find a person as patient as a tree," Anger wistfully concluded.

To raise money, Vaughn arranged for Anger to strike "a Faustian deal. I agreed to do this interview for German TV and in return they would pay me twenty thousand pounds so I could do my feature, as long as they got the rights to show it on TV." While filming, Anger was uncomfortable, but remained polite. Initially, he called the documentary's director, Reinhold Thiel, "a great artist, a religious man. He regards each film almost as an icon, and making it as an act of worship."

When the documentary, *Kenneth Anger, or Film as Magic Ritual*, was completed, Anger howled and bitched like a cur. Like Kinsey, he hated losing control of his media image. People using his method of communication—film—to document him was intolerable. The crew had jangled his nerves. "I detested that man who interviewed me. He offered me a joint at the beginning, as if to say, 'Here, take me as I am,' and I said no thanks. I refused."

Anger continued on his 1970 vindictive streak against Beausoleil in the press, still screaming that Beausoleil stole the *Lucifer Rising* footage. Anger would flash a locket to any interested party. Beausoleil's portrait was on one side and a gold toad was on the other. The inscription around the rim read "Bobby Beausoleil, who was turned into a toad by Kenneth Anger."

On April 21, 1970, Beausoleil was sentenced to die in the electric chair. Beausoleil's attorney attempted a new trial, but the prosecutor won again. Beausoleil was sent to California's San Quentin Penitentiary to await his execution.

In public Anger expressed sorrow but wasn't surprised at Beausoleil's fate. Anger gave interviews in which he detailed his unique situation. "My second Lucifer, a Scorpio, was Bobby Beausoleil, who was one of Manson's family. He's presently in San Quentin on death row. He freaked out after he left me. I never met Manson and don't know what Bobby got into with him, obviously Bobby had his dark side and that took over. I'm sorry about it, as I chose him because he was a powerful cat, he has that kind of extra dimensional quality that comes across on film. But Bobby got the message wrong. He went on an ego trip and I just couldn't handle him."

Anger was still hung up on Beausoleil, and the fact that he was a murderer made him all the more desirable. Anger now felt Beausoleil was finally in the position to appreciate his guidance. As time went on Beausoleil would become desperate and thankful for his one link to the legitimate artistic world.

In the States, Anger and Anton LaVey were playing on a fetish double bill. Sherpix packaged a documentary about LaVey, *Satanis— The Devil's Mass* with *Invocation of My Demon Brother*. The films made good grindhouse fare, the perfect item for those big old theaters in Tenderloin areas. Together, they formed a virtual *Mondo* movie depicting rituals of active San Francisco occult circles at the close of the sixties. *Satanis* was slight but certainly entertaining for those with an interest in the devil, witches, hedonism, cults, and the pesky problem of nosy neighbors. *Invocation* was utilized as the short film to spice up a sexploitation bill, a prevalent practice at the time. These shorts could be jarring, insomuch as they focused on a sexual kink you may not have wanted to see, or they would give unwanted self-realization. Anger's aggressive homosexuality and sadism in *Invocation*, along with the presence of Beausoleil, were a heavy number to lay on the sexploitation crowd.

In September 1970 Anger gave an outrageous interview to the English magazine *Friends*. He was now forty-three and working his way through a "you're too hip, baby" stage. His hair was cut in the swinging executive mode. He wore tight jeans and a button-down, skintight white polyester shirt. He spread the shirt for the photographer to show off his LUCIFER chest tattoo. Two conflicting sides of Anger's face were becoming more apparent. While the left looked relaxed and subdued, the right looked buckled up and intense.

Anger was still attempting to retain Jagger's interest in *Lucifer Rising*. Richards and Pallenberg, along with Faithfull, were still on Anger's side, but Jagger started to back away, offering his brother Chris Jagger for the part of Lucifer. Anger reluctantly accepted and continued gathering a volunteer cast. Faithfull, who had been in numerous commercial releases like *Girl on a Motorcycle* (also known as *Naked Under Leather*), agreed to play Lilith, the kabbalistic goddess of destruction. Faithfull's brother, Chris, was hired to do the photography. Donald Cammell, whose film *Performance*, starring Jagger and Pallenberg, had finally gotten released, was cast as Osiris. Michael Cooper, the Stones' personal photographer, was also to assist in shooting *Lucifer*.

Anger's act again began to play well to the Brits, like in "Pretty, Sexy and Satanic," a piece in the Sunday *London Times* on designer Laura Jameson. Jameson was supposed to create the costumes for *Lucifer* and play a priestess. A photo shoot was arranged at Anger's basement flat. Other film directors, including Donald Cammell, arrived. Old boho cohort Dennis Hopper, riding high from *Easy Rider*, was accompanied by the legendary filmmaker, Panic Theater innovator, comic strip artist, and magician Alejandro Jodorowsky, who had just finished his film masterpiece *El Topo*.

Hopper recalls that "I always got the impression that Ken was very intelligent, that he was on the scam. He was always having a struggle making it. Not that he showed this, but that he was always scamming ideas, and that's a very tough way to live. It's a lot of pressure to have on yourself all the time. I recognized it. We had chosen for ourselves a way of life that has no job security at best and most of the time you're in dire straits. Not just economically, but spiritually, in not being able to create the things that you want to create. We're full of creative ideas and it's very difficult to get them to actually happen. So I always felt that kind of pressure from him. Not on me, but just the pressure—his internal pressure and anxiety—about wanting to create things, wanting to make things, his ideas, and so on."

Anger shot eight minutes of film and called it *Lucifer Rising, Part I*, utilizing the serial format he had first experimented with in *Prisoner of Mars* and *Escape Episode*. He played the magus, and the clip shows him dancing around a magic circle. On the basis of this footage, the British government, through its National Film Finance Corporation, fronted fifteen thousand pounds for *Lucifer Rising*. This prompted an outraged headline in the London *Sunday Telegraph* on March 28, 1971: DEVIL FILM TO GET STATE AID.

Anger played this publicity for all it was worth. He had time, money, and attention. He moved out of Vaughn's place to his own apartment, and flew his cast to Egypt and Germany for shooting. Anger's trip to Egypt garnered some good press. In July 1971 the *Evening Standard* proclaimed that "at 4 AM in the desert . . . it's Marianne Faithfull and Sphinx" above a photo of Anger gently touching up her makeup in front of the pyramids.

Anger was happy with her performance. Faithfull commented that Anger "created atmospheres" on the set to which the cast members responded. "He made every one of us who worked on the film more or less, without knowing anything about it and without having read a script, want to do it, and do it completely seriously."

Anger wanted Faithfull to get into Crowley, but she refused, finding Anger himself frightening. She recalls him on the *Lucifer Rising* set, "completely freaking out, completely carried away."

Anger has called Faithfull "one of the six women in my whole life that I have loved. Marianne has a strong streak of self-destruction. Marianne is half-Jewish. In some ways, she hated the part of Lilith, but when she got it all objectified, it helped."

Anger was unsatisfied with Chris Jagger. They clashed, and

eventually the friction between them led to an on-set row culminating in Anger firing the mouthy Chris. Anger wanted Mick, not his nobody brother. Meanwhile, Mick Jagger had married Bianca and made himself all but inaccessible to Anger.

It was inevitable that Anger would cross paths with Jimmy Page. Page was at his peak. Immersed in demonic folklore, Led Zeppelin's mythology was a pact with the devil in exchange for success.

More than any other rocker, Jimmy Page was fixated on Crowley. His millions afforded him the Great Beast's Loch Ness residence, Boleskine. He would buy anything associated with Crowley, owning the second-largest Crowley library in the world. Page even had groupie minions scouring dusty occult bookshops in Hollywood for manuscripts.

Page put his knowledge of Crowley to good practical use. He inherited the Beast's gift for wordplay as a lyricist, and was able to integrate multiple, numerically complex musical scales in one moment. The Crowleyan eucharists of heroin and cocaine unleashed Page's creative powers.

Crowley artifacts were occasionally up for sale. Anger turned up at Sotheby's to check out who would be bidding. Anger was outbid at the auction by Page.

After they met at the auction, Anger stunned and astonished Page with tales of the Master Therion. Anger had extraordinary knowledge he could share.

Shortly after this, Anger began spending time with Page at his damp, creepy Boleskine castle. Page believed the place was haunted by the ghost of a headless man, and Anger was helping him deal with it.

Around the same time, Anger had had it with Jimmy Vaughn as his distributor. Anger had just filed suit against Impact Films, the American distributor who supplied Vaughn with films. Vaughn even committed the cardinal sin of distributing the movies of Anger's nemesis, Andy Warhol.

Anger planned something for Vaughn. Nothing terribly heavy, but enough to throw a good scare his way. He arrived at Vaughn's Carnaby Street office with a valise in tow. Anger stayed on after the staff had gone for the day. Vaughn arrived the next morning to find what was described as "fragments of a charred altar, specks of blood and traces of burnt-out candle. Scattered around were weird curses and a singed likeness of 'the Beast' himself," Aleister Crowley. Vaughn became terrified and freaked out, believing Anger had cursed him. To soothe his nerves, he employed a West Indian witch doctor to sweep out the evil spirits—much like hiring a ghostbuster.

Shortly afterward, Anger persuaded Page to compose and perform the music for *Lucifer Rising*. He moved into the basement of Page's London mansion, where he continued to tinker with his *Lucifer* fragments on an editing table Page had installed.

The world's biggest superstar guitar hero was working for Anger, gratis. Anger was indeed a magician.

Part III

Decadence

Chapter 13

Bootlegged Babylon

by 1971 Anger was considered a hip, powerful force in the underground. He began flying back and forth between England and the States, appearing at colleges, presenting his films, and performing speaking engagements. Audiences were very anxious to hear what he had to say. Having stayed out of the United States so long, Anger had the added charm of being a visiting expatriate.

A year earlier Anger had requested the footage he stored for *Les Lunes des Lapins* from the Cinémathèque Française. He transformed it into his first version of the balletic *Rabbit's Moon*.

Anger remained as expert as ever in his use of music. The oldies he picked for the soundtrack go for the slow, aching emotions. The Flamingos' "I Only Have Eyes for You," the Dells' "Oh, What A Night," the Capris' "There's a Moon Out Tonight" and Mary Wells's "Bye Bye Baby" venture into the heartbroken world of doo-wop. The passionate romanticism reflected Anger's angst over Bobby Beausoleil's impending execution.

This version of *Rabbit's Moon* is visually a throwback to the *Midsummer Night's Dream* set of Anger's childhood, with its silver tinsel forest. *Moon* is softly, rhythmically edited, with occult symbols for the sun and the moon intercut indicating a heterosexual "working" in Crowleyan terms.

Anger also revived *Puce Moment*, which he had withdrawn from public viewing at the closing of Cinema 16 in 1963. A great psychedelic-tinged soundtrack by Jonathan Harper was added.

Both *Puce Moment* and *Rabbit's Moon* were well received in the States. Anger frequently appeared with the films as a guest lecturer at the Art Institute of Chicago. The films were seen as proof of his creative resurgence.

Taking advantage of Anger's new fame, publisher Marvin Miller, in a stroke of his own unique business acumen, thought he could squeeze more bread out of *Hollywood Babylon*. Instead, he got the gasface.

Using his Institute for Adult Education, which had a Los Angeles post office box for an address, Miller put *Hollywood Babylon* on the big screen. Before it was even completed, Miller, huckster supreme, promised a spectacular. A *Variety* piece mentioned a planned national tour of its star-lookalike cast members, culminating in appearances on the Merv Griffin and Dick Cavett shows.

Anger had been furious for years that Miller had shafted him out of any royalties on the *Hollywood Babylon* paperback. He stated that "all the charm is gone out of it and all they've done is to make it as sensational as possible. I've tried to sue the publisher, but, unfortunately, he doesn't exist; he has a synthetic address in Phoenix." Miller had managed to elude Anger and numerous other foes with the post office box for his company, Professional Services, Inc., which folded in 1968 for failing to file annual corporate reports.

For this venture, Miller had assembled a consortium of sexploitation veterans. Van Guylder directed; George "Budd" Costello, who had production-managed Russ Meyer's films, was Miller's assistant; Henning Schellerup, who had shot dozens of exploitation films of every variety, operated the camera. Miller billed himself as executive producer.

The resultant product was painful in the cheapest, blunt softcore way. It has the look of a gross, sweaty quickie. Everything is padded out with interminable old footage, a hodgepodge of clips of stars from Charlie Chaplin to Marilyn Monroe. The actual cast of the movie is populated by L.A. bust models like Uschi Digart (again, a veteran of Russ Meyer productions) and unemployable Hollywood Boulevard actors. Narration from Anger's book is nakedly blurbed over the proceedings like loud *Variety* headlines.

A Charlie Chaplin impersonator issues demands for blowjobs. Fatty Arbuckle is incarnated by an overweight Junior Samples *Hee Haw* lookalike who seemed to be in a pathetic barbiturate fog. Erich von Stroheim, "The Hun," is a bald, monocled man in jodhpurs who whips women. The Hearst shooting gets played out on a tugboat instead of a yacht. There's a gay bar scene with Valentino. Period detail is supplied by a rented antique car driving up a street in what is obviously early seventies L.A. Like an endless loop, the same nude extras appear in the background of several scenes.

What sounds funny in retrospect or description is not always laughable if you have to sit through it. The movie is incredibly lewd and unwatchably wooden. There is nothing shocking or sexy about it; it's all very tawdry and ugly and makes one think that gossip like this doesn't need to be acted out.

A movie that had given Miller the idea to produce *Hollywood Babylon* was Bill Osco's enormously successful *Hollywood Blue*, itself the first pornographic knockoff of Anger's book and still playing at that time. It cut to the prurient core of Anger's subject matter. This film showed a few loops purporting to star famous personalities. A Marilyn Monroe imitator is shown in "Apple Knockers and Coke Bottle," a piece of fifties cheesecake. A hard-core gay clip featured a TV cowboy star resembling the late Chuck Connors in Marine drag, receiving fellatio from and fucking a hapless Army private. A freshly shot interview with Anger's old pal Mickey Rooney is used; Rooney later called this the low point of his career. Most shocking was the clip of the girl with the German shepherd, which got quickly snipped from widespread release prints but remained in the movie's trailer.

Miller's dirty-movie version of *Hollywood Babylon* got a splashy campaign. Its pressbook looks more expensive than the film and tauntingly includes a still of the *Midsummer Night's Dream* premiere, as well as liberally quoting text from Anger's book. Large newspaper ads were taken, which committed the most hurtful act of all—not mentioning Anger's name. Unlike *Hollywood Blue*, *Hollywood Babylon* wasn't technically hard-core, so it could play in grindhouses, drive-ins, and small neighborhood theaters that shunned porn. Its New York City release was handled by Aquarius Pictures, a bottom-of-the-barrel exploitation distributor with an office on Forty-second Street.

In February 1972, a *Variety* reviewer caught *Hollywood Babylon* on Forty-second Street, where it was playing with *The Grissom Gang*, a violent *Bonnie and Clyde*–era thriller. As was the overwhelming case with the scant reviews of the film, it was negative, but concluded that "the release will make two things: mischief and money." Miller had taken Anger's book to create an embarrassment in the only medium Anger truly cared about—film.

A week after it opened Anger sued. Backed up by *Hollywood Babylone* French publisher Jean Jacques Pauvert, Anger demanded:

$1 per copy of the bootleg *Hollywood Babylon* found on Miller, $5,000 in statutory damages, $25,000 for using Anger's name on the bootleg paperback, and $500,000 for using Anger's name in connection with the unauthorized movie version.

Anger called Miller a cheap pornographer, using as an example a film Miller released through his Institute for Adult Education, *The Sensually Liberated Female*. This was a hard-core sex-ed film made by Matt Cimber, who ironically had been the ex-husband of *Hollywood Babylon* cover girl Jayne Mansfield.

Miller's attorneys attempted the defense that the events were so far in the past that they were public domain. Anger didn't own the gossip stories; they existed as so-called comments on facts and anyone could tell them.

This lawsuit would linger in the courts for over a year. However, the movie was yanked after a mere four-day run at grindhouses pending the litigation.

Eventually Anger won a small judgment in his favor over the unauthorized Miller *Hollywood Babylon* book and movie, and the prints of the film were ordered destroyed. Slippery electric eel that Miller was, Anger never collected a cent. Anger later had some solace when he learned that Miller had been sentenced to eight years in prison. However, no one seems to know or want to acknowledge the real fate of Miller. One rumor has it that he was found dead while on the lam from the feds.

For several years, prints of the bootleg *Hollywood Babylon* sat in the attics of questionable exploitation film distributors. It now occasionally surfaces at East Indian–owned video stores in Tenderloin districts for about $10 a copy.

On February 18, 1972, the California State Supreme Court voted six to one to abolish the death penalty on the basis that it was cruel and unusual punishment. One hundred seven humans living on California's death row were not to be murdered. Bobby Beausoleil was given his life back.

Anger used *Variety* to spotlight *Lucifer Rising*. In the February 23, 1972, issue, he claimed that the film was near completion, mentioning Marianne Faithfull as star, with music by Jimmy Page. In reality, the movie was far from any kind of finished form.

Lucifer Rising footage was shown on a sweltering night in April 1973 when Anger made an offbeat public appearance at the State University of New York at Buffalo. Stan Brakhage introduced him, and Anger took the mike and admitted that he hadn't slept for two weeks and that the only meal he'd had all day was a spartan cup of coffee. He was wearing his LUCIFER jacket, a satin rainbow affair.

Anger's talk was highly animated and free associative. He showed clips of *Kenneth Anger, or Film as Magic Ritual*, the German documentary he had loathed making so much. He apologized for the splices in the film: he had schematically taken the scissors to himself. The interviewer in the film would ask Anger a question, Anger's face would be visible for a second, and BLIP!—his subsequent response would be hacked out. The audience was jarred. Anger spoke loudly throughout the film, voicing his distaste for its creators, no longer in control of his tongue.

He lashed out at Jagger for backing away from him and the *Lucifer Rising* project, railing that "Mick got his idea for 'Sympathy for the Devil' from my idea for the film. He stole it from me." Bianca had apparently been instrumental in banishing Anger from the Jagger camp: "I didn't dig Mick's marriage to Bianca." Faithfull, whom Anger was still friends with, "had a hard life when she was with Mick. He is a very sophisticated sadist."

"Venereal disease," Anger blurted, "may be the subject of my next film. Two or three people in this room right now will get clap at some point in their lives. There is a new strain of gonorrhea that has come over from Vietnam and it is a killer. It hibernates in your brain for years and years and then one day it takes over your body and kills you. The B-girls in Vietnam spread this disease deliberately to our boys." The audience was startled.

Anger was all keyed up and began talking about his new rock and roll associate, Page. He knew how absolutely mind-blowing it was for a bunch of college kids to hear that Page would be doing the music for the film he was premiering. "He began it," explained Anger, "when he was on the road with that teeny-bop group Led Zeppelin. He's using nine instruments." Some silent rushes from

Lucifer Rising were shown. The SUNY students found Anger's frankness startling and his films fascinating.

In a less academic realm, the homosexual pornographic cinema Anger had given birth to was flourishing. Many filmmakers were now using the segmented format Anger had established with *Scorpio Rising*—Wakefield Poole in *Boys in the Sand* and Toby Ross in *Reflections of Youth* and *Boys of the Slums*. The most unusual and publicly visible of these directors was Fred Halsted, a heavy user of Tuinals and acid who had been around the L.A. leather scene since 1960. His movies were far from the norm, defying many of pornography's strictures, and he was heavily influenced by Anger. For example, *Sex Garage*, his variant on *Scorpio Rising*, was, unlike other films of this genre, shot in black and white. A blond kid has sex with a girl, then a guy, culminating in the appearance of a leather guy who proceeds to have sex with his own motorcycle.

Halsted paired the half-hour *Sex Garage* with his own variation on *Fireworks*, a film called *L.A. Plays Itself*. In this explicitly autobiographical statement, Halsted plays his own protagonist, who cruises L.A. meat markets looking for young guys to beat up. Creepily mixed on the soundtrack are tapes of a kid warned of the unkindness of strangers. When Halsted's double bill of *Sex Garage* and *L.A. Plays Itself* premiered at New York's 55th Street Playhouse, police busted the movies on the basis of complaints by homosexuals. Gay libbers were both attacking and championing Halsted's identity stance of sadomasochism, which not only had its roots in *Fireworks* but was also now overtly applicable to straight people with the same bent. Ironically, the arresting officer made out his report on the basis of the motorcycle sex scene in *Sex Garage*.

Halsted's other work at this time included *Truck It*, in which a middle-aged businessman voyeuristically savors the sexual activities of the hitchhikers who ride in the back of his van. Every form of sex, from straight to gay to S&M to autoerotic, is shown. The movie is, again, highly influenced by Anger, using pop tunes like "The Happy Organ" and recognizable L.A. billboards and locations as a running commentary on the action.

Halsted donated prints of *Sex Garage* and *L.A. Plays Itself* to the permanent film collection of MOMA, New York City's Museum of Modern Art. In March 1974 both he and Anger participated in a "Cineprobe" series where filmakers appeared in person to screen their work.

Anger arrived with the Magick Lantern Cycle in tow. It concluded with a showing of the still incomplete *Lucifer Rising*. At this time Anger was using at least three different soundtracks for this film. For the MOMA showing he used the music of an ensemble called the Alternative Enlightenment System, which he experimented with only briefly. Other screenings featured Jimmy Page's soundtrack, which was appropriately eerie and heavy, reminiscent of the instrumental portions of the darker Led Zeppelin tracks. This soundtrack naturally wound up on Page and Zep bootlegs, but was eventually officially issued on a collection of Page's solo works. For souped-up psychedelia, Anger would wed the film to Pink Floyd's *Atom Heart Mother* album.

Halsted represented himself at the MOMA Cineprobe series with *L.A. Plays Itself* and *Sex Garage*. It was clear that he had usurped Anger's position as the most outspoken filmmaker from the homosexual and S&M orbit. Halsted's way wasn't the old-fashioned guilt trip of reliving traumas. He enjoyed his ride, reveling in his outrageousness. His lifestyle involved open drug use, fist-fucking, and, at its most shocking, a proud recollection of a scat episode with his male wife, which he recounted to Al Goldstein in *Screw* magazine.

Halsted wasn't about to hide. He looked like a middle-aged Tarzan, even appearing in hard-core movies other than his own. He narrated *Erotikus*, a history of the gay porn movie from its posing-strap origins to 1974. By the end of the film he was nude and good-naturedly stoned.

Personally, Halsted was the diametric opposite of Anger: a physical sadist but a mental masochist, held together by Joey Yale, his partner. When Halsted would lose it a bit from his heavy drug use, Yale expertly handled his business transactions.

Anger himself was gaining weight and his hair was obviously colored in the manner of Aschenbach in *Death in Venice*. The years were pressing on his psyche and vanity, so to see another director who was so out-front clearly unnerved him. He stated, "I know Fred. He's on a colossal ego trip and he thinks he's the most beautiful hunk around. He will have to go through the same changes like John Rechy of *City of Night*, because it's terrible how—well, I was never a narcissist and it's very hard for those who are hardcore narcissists to see that they go into a bar and people's heads no longer turn. So that's why I just wait." Anger chuckled. "No, I don't dislike Fred."

After appearing at MOMA, Anger returned to San Francisco. He subsequently wrote a piece for San Francisco's *City* magazine about an art deco show, but his byline was left off. This caused Anger to have a severe temper tantrum. On July 29, 1974, he stormed into editor Hal Aigner's office, threw a typewriter to the floor, and then hurled it out a closed window.

Years of stimulants and hallucinogens, coupled with the exhausting struggle of surviving without the security of a regular income, had taken their toll on Anger. The line between socially acceptable and unacceptable behavior was becoming blurred.

Adding to Anger's insecurity was the fact that John Waters had also toppled him off the throne of outrageousness. *Pink Flamingos* had become a runaway midnight cult hit. Too mockingly perverse to be considered conventional pornography, too narrative-structured to be pigeonholed as free-form underground, the movie shattered distinctions generally thrust upon independent films. The success of *Pink Flamingos* enabled Waters to gain the notice of a commercial independent distributor, New Line.

Waters was admittedly extremely influenced by Anger. As a sixteen-year-old boy, he'd hitchhike from Baltimore to Manhattan, where he'd catch Anger films like *Fireworks* and *Scorpio Rising* at a time when they were still considered sexually shocking. He had also been influenced by the tabloidism of the Miller *Hollywood Babylon* bootleg paperback.

Waters was also obsessed with the Manson family, going as far as attending their trials. *Pink Flamingos* was explicitly dedicated to several Family members and "Free Tex Watson" appears in the film as graffiti across a wall. At first through correspondence, then with meetings, Waters developed an enduring friendship with Watson.

From time to time, Bobby Beausoleil was in touch with Anger. He even did some artwork for him, including a stationery design for Anger's Puck Productions. The Puck Productions stationery became Anger's standard format for issuing proclamations from the Kingdom of Anger.

The stationery is extremely unique and striking, lavish and impish at once. The crying and laughing faces of theater are in each corner. Sandwiched between is BEAU and SOLEIL, like the banner surrounding a tattoo. A little caricature shows Beausoleil as Puck, with elaborate cape, tights, boots, magical top hat with stars and a big plume, the curls of his hair forming two tiny horns. He's holding a sword and standing on a wooden stage. Long curtains lead to coiled dragons. PUCK PRODUCTIONS is written in gothic letters, with a lantern. KENNETH ANGER, RESIDENT MAGUS, is above the dragons; SPRING 1975 is below them.

Chapter 14

The Gossip

If you are a member of the media, you belong to the public.
You've made that Faustian bargain with your public. Take
me—all of me—I'm yours.

KENNETH ANGER

anger had gained nothing from his lawsuit against Marvin Miller. However, he became aware that there was still domestic interest in *Hollywood Babylon*. This propelled him to seek out a publisher for a legitimate version. All that would be required was the translation from the French, an editorial overhaul to Americanize the text, and the addition of new Hollywood deaths. Several publishers expressed interest in the project. Finally, a deal was struck with Straight Arrow Books, a subdivision of *Rolling Stone* magazine.

Released in 1975, the American *Hollywood Babylon* was a festival of rot and decay. A lurid shot of Jayne Mansfield under the crumbling Hollywood sign provides the cover. Inside, one finds the shattered mirror of Anger's mind, a Rubik's cube of his obsession with Hollywood's seamier side.

Anger uses Aleister Crowley's writing as a literary model and some chapter titles are direct homages to Crowley, such as "Heroin Heroines." Like Crowley, Anger emphasizes the stories' ambiguities, yet has them function as parables as much as enigmas. But Anger is a poet of pictures and Crowley of words; thus, Anger's sentences can sound ham-fisted, while Crowley's had the flow of musical cadences.

Since Anger communicates through the eye, he was credited as visual director of the book. *Hollywood Babylon* became his *That's Entertainment*, his quick-cut film editor's sensibility ever-present. Some of the photos gave the book the push into myth he was desperately straining for.

The opening still photo of costumed extras from D. W. Griffith's *Intolerance* is Anger's view of a pagan paradise afterlife. Unrestricted libido-driven clothing, perfect corpse makeup, all sexes joined in a somnambulistic ritual. The photo that follows is a post-Christian version of the streets to heaven being paved with gold. Falsely smiling, nasty, constrictedly attired cast members are in the forefront of a musical set. The men, though wearing less makeup than in *Intolerance*, look asexual and artificial. The women look like frigid forties good girls with their legs slammed shut. The Saturn looming in the background indicates, by Anger's own auto-hagiographical statement, everything Anger stands against. A fake star is off to the side, and the quote from Crowley's poem "One Star in Sight" in *The Book of the Law*, "Every Man and every Woman is a Star," is at the bottom of the page.

Two shots of nighttime Hollywood follow. One is of Grauman's Chinese Theater, with a spotlight illuminating Anger's dedication "To the Scarlet Woman"—his old pal Marjorie Cameron. The next photo prominently features a neon sign spelling out DRUGS.

Everything in Hollywood after the opulence of *Intolerance* becomes fair game for Anger. A shot of shabby houses behind the dismantled *Intolerance* set. It sets up the vantage point of *Hollywood Babylon*, suffusing it with the snickering rage of the have-nots. Everything spirals from the fan to the star to the studio head and then back to the fan, who keeps it all going by buying a ticket to a movie—or by purchasing a tabloid to rip the star down.

Disasters, heartbreak, sexual dysfunction, premature deaths, suicides, drug addiction, and nervous breakdowns fly at the reader like shit hitting a high-powered fan. What Anger tends to imply is that all of these individuals, whether consciously involved in the occult or not, have made a Faustian bargain. In exchange for wealth and fame are drug addiction, scandal, and death.

As *Hollywood Babylon* progresses, it assimilates seventies junk culture and becomes more lurid. The mentions of snuff movies, of an exploitation film calling itself by that name, and magazines like *Violent World*, which included photos of bloody deaths, were all part of the sleazoid aesthetic climate of the time. *Hollywood Babylon* becomes a snuff scrapbook of famous people. Paul Bern, Jean Harlow's husband, has his corpse and suicide note pictured. There's a photo of Marie Prevost's body partially devoured by her dog. Lupe Velez's corpse lies in state. Bugsy Siegel's eye is shown shot out in a *Godfather*-like photo. Anger seems genuinely disturbed by Siegel, who comes across as a Marvin Miller out of control, a bully feared by all stopped only by death.

As Anger's opus grinds to a halt, pieces of him are found strewn across its mosaic. Silent screen lover John Gilbert offs himself after talkies make him sound screechy. F. W. Murnau, the German expatriate director, dies in an auto accident as he's giving a blowjob to his Filipino houseboy. Mae Murray, who's posthumously thanked at the end, gets picked up by cops after she passes out on a park bench.

Things reach an extreme with Erich von Stroheim, whom Anger dubs "The Dirty Hun." But when he sees von Stroheim, does Anger see himself? Von Stroheim was a filmmaker whose budgetary extravagances and sadomasochistic escapades were cruelly misunderstood by small-minded front office men. Anger feels that Hollywood made this genius a broken man.

Anger concludes his treatise with "Hollywoodämmerung," which includes all the gory shockers that had occurred since the publication of the Miller bootleg. Lewis Stone is seen in throes of dying of a heart attack after chasing stone-throwing boys away from his house. There's a triple spread on Ramon Novarro: head shot, corpse, and the hustlers who killed him. They had stuffed a Valentino-autographed dildo down his throat on Halloween night, choking him on his own blood. Albert Dekker's autoasphyxiation suicide in drag is briefly detailed. The blood on Sharon Tate's doorstep is shown. A photo of Tyrone Power's grave is on the back inside jacket.

Anger has half jokingly alluded to a secret code in the book. He offered the lucky reader who broke it a grand.

Unlike Anger's movies, which are always masterful, *Hollywood Babylon* tries hard to be art, but only occasionally succeeds. It is valuable primarily in terms of being an abstraction of hate. Anger has succeeded in documenting the most foul, rank, vicious, manipulative, and mentally damaging behavior of which humans are capable.

Hollywood Babylon received several favorable reviews. Jack Kroll, who had captured Anger during the sixties with his "Up from Underground" piece, gave the book a rave in *Newsweek*. Rex Reed loved it, lending a substantial blurb to its back cover. Michael Perkins in *Screw* honed in on the forbidden erotic quality of Anger's Hollywood tales.

Not all the notices were positive, however. The *New York Times* found Anger an effective melodramatist and felt that the book could supply the reader with a year's worth of barroom stories. The *Times* ultimately concluded that Anger had pandered to everyone's lowest common denominator.

Hollywood Babylon created a cartoonish public image for Anger. He had finally made that Faustian pact for fame he had wished for for so long. Anger would now have to live with the persona it created.

At first, Anger enjoyed the attention. The book made him a noted expert on Hollywood. He had finally been granted space in a world that he had been obsessed with and that had denied him admittance up until now.

Initially, he was invigorated into a surge of exhibitionism, becoming as outgoing in public as he had been with Beausoleil almost a decade before. In September 1975 Anger put on a straw hat, grabbed his cane, and took *Hollywood Babylon* on the road. Seven hundred curious individuals, mostly college students, showed up at the Pacific Film Archive in Berkeley to witness "The Hollywood Babylon Show."

The aroma of incense knocked the audience sideways. Anger was onstage in his "Mr. Anger" director's chair. A too-tight, white double-breasted suit, a red tie, and a purple shirt rounded out his ensemble. The Kinks' melodramatic "Celluloid Heroes" played as Anger knelt before tacky icons of dead celebrities. At the end of the song he leapt to his feet. Like a mechanical toy that was too tightly wound, Anger raced back and forth, brandishing the neon violin that Mickey Rooney had given him from *Gold Diggers of 1933*. Anger's impromptu free-style moves ended with him screaming "THE SIDE SHOW!" He dropped to one knee like Al Jolson and pantomimed Blue Magic's smarmy falsetto soul hit, "Sideshow."

Fervent, impassioned readings by Anger ensued. Next he showed some early exploitation movies. Curious drug or scandal items, mostly in the public domain, this type of fare used to play on multiple feature bills at theaters like the Thalia or the Elgin as *Reefer Madness*–style laugh fests. The movies Anger showed starred some of the people mentioned in his book. He kicked things off with *The Mystery of the Leaping Fish*, starring Douglas Fairbanks, Sr., injecting himself with enormous syringes of cocaine. Exemplifying *Hollywood Babylon* excess, he discards the empty set of works like a beer can and grabs another from a bandolier of a dozen more syringes across his chest.

On the opiate side, Anger showed *Human Wreckage*, featuring morphine shooter Wallace Reid's greedy professional widow. In a moment of excitement, Anger smiled and exclaimed, "I'm gonna show it to you all! All seven reels!" The audience groaned and grew restless. Anger also screened *The Red Kimona*, which involved underage girls being used in white slave traffic.

Anger had done his wild shimmy for the evening. Reviewers were entertained, though disconcerted about how into the part he was.

Around this time Anger began sporting what would become a highlight of his wardrobe: a New York Rangers' hockey shirt with the R and S removed, spelling ANGER diagonally across his chest. Another wardrobe prop was the ANGER turtleneck, which spelled the letters of his name out, red on red, straight across his chest. Skintight bluejeans, one pair studded in a disco era manner, completed the ensemble. The hair-coloring process that Anger had initiated many years before was heightened with a severe raven black.

An appearance at a college or film society no longer became merely a talk with a director showing his films. Anger felt he had to live up to the new persona he had created. Copies of *Hollywood Babylone* in French were frequently available for $300. Anger would exhort audience members to buy the Straight Arrow *Hollywood Babylon* and offered to sell autographed copies. He'd have stacks of them for sale at a markup over the cover price.

Anger was also becoming well known on the Hollywood memorabilia collecting circuit. Anger was so noted for his Valentino paraphernalia that, like other persistent individuals of this ilk, he managed to derive an income from his collection. Newspapers seeking to photograph Valentino items would inevitably seek him out as a source. The publicity from *Hollywood Babylon* kept this weirdly cannibalistic cycle going.

The saddest impact of the *Hollywood Babylon* fallout on Anger was the inevitable fulfillment of the Faustian pact. He had exchanged the respect of being a world-class, internationally known director for the larger-than-life image of a famous gossip. Outside of large metropolitan areas where his films were revived, he wasn't known as a director at all, but as a professional gossip, retelling reminiscences about Valentino and Butterfly McQueen.

The bicentennial year saw Anger commuting back and forth between a tiny hotel room in London and a sublet in New York City on West Ninety-ninth Street off Riverside Drive. The apartment was dark and gloomy, facing an alley. It soon became a warehouse for memorabilia. A life-size portrait of the Frankenstein monster hung next to an enormous French poster for *Rebel Without a Cause* featuring an over-Gallicized James Dean. Marbles sat in a jar, peacock feathers were placed in vases. Flying saucer newsletters lay next to a thirties French version of *Photoplay*, a magazine called *Pour Vous*. Anger would admonish guests to handle *Pour Vous* "as delicately as you would the Dead Sea Scrolls."

Interviewers from both sides of the Atlantic sought out Anger, the famous gossip, the man with the real dirt on Hollywood. With each interview, Anger formed more of a hard candy shell to obscure the facts of his childhood. He made himself five years younger, moving his birthdate to 1932. Beverly Hills became his hometown instead of Pacific Palisades, which would mesh better with intimate stories he'd tell about silent stars.

Anger told interviewers of being conductor of a toy orchestra as a child that featured "André Previn on wood blocks." Adorable, if it were only true—Maestro Previn didn't spend his early childhood in the United States. While they attended Beverly Hills High at the same time, Previn never worked for or met Anger at any time in his life. Still, he found Anger's statements charming and flattering. These kind of tall tales didn't hurt anything, except Anger's own emotions, being an expression of desires that can never be fulfilled.

In June 1976 Anger made the New York City tabloids. The *New York Post* published "The Return of Kenneth Anger." A recent photo of a disheveled Anger is laid out next to his child face in *A Midsummer Night's Dream*. Anger seemed disjointed and confused in the text. He obviously felt people were doubting the authenticity of his *Hollywood Babylon* stories. For no apparent reason, he brought up a dislike for pornography, a statement he'd often repeat during the mid-seventies.

The New York *Daily News* then ran a feature on Anger entitled "Looking Back at Anger." It kicked off the use of puns on the John

Osborne kitchen-sink play *Look Back in Anger* as a perpetual moniker for Anger interview pieces. A curious photo of Anger smiling by a typewriter, sporting a sparse mustache, was included. Anger talked of another exposé called *Washington Babylon*, which he was supposedly finishing. He repeats the mantra of Beausoleil stealing the *Lucifer Rising* footage. At the end of the interview, he shocks journalist Ernest Leogrande by saying, "I'm the only director who has the title of his movie tattooed on his chest." Anger grinned, opened his shirt, flashing his tattooed breasts, laid down on a bed, then got up. "*Lucifer Rising*," he said. "Get it?!"

Writer John Calendo was working for *Oui*, a kinky offshoot of *Playboy*. Impressed by both *Hollywood Babylon* and Anger's films, he had always wanted to meet Anger. In the manner of seventies men's magazines, *Oui* was trying to be hip, so Calendo used the fresh notoriety of *Hollywood Babylon* as a reason to interview Anger. Anger gave him such a difficult time that the piece wound up being subtitled "Is the gossipy occultist who wrote *Hollywood Babylon* really an agent of Lucifer? Or is he just a deviled ham?"

Calendo had enjoyed the Miller bootleg paperback of *Hollywood Babylon* and found the Straight Arrow edition a watered-down version of its "fabulous purple excesses. More of Kenneth Anger's pettiness and viciousness came out in such a naked way. Surprisingly petty. When you know that, the stuff is less charming. He picked on people with a gay quality about them. It's animated by a kind of revenge, by someone who feels wronged by famous people and is going to get them.

"It was only after I met him that I realized he had no sense of humor about what he was writing. I thought he was in on the joke. I thought he was celebrating depravity. This is a man who is worshiping Satan and he's coming on like morality is being corrupted because an actress is getting fucked by five guys at once. You can't have it both ways."

Expecting to meet the leatherman in the Chester Kessler stills, Calendo was surprised at Anger's weight when he met him. "What he reminded me of is one of those castrated cats that had ballooned up. Kind of a pampered quality where he could be malicious."

Anger brought up the supposed secret code in the book, claiming that two Egyptologists had hipped him to it. "In other words, the real dirt is in code! I wrote *Hollywood Babylon* for one reader in a thousand. The code is a challenge to his ingenuity and diligence, either subliminally, when they skim along the top layer of print, or actually, when they dig down to solve the puzzle." Calendo could never uncover any code. He found Anger's talk "like a guru who lies and says it's divine. Now, as a forty-year-old man, I find it obnoxious."

Anger described the men who came into his life to Calendo as "elementals. Oh, they were human once, but at some stage, a demonic force moves in and sits there." He had trouble photographing them because "they come and go so quickly."

Anger remained insistent that Beausoleil had robbed him and that his curse on Beausoleil had worked. "It's like the old fairy tale in which the toad turns into the prince; I turned the prince into the toad. His dark side took over—with considerable help from Charlie M. Now, like the toad, Bobby sits in the well, in prison."

Calendo initially felt that the interview was enjoyable and Anger had acted pleasantly. Anger had originally sent Calendo a letter praising a piece he did on movie star gravesites, writing, "I can't think of anyone more qualified to review *Hollywood Babylon*." He did a complete 360-degree turn when Calendo sent him a copy of their interview and an Anger-inspired bit he did for *Interview* magazine. In it Calendo nominated Jayne Mansfield for sainthood, satirically stating that she died in a car wreck after getting cursed by Anton LaVey for refusing to worship the devil.

Anger showed this piece to LaVey. Anger wrote Calendo that "never have I seen him roused to such a towering fury!" Anger and LaVey laid a curse on Calendo. "This will be a lesson to you to never print an unsupported rumor." Anger also didn't want the interview with him to run in *Oui*.

Subsequent to the curse, Calendo came down with what initially felt like hepatitis, complete with brown urine. He did his own *Exorcist* number with rosary beads and a scapular while burning Anger's writings, chanting, "Die, you bastard. I probably did have mono, which has nothing to do with Ken Anger. When I got sick, I did not feel it was in any way related to the curse."

Calendo's piece placed Anger as the precursor of John Waters and Fred Halsted. Calendo recalls: "When you read the piece, not only is it perceptive but it's from someone who likes his work. That's the killer. What about the people who dismiss him as a kook?

"Years go by. I go out to Hollywood. I happened to meet someone I used to know. He said, 'I ran into Kenneth Anger the other day. I said I'm a friend of John Calendo's. That's the worst thing I could say. Anger went on about how he hated you for twenty minutes.'

"Look at the name he picked," Calendo says exhaustedly, "he's been trouble from day one."

During this time in 1976, Anger began actively flirting with journalists over a special photo he had in his possession. Sometimes he'd coquettishly slide it out and show it. The photo revealed what Anger claimed to be Marlon Brando in a sexual act with another man.

This photo can often be found in private pornography collections. It has even been published in a censored version in *Hollywood Hotline*, a one-shot magazine released without publishing or copyright information that also offered such gems as nude photos of stars and lists of circumsized and uncircumsized actors.

Anger has never given an explanation about how this photo filtered into his hands. He complained loudly about not being able to include it in *Hollywood Babylon*, griping to Calendo that "I fought with the lawyers at Straight Arrow Books to let me include a compromising snapshot of a certain very important actor. But the lawyers insisted it was an invasion of privacy, and so the photo was surpressed. It's not that I want to *hurt* him; I just think it's time he came out of the closet."

"It was a pity," Anger told *Crawdaddy* interviewer Mick Brown, that he couldn't publish it. "It's a terrific photo. I guess it was a dare or something but the idea that it's right out there in front of the party." The accompanying photo showed Anger wearing a denim jacket and a Vegas-sized pentagram medallion, beaming admiringly at a Brando beefcake still. The caption read: ANGER CAUGHT BRANDO WITH HIS PANTS DOWN.

Anger passionately describes the "Brando" photo as an artfully composed pornographic photo, not a keyhole shot at all. It became the picture that would not go away, a conversation piece that was to be revived ever after. The object of this wild peep fetish, Marlon Brando, has never commented on its existence one way or another.

By the end of September 1976 Anger was spending a lot of time in London. He was out to make the papers. And there was unfinished business to attend to.

Anger's first newsworthy action was to purchase Cagliostro's baroque eighteenth-century mirror at a London auction. The auctioneers were shocked to receive seven thousand British pounds above what they expected. Anger had paid a total of ten thousand British pounds for the mirror, or US $16,800. He told *Variety* that he was going to use it as a prop in *Lucifer Rising* and also planned to keep it in his London flat as a hedge against lean times. Whether Anger popped for the mirror out of a particularly juicy *Hollywood Babylon* royalty check, investors' money, or was on a buying mission for an anonymous, moneyed associate remains ambiguous. The mirror is considered to have great sex magick value. During his Inquisition trial, Cagliostro was accused of flashing his maid, tying a bow on his cock, and putting an egg cup on his "bishop," as he referred to it, before this mirror.

But there was another pressing matter Anger had to attend to in London. The matter of Jimmy Page.

The Public Humiliation of Jimmy Page: An Interlude

The Jimmy Page debacle had been dragging on since the outset of the decade. It would prove to be the last big bang of Anger's involvement with the top echelon of the English rock crowd.

Page had given Anger an album side of great music for *Lucifer Rising*. He had enabled Anger's perpetual tinkering with the film, allowing Anger to use an editing table in the basement of his London townhouse. The table had been installed to cut concert footage into the Led Zeppelin feature *The Song Remains the Same*.

In October 1976 Anger went to the Page abode in London. Page's wife, Charlotte, argued with him, called the cops, and booted him out of the house. Though the door was bolted the following day, by week's end Anger was collecting his belongings—props from *Lucifer Rising* such as Egyptian statuettes and the crown of Lucifer, which was studded with paste rhinestones from a Mae West dress.

Photos of this momentous occasion appeared in the British rock newspaper *Sounds*. The pictures have a filmstrip effect, since Anger is glimpsed walking from behind a wall clutching Orientalia trinkets. He appears extremely uncomfortable, clearly perturbed in some of the photos and forcing a smile in others.

Anger called a press conference. The press responded, thinking that anything out of Anger's mouth could be juicy gossip. Anger proceeded to pick on every delicate flaw a man could possess. Jimmy Page had domestic problems with some sort of dominant girlfriend. He couldn't hold his drugs. The drugs had ruined his music. On and on it went. To top everything off, there was the most cutting blow: He said Page wasn't a true magician.

"I'm beginning to think Jimmy's dried up as a musician. He's got no themes, no inspiration, no melodies to offer. I'm sure he doesn't have another 'Stairway to Heaven,' which is his most Luciferian song. *Presence* was very much a negative, downer album." (*Presence* sold well like any other Zep album and utilized some of the eerie textures that Page had developed with the *Lucifer Rising* sound-track.)

Anger believed he had a gentleman's agreement with Page, so nothing was ever put in writing. "The whole idea behind the film was that it should be an offering of love," Anger demanded—this love clearly being under his will. "The idea was to go 50-50 on the film's profits and that Jimmy should have all the proceeds from any soundtrack album that came out of it."

Journalists asked Anger if he felt vindictive toward Page. "You bet I do. I'm not a Christian, turn the other cheek kind." A thin smile crept across Anger's face. "In fact, I'm all ready to throw a Kenneth Anger curse."

Magus Anger hath spoken. However, Anger seemed quite peeved over a worldly matter—that Page had not selected him to direct *The Song Remains the Same*. "He could have got me to make the film. Instead he chose some arsehole. I refuse to see it. Rock fans will see whoever they're hot for in the poorest trash."

After Anger had played his last nasty trick, he felt no wrath from the rock crowd. They all had the classic junkie attitude of get out of my face, you're not worth the trouble. The minute Anger ceased to be entertaining and turned demanding, they dropped him like a hot potato.

Predictably, Page ignored him.

Anger now began mouthing off about Page and Jagger any-where to anyone, calling them creeps, losers, junkies, and, the ulti-mate spiritual insult, spent forces. What could they do? Sue him? They knew all too well Anger's financial impotence. If they tried to retaliate in any way, they'd look like fools. They'd look like chumps.

Chapter 15

A Swastika of Desire

after Jimmy Page was ousted by Magus Anger in that loud public display, Bobby Beausoleil wrote to Anger, proposing that he do the soundtrack for *Lucifer Rising*. With the help of a prison teacher, Beausoleil began sending for musical instruments and the necessary parts via mail order. He also began assembling his behind-bars Freedom Orchestra.

On November 17, 1976, *Variety* announced MANSON FOLLOWER TO SCORE ANGER PIC WHILE IN CAL JAIL. It reported that "Bobby Beausoleil, onetime associate of the Charles Manson 'family' and convicted killer of fellow musician Gary Hinman, has replaced Jimmy Page in composing the soundtrack for Kenneth Anger's upcoming film *Lucifer Rising*."

A forty-nine-year-old Anger arrived at Tracy Prison, California, in a three-piece suit. It was the first time since 1967, when Beausoleil was still a teenager, that they had seen each other. Now twenty-eight, Beausoleil had wiled away the time in stir by tattooing his entire upper torso. He also had been pursuing the art of erotic drawing.

The combative decade that both Anger and Beausoleil had endured had left irreparable scars, which in one way made it easier to relate. Beausoleil felt that Anger "had mellowed out. I understood that he had suffered." They both had. "We just kinda talked about old times and whatnot. He did tell me—he said that nobody ever replaced me. He did say that."

After the visit, Anger waxed enthusaistic about the Freedom Orchestra to Bay Area newspapers. He claimed that his falling out with Beausoleil was about "who was to be boss," but that it hardly mattered now. Under these circumstances, Anger changed the story from Beausoleil being a thief to one that had anonymous kids crashing at the Embassy as the culprits for the *Lucifer Rising* rip-off. Meanwhile, Beausoleil submerged himself totally in composing the soundtrack.

Back in New York, Anger was doing some mixing and mingling. At this time Anger hooked up with a public relations service in Manhattan. The firm sent out a press release littered with Anger projects that would never see the light of day: Anger's movie version of *Hollywood Babylon*; the Crowley biopic, now titled *Wickedest*

Man in the World; *Blue Rats*, a Crowley anthology; and *Applied Cruelty*, Anger's verbal musings on S&M. To top it all off was Anger's confessional, *Airborne with Titania*, which was described as "a simply monumental autobiography."

Of course, the press release had something definitive to sell to interested investors or obsessive collectors: private Anger films. *Senators in Bondage* was supposedly Anger's bicentennial ode. The Anthology Film Archives includes it in a semiofficial listing of Anger's films, but declines a definitive answer about possessing a print.

Shortly afterward, another press release declared that all prints of *Senators in Bondage* had been sold; one of the prints had supposedly been acquired by J. Paul Getty, Jr. A second limited edition from Anger, *Matelots en Menottes* (loosely translated as *Sailors in Handcuffs*) promised to be "a return to the subject matter of *Fireworks*." Twelve boxed, numbered, and signed 16mm prints would be available at $1,200 each for June 1977 delivery. Apart from this press release, there is absolutely no evidence that *Matelots en Menottes* exists anywhere.

In 1978 Anger moved out of his West Ninety-ninth Street sublet to 354 East Ninety-first Street, Apartment 9. This would become Anger's permanent residence for the duration of his stay in New York City. The area around Ninety-first and First Avenue, where the apartment was located, had traditionally been a German-Irish neighborhood, one of the last white bastions before Spanish Harlem. The building was a tenement with a huge spark plug ad painted on its side. The apartment itself was a four-room railroad flat with a bathtub in the kitchen and was a shambles when Anger moved in.

Anger set to work decorating the apartment in his own overpowering style. Rooms were painted either glossy blood red or black, the windows were sealed shut. The entire place was transformed into a sarcophagus of old Hollywood memorabilia and occult paraphernalia.

On July 8, 1978, at ten in the evening, Anger was mugged in the doorway of his building. He variously described the assailants as teenage Irish boys from the neighborhood—or a group of queer bashers who had been prowling the Central Park Ramble. Anger was knocked out for an hour and a half and came to in Metropolitan Hospital as stitches were being applied to his head.

Shortly afterward, Anger had a roll of snapshots taken of his bandaged face, captioning them "After the Mugging." He'd whip them out for acquaintances. These muggings would increase in frequency and severity during his stay at this apartment.

From 1978 through 1979, Anger's Scorpio, Bruce Byron, was living a bi-residential lifestyle, knocking between Manhattan and Hoboken, New Jersey. He was still not enjoying any kind of attention that was being lavished on the Warhol superstars, who at least had admirers who would treat them to dinner and a movie. No august institutions were extending invitations to Byron to speak before screenings of *Scorpio Rising*.

Byron was still pathologically following every public showing of *Scorpio Rising*. The need for narcissistic gratification had become overwhelming, causing Byron's psyche to wander into painful self-examination. The only manner in which the narcissus could be fed was by the mirror image, complementing and congratulating the gazer, and virtually the only expression of this primitive need was his cab.

Byron still earned money as a taxi driver in Manhattan, operating an old yellow Checker. For the few hours he occupied the vehicle it was transformed. It was a shocking drumburst of emotion. Every available inch of space in the driver's compartment was taken up by an embarrassingly huge array of photos and clippings of himself and his idols, James Dean and Marlon Brando. Buttons and pictures of Dean loomed everywhere. One would plop down in his cab and be greeted by the sight of this display, although the grizzled driver bore little resemblance to the man in the photographs.

Byron remembers picking up many famous people at this time. He had to correct all of them. They were all wrong. "They all said, 'Kenneth Anger's *Scorpio Rising*' and I said no, I thought of the film before Kenneth Anger. People would look at the photo of me in the film and say it was Kenneth Anger. Kenneth Anger stole my identity. People think that guy in the film is him."

Byron was circulating flyers, which were also sent to any writer interviewing Anger and anyone presenting Anger's films. Some of these flyers consisted of the words BOILING ANGER over a profile shot of Byron from the late fifties and what resembled a police ID sketch of him.

No one in what remained of the underground film world wanted to hear about Byron. He was known for getting up before screenings of *Scorpio Rising* and screaming a rant that had scant basis in anyone's reality and that gave the audience an unwanted jolt in the process.

As a trend in the commercial cinema, underground film had become a fixture of the past. Warhol, its best-known exemplar, had totally gone the exploitation route, with features like *Frankenstein*, *Dracula*, and *Bad*, which were centered around blatant sex and violence.

The audience that had previously sought out underground films as an alternative to Hollywood conventions were now increasingly drawn to midnight cult movie showings. *Pink Flamingos*, *Night of the Living Dead* and Alejandro Jodorowsky's *The Holy Mountain* and *El Topo* all shared traits with their underground predecessors. Sex was surreal, camp spectacle; the films reveled in their outrageousness. Unlike the underground film, which tended to be either overlong or fragmentary, the cult films were accessible, narrative-length features. The viewer's head was also no longer broken by outbursts of Brechtian declarations of the "it's only a movie" sort.

The sexual shock value of underground movies had been subsumed by hard-core pornography. The explicitness hinted at by the underground had been reduced to a commercial formula in which sex was bluntly sold to a horny viewer, no strings attached. Human nature was revealed, because a lot of the underground's audience had been going merely to see sex.

Underground films had been notoriously hard to book; most of the time they had to be packaged into a program of shorts for specialty houses. The feature length of cult and hard-core porn movies made them easy to place. By 1979, these genres were established phenomenons, running not only at specialty theaters but neighborhood outlets.

Underground films had drifted into the hands of the archivist; even in New York City, there were fewer places to view them. Apart from small screening spaces and museum showings, the only regular venues were folding-chair arrangements at the Collective for Living Cinema on White Street in TriBeCa, the Millennium on East Fourth Street in the East Village, and Mekas's Anthology Film Archives on Wooster Street in SoHo.

The minuscule amount the filmmakers made from rentals had never been enough to sustain them, even in the movement's heyday. The most financial return they could expect was a lump sum in the form of a grant or award, certainly not any steady cash flow.

Many underground filmmakers, like Stan Brakhage, drifted into teaching. Brakhage remained the underground's conscience. He had stuck to his guns and gone totally into abstraction. Brakhage's best-known film of this time, *The Text of Light*, is an hour-long meditation on color patterns formed in an ashtray.

At the close of the seventies, Brakhage, Anger, and Warhol continued to be the most visible of the undergrounders. Their films were the most frequently revived and best attended. Unfortunately, a severe and final split between Anger and Brakhage occurred.

As with all such deep personal conflicts between longtime friends, there are various accounts and interpretations as to what happened. One version is that Brakhage won Mekas's *Film Culture* annual award for best independent feature. Anger was one of his competitors. Brakhage felt that Anger deserved the award and would have gladly conceded it to him, but he did need the prize money, since academia barely provided enough income to support his family, let alone his distinctly uncommercial artistic ventures.

Anger was furious about the loss of this award. Using his Puck Productions "Beau Soleil" stationery, Anger announced his new private collector's film, *The Denunciation of Stan Brakhage*. This proclamation was written by Anger in Magic Marker. To make it all the more ominous, a hawk representing Horus the Avenger loomed over the title. Anger included the name "Robert K. Beausoleil" on the flyer, and aped Beausoleil's style, calling himself

"Kenneth R. Anger" for further shock effect. The overall visual impact suggested that Anger was flinging a curse at Brakhage.

The flyer described *The Denunciation of Stan Brakhage* as a fifteen-minute, black and white talkie. Five hundred prints, each costing $800, were offered for sale. Copies of its flyer do exist in the Anger files of the Museum of Modern Art.

Brakhage believed its basic activity consists of a disgruntled, sour Anger expressing his disgust at many of his old friends, especially Brakhage. Anger accuses them of turning their backs on him.

Exacerbating and underlying this conflict was the lectures Brakhage had given about Anger. Anger is not the type of man who opens up easily, and he had confessed private, pained details of his life to Brakhage in times of great emotional stress. Anger became quite perturbed that his statements were providing fodder for Brakhage's lectures and essays. Anger was also an individual who hated having his aura of mystery dispelled. He wanted to be known as a magus of cinema, a sorcerer who used film as his medium.

Anger's *Denunciation* flyer struck Brakhage like a lethal paper plane. It also facilitated Anger's use of censorship over anything Brakhage attempted to publish about him. When Brakhage was assembling *The Brakhage Scrapbook*, a personal volume reflecting his life in the underground film world, Anger went wild. He lashed out every way he could. Letters were sent to everyone who mattered in the assembly of the book, including Brakhage's editor and his wife. Anger's threat of a promised legal proceeding was something Brakhage could neither afford nor want to endure.

Around this time the American Federation of the Arts had acquired prints of Anger's movies for distribution. AFA head Steve Aronson had managed this by getting Anger's films out of a sticky in-hock situation in England.

A safe haven was provided for Anger and his prints. The AFA had a beautiful townhouse on a tree-lined Upper East Side street, elegant in a quiet, comfortable way. The staff was always polite and friendly, extremely nice to everyone they came in contact with. As a distributor, the AFA was on a museum level, with respectability of the highest quality. It provided Anger with a steady stream of royalty checks and advances that could be written off against current screenings.

Anger began turning up at the AFA building to once again touch up the gold fan in *Eaux d'Artifice* by hand. Around this time he also added the Electric Light Orchestra soundtrack to *Pleasure Dome*, which was not as bad as it initially seemed when hearing it. The music was highly melodramatic, yet was well timed with the ebb and flow of the action.

Anger also produced what he calls the 1979 "kiddie version" of *Rabbit's Moon*. The film was compressed virtually in half, into seven minutes, and pops out at the viewer like an angry accordion. All the romanticism is gone. The complex sadomasochistic triangle involving Pierrot, Harlequin, and Columbine was transformed into a fast-paced slapfest à la Charlie Chaplin. The film's major symbol of narcissism—the little boys holding the mirror to Pierrot—is now barely present. The images are even speeded up at points. All this is set to a grating, incessant, repetitive, British teeny-bopper tune by Andy Arthur.

Around this period, the slick hard-core porn magazine *Puritan* did a feature on Beausoleil's erotic art. It was the first time his artwork had appeared publicly. A one-page essay written by Anger was included. It was highly reminiscent of Cocteau's description of past sexual conquests in *Le Livre Blanc*. Anger is slavish in his worship of Beausoleil, calling him a genius, comparing him to de Sade and Genet. Anger lets loose with an impassioned swoon over Beausoleil's "rampant stiff cock" and "smooth male balls." He explained Beausoleil's art as being based upon "a swastika of desire."

The girls in the Beausoleil artwork are either Sweet Gwendoline, pubescent blond nymphs, or slightly older, maternal dark-haired women. Three panels show a girl worshiping a disembodied cock. Beausoleil is quite proud that the male genitals portrayed are his own. One surrealistic drawing portrays a cock and an ass, with two blond twins, one sucking, the other rimming. Another shows a woman fingering his ass and sucking his cock. A highlight is Beausoleil's self-portrait: he's embodied as a satyr with goat's legs, leaving his mark on a nymphet's willing buttock.

The article was surprisingly good for a men's magazine, daring in a genuine way. Anger was sexually open and romantic in his description of Beausoleil; it seems the most honest representation of his feelings that he's ever given.

Other than that, Anger was strictly a junk culture influence in 1979. A European sexploitation movie known domestically as *Smooth Silk and Raw Velvet* mimicked the scenes shot at the pyramids for *Lucifer Rising*, with cast members attired as gods performing sex magick rituals. The book *Too Young to Die* imitated *Hollywood Babylon*, covering recent deaths of celebrities like Lenny Bruce, Duane Allman, and Cass Elliot.

Scorpio Rising played the Film Expo at the New York Coliseum. Prints were being sold there, and the Anger film was one of the products offered. It was shown in a tiny, cordoned-off tent, with folding chairs in front of a screen. Nonetheless, the movie remained powerful, a knockout even under those circumstances.

At the close of the seventies, Anger's personal appearances unfortunately were not holding up as well as his work. He had become a familiar yet depressed sight at screenings of the "Magick Lantern Cycle" at college campuses and the scant venues for underground films in New York City.

At a showing at the Millennium, Anger was especially despondent. He was broke. A lonely hearted table was set up with memorabilia from his own films for sale. First editions of the French *Hollywood Babylone* went for $300 each. There were the omnipresent ANGER jerseys. Anger was even trying to sell the *Lucifer* jacket. Perhaps he felt he'd never find another Beausoleil or Huggins to fill it, and the search had wearied him. Despite his malaise, a flash of Thelemic pride suddenly seized Anger, and he yanked up his jersey to reveal his LUCIFER tattoo to the audience.

Chapter 16

I Love Lucifer

1980. It was a new decade and Anger was off to a hostile start. It began on a paranoid note for Anger's old nemesis Andy Warhol. On Wednesday, January 2, Warhol complained to his diarist Pat Hackett that "Whitney Tower called and said that Kenneth Anger threw paint at Fred's [Hughes] door up on Eighty-ninth and Lexington. He must think I still live there. He's been saying I'm the devil or something, I don't know what the problem is." As with anything that disrupted Warhol's routine at this point, it jangled his nerves.

On Saturday, March 1, Warhol went to dinner at William Burroughs's bunker at 222 Bowery. Also present were Victor Bockris, Mick Jagger, and *Wet* magazine photographer Marcia Resnick. Resnick told Warhol about her experience shooting Anger for *Wet* at Anger's pad. Warhol begged her not to mention his name to Anger, saying, "He might beat [you] up, he thinks I'm the devil." Resnick described to Warhol the blood-red motif of Anger's Ninety-first Street digs and how he was putting everyone down.

That same month the *Wet* interview hit the stands. The photos were startling. Anger was gaunt, hollow-cheeked, his appearance harkening back to his soda straw look in *Fireworks*.

Anger's rap in this interview was tangential and slightly off kilter. He bitched about his nearly decade-old uncollected judgment against Marvin Miller, making it sound like a landlord-tenant dispute going nowhere. He accuses members of the Hollywood establishment like Dennis Hopper of stealing from him.

Anger seemed bored and petulant. He complained that LSD wasn't working like it used to: "I used to see real Technicolor trips with the waltz and the rhumba. I mean very colorful, bright colors. Maybe the quality of the stuff is so bad now that it doesn't do what it used to. I guess you can't get the real thing anymore. I used to see things like a desert sky with stars and the stars would turn into showgirls and diamonds and things like that. It was something to have fun on. I don't know whether my brain burned out or what, but it doesn't register anymore."

Anger's disillusionment with acid was obvious. He needed to *feel* something. The conversation turned to SS atrocities, which he explained as methedrine freakouts. Turning personal, Anger confided that "speed brought out the killer in me. It began to do nasty tricks to me. The fantasies got too ugly. I would begin to see people, maybe more accurately, but in a very bad light and I would feel like attacking them."

Anger then went off on a Ramon Novarro–style tangent about having no family or friends, only "associates." He mentioned his recent trip to the hospital, jealously stating that a certain New Yorker refused to pick him up because "he was smoking grass in his apartment with some trick."

Back at Anger's home, his gramophone crooning in the background, Anger was trying to be social, entertaining two ladies of the press, interviewer Ann Bardach and photographer Marcia Resnick. They brought up his sexuality, asking if he was gay. "Ugh, I hate labels. I am not gay in the sense that most of the time I am mean and gloomy because I am a manic depressive."

Anger ended this treatise on a note of isolation. "I have deliberately blocked out the outside world. It's so noisy I've sealed the windows. I've sealed myself away. From this room you could never tell this is New York City. It could be anywhere. The thirties was my childhood. That's the period that fixates me. It's the only time I relate to."

He spoke of possible future projects in the interview: *Anger's Autographs* and *Unknown Marilyn*, which would contain unpublished photos of Marilyn Monroe. They never came to light. *Hollywood Babylon II* was scheduled for release in early 1981 by Times Books. It would be three years and at least one other publisher before this would happen.

However, soon after the wet interview, Anger's movies suddenly enjoyed multiple New York City revivals in highly varied contexts. The Collective for Living Cinema ran *Fireworks* with Jean Genet's *Un Chant d'Amour*. It was extraordinary that in the screen freedom climate of the early eighties both films retained their shock value. The double bill was also aesthetically perfect in the sense that both films shared a dream fulfillment quality of the erotic imagination.

Anger appeared with the "Magick Lantern Cycle" at Club 57, a tiny East Village nightspot located in a church basement on 57 St.

Mark's Place. The club featured various performance pieces and screenings of offbeat movies and drew a crowd that included burgeoning downtown diva Ann Magnuson, animator M. Henry Jones, artists Keith Haring, Kenny Scharf, Scott Covert, and performance artist/dancer John Sex. The Club 57 crowd was united by a post-punk aesthetic that was deeply rooted in the sixties. They wanted to see the old guard, such as Warhol superstar Ondine, who showed up with his prints of *Vinyl* and *Chelsea Girls*. Anger was considered as much of a stylistic harbinger, with the leather iconography and theatrical masochism he immortalized in *Scorpio Rising*, as well as his introduction of the first punk rock name, Anger, so it was only logical that he should appear, too.

The showing of the "Magick Lantern Cycle" got off to a bang. The Club 57 ad was a bold visual statement, featuring a nude, *Kustom Kar Kommandos*/Dick Dale–era beach boy with an erection. Wheat-pasted all over the East Village, the flyer gained instant infamy.

Club 57's teeny space, which broke fire safety codes with a crowd of a hundred, was packed with hundreds of people anxious to see Anger present his films, some traveling from as far as upstate New York college campuses. As always, Anger set up his "Buy Direct from Anger" table at the entrance where admissions were sold. Anger was gratified with the size and excited enthusiasm of the crowd. He responded by digging deeply into his purse of gossip tales. *Hollywood Babylon* stories were told, followed by Anger ripping deeply into Jagger, stating, to the amusement of all, that Jerry Hall made a great dominatrix for him. Anger was pleased that he had made a nice, fun appearance.

Anger's subsequent appearances at SoHo's Performing Garage were more restrained. Anger was far less outgoing and humorous than he had been at Club 57. He preceded each film with a little story, such as the sailors being "real ones" in *Fireworks* and how he met the "bikers" in *Scorpio Rising*. During this screening a playfully tipsy John Sex walked up to the "Buy Direct from Anger" table, stared at Anger's portrait photo on the back of *Hollywood Babylon*, looked at Anger and clucked, "You were a handsome man—twenty years ago!" Anger stood in shocked silence.

A standard item that was now featured for sale at the table was Robert Haller's monograph on Anger. Haller worked for Anthology Film Archives, and the monograph took an academic slant on the highlights of his career and included a few stills, a filmography, and a short chat with the artist.

I met Anger on April 30, 1980, to interview him for the *Soho Weekly News*. In person he seemed a kind, gentle, intelligent man. Anger also seemed to be lonely and isolated, with few friends, and painfully aware that he had aged. His apartment had a museum-like, pristine quality, although it seemed somewhat ominous with all the red and black decor. The interview was enjoyably detailed, with Anger telling many anecdotes about making his films, and we agreed to continue it the following evening.

At five the next night, Anger greeted me at the door of his apartment. Unlike the prior night, the place was a shambles. Sex tabloids like the multisexed *Screw* and the gay *David* were strewn all over. Anger mentioned that we would be on limited time this evening. He had called one of the escort service ads and was expecting his date, who would be attired in an Air Force uniform, to arrive shortly.

Anger unfolded a rather long story about Bobby Beausoleil, the major thrust of which was that Beausoleil was a thief, that he had talked Anger out of money in order to front a pot-selling deal, and that he lied. This night's Beausoleil sonata concluded with Anger saying, "I still love Bobby and the fact that he's a murderer doesn't change anything." He insisted that his feelings were different from Genet's lust for rough trade killers but did not elaborate as to how.

Anger talked a great deal about S&M, brilliantly detailing what he felt were the nuances of its homo- and heterosexual realms:

"They're totally different. In the first place, straight S&M is much more secret than gay S&M because in gay S&M both parties are male, and men, whether they're passive or active, are much more apt to be open and aggressive about their tastes. When one of the partners is a woman, it implies reticence and really being in the closet much more than the— I hate the term gay and I never really do use it. I use homosexual and reject the term 'gay.' It's a term I don't like. It's a distortion of language. The homosexual scene is much more liberated. In other words, they're not into wasting time. They want action. They want something delivered.

"But a heterosexual who is interested in a woman who will whip him or dominate him or treat him like a bad baby or any of those variations on that trip, which can go from very heavy to just psychological titillation, is in for a much harder time. In the heterosexual scene there are correspondence clubs and under-ground networks and things. But even today, in the so-called liber-ated eighties, or whatever it is, it's still a much more difficult trip. It's much more difficult for a man who is oriented, a submissive man . . . to find a dominant woman. . . . much more difficult to find one who is genuinely into that than . . . if he were gay to find a dominant man. I talked to Dr. Kinsey about this at length and he said, 'There are very few.' It's almost like trying to find a needle in a haystack."

Anger vacationed in Key West that spring, staying with his old friend, Tennessee Williams. The tropical humidity was asphyxiat-ing, so Anger sought relief in a bar where he cast his eyes on a new fallen angel. He had found a fresh Lucifer.

Alan French was originally from a small town in Massachusetts. Having knocked from coast to coast, he spent some time with Anger.

Anger was very excited, but all too soon it was time for him to return to New York. He promised to send for his new Lucifer when the proper funds were conjured.

Back in the city, Anger would sit brooding in his glossy red tomb, scheming about how to assemble the bucks to get Alan to come north. After getting the necessary cash, Lucifer was brought onto the scene, in cutoffs.

Anger was a proud man. Alan would be the perfect escort for the upcoming premiere of *Lucifer Rising*. Anger had again proved to the world that he could still attract a good-looking young study.

Alan was to be pacified at any cost. Anger loathed television, but Alan was bored. Soon a black and white TV was blaring in the background during phone conversations with Anger. Alan was a quiet doper who, according to Anger, had a $100-a-day habit.

I continued to remain friendly with Anger. Along with Alan, he attended the screenings I presented at Club 57 of the exploitation documentaries *Mondo Cane* and *Manson*. During the latter film, a still of Beausoleil flashed onscreen, and Anger winced in dramatic emotion.

Photos of both Anger and Alan were taken by the late Jimmy De Sana to accompany my *Soho Weekly News* interview. De Sana was known for his photography book *Submission* and his sado-masochistic take on reality. The shots showed Anger shirtless and sassy under pounding red and yellow lights on a color cover, a scowl filling his face. De Sana also took some provocative stills of Alan in cutoffs.

Originally, Anger's LUCIFER tattoo seemed to be a pun on Cocteau's Pas de Chance character in *Le Livre Blanc*, the sailor with OUT OF LUCK across his chest. Now the tattoo seemed shocking. More than its occult overtones, the tattoo looked like something you'd see on a hard-core street kid. It seemed that Anger wanted to be linked to that sort of gray world so badly he'd mark himself to be part of it.

Anger enjoyed attending the tattoo parties at the infamous and sexually decadent Hellfire Club, located in Fourteenth Street's meat-packing district off the West Side Highway. At night this area metamorphoses into a Tenderloin district for drag queens, S&M devotees, and leather enthusiasts. The Hellfire get-togethers gave Anger the opportunity to display proudly the proclamations of this most permanent of personal expressions. He could mix and mingle with tattoo freaks, premiere tattoo artists like Spider Webb, and sex movie stalwarts like Marc "10-1/2" Stevens and Jamie Gillis. Along with other post-party revelers, Anger was a frequent house guest at Stevens's relatively luxurious high-rise digs in Gramercy Park.

Gillis, a veteran sex performer and S&M enthusiast, had seen *Scorpio Rising* as a teenager when Anger's films played the male adult theater circuit in packages like "The Fabulous Anger Trilogy." He found the atmosphere at Hellfire stimulating, describing it as "a free-for-all, but it didn't mean you had to participate. You could go in and watch. If you were there, you could sit at the bar and have a drink and do nothing. Or you could get gang-banged by twenty guys."

According to Gillis, the scene at Hellfire was so base that people were known by reputation, not name. "It was a very vital, exciting, strange kind of place with all kinds of madness going on. Sexual stuff in the pre-AIDS days that people were happy to do. Lots of gang-banging and fist-fucking. Whatever you can imagine went on."

At this time, Alan French's signature was proudly added to the indelible roll call of inamoratas tattooed down Anger's arm, after BOBBY and JERRY (Main from *Kustom Kar Kommandos*). As Anger walked through Hellfire displaying these tattoos and the omnipresent LUCIFER, which through the aging process had started to sag, he was waving his freak flag high.

After my *Soho Weekly News* interview, Anger's reputation as a major American artist was reinforced by *Kenneth Anger's Magick*, a PBS documentary. This reverential short film is academic in the sense that it explained Anger's achievements to a mass audience. It was enormously satisfying to see an underground filmmaker of Anger's stature getting this sort of television exposure. The format was a filmed version of a polite chat with the artist in his living room, punctuated by cannily selected film clips.

Director Kit Fitzgerald knew what she wanted and executed it well. The documentary relies on Anger's myths, but uses them to highlight some of the best scenes from *Fireworks*, *Rabbit's Moon*, and *Scorpio Rising*, replete with the male nudity that had prompted the *Scorpio* obscenity trial. Anger appears remarkably relaxed and composed.

It wasn't easy to reach this level of professionalism. Fitzgerald recalls shooting "on a very hot July evening. He had to sell his air conditioner recently because he was so broke. The windows are sealed there. So there's a lot of sweating going on. As we were shooting, we were kind of stopping and wiping him off and giving him some water. I kept it at a very small crew because I always think it's easier—very personable, very intimate. Afterward, we went to a restaurant. I remember that as one of the most wonderful times I've ever had. He was just completely comfortable and sympathetic. We stayed a long time and talked and talked.

"I worked so hard both in the studio and the editing. I did a lot of audio editing, more than any work I've ever done. The audio is edited to be continuous because he can speak very rapid or low. Sometimes he speeded up, then it's—pause—'Ken, where's the next word. Hello, are you there?'

"He's isolated. He seemed very lonely. He kind of wants to keep up the image of the *enfant terrible*. In America, middle age for artists is difficult because in Europe there is a greater connection with the arts and a greater appreciation of artists. Here you may be the *enfant terrible*, which he was, then you move into your thirties and forties, and there's another generation, a new concern. So this is a very lonely time for artists."

Alan and Anger continued to be seen together at public events. Anger seemed to have an insistent need to be viewed in Alan's company, taking him to virtually everything Alan would allow.

Alan would take off every now and then. During one of these absences, Anger socialized with Larry O'Toole, a good-natured teenage punk rock enthusiast from Staten Island. Anger and O'Toole saw Martin Scorsese's *Raging Bull* at the huge Cinerama Theater in Times Square. Anger sat spellbound by the story of an aggressive man who couldn't control his temper.

In November 1980 I accompanied Anger when he met with Ava Leighton, president of Audubon Films. She was a no-nonsense woman who had been a major pioneer in the distribution of sex-ploitation films before they became totally legal. At this time she was occupied with marketing Radley Metzger's pseudo-art softcore, movies like *The Lickerish Quartet* on videotape. Videotapes then were a luxury item, selling in the $100 per cassette range.

Anger had worn his cream-colored suit to Mrs. Leighton's office on Fifty-third and Seventh Avenue. He had brought his prints and appeared extremely depressed. Alan had been giving him a hard time at home.

Perhaps Anger suspected that video would be, in effect, a final sale. No longer would collectors need to go through the costly process of duping prints. The low-cost piracy inherent in the video business meant that anyone could copy a tape and bootleg it. He would no longer have control over where his prints were shown. There would be no more left-handed fanatical craftsman work on individual frames, adding or removing things, making each print unique.

Despite her gravelly voice and cold manner, Mrs. Leighton could be very kind if she liked you, and she had an honesty that was rare in the exploitation movie field. She was polite to Anger, but he remained somber, knowing that she was a businessperson who would be analyzing his films from a monetary standpoint.

Silence fell over the office as the "Magick Lantern Cycle" moved through the projector, threading itself. The room was lit with *Scorpio Rising*, the film which Mrs. Leighton later remarked as being the most commercial. Anger sat frowning, holding his head.

Under these circumstances, *Pleasure Dome* was especially interminable. No one noticed that the film was accumulating on the floor instead of on the spillover reel. About halfway through it Anger snapped alert in his chair. He began screaming, "MY PRINT! MY PRINT! This cost A THOUSAND DOLLARS! Oh, I just want to get out of here! Bill! I just want to get out of here!"

Anger began intimating that Mrs. Leighton would be financially responsible for the damage to the print. Mrs. Leighton, in her businesslike pragmatism, thought he was full of shit and that no 16mm one-reeler could have cost a grand to strike.

After rethreading the film by hand, with the deal blown to hell, Anger beat a hasty retreat. When we had a snack in the Stage Deli afterward, he calmed down a bit but his mood remained foul. He was distrustful of Mrs. Leighton, of anyone controlling his films.

I called Anger a few days later. He was hysterical. "John Lennon's been shot. He was a very good friend of mine. I'm on my way up to the District Attorney's office because Mark David Chapman came up to me at a screening in Hawaii and handed me a fistful of bullets. He said, 'These are for John Lennon.' And if that lady [Mrs. Leighton] doesn't want to give me a deal, she can go fuck herself!" He slammed the phone down.

Anger was about to receive a lot of shocking publicity. He told the press about Chapman: "He came to my film show but instead of moving on, he kept asking me, 'You know Anita Pallenberg? You know Mick Jagger? You know John and Yoko? How often do you see them for dinner?' I said, 'I live in New York.' 'They live in New York.' He kept bugging me. He went down the list of rock stars I knew." After shaking Chapman's hand, Anger was given two 38-caliber cartridges.

Chapman has told me by letter that he did, in fact, meet Anger and that there were three parts to their meeting. He also asked me for a copy of the Koran and, like every modern-day murder star, had his hand out for money to tell me about it. I declined.

After the Lennon shooting, Anger held a press screening of *Lucifer Rising* at the Whitney Museum. Anger appeared exhausted, beat and very upset. He was wearing an old Navy peacoat and his hair was showing signs of gray, not having been dyed for a while. Yet he was extremely gracious, apologizing to me for his outburst on the phone, emphasizing that he had just been very upset.

Lucifer Rising opens with the Puck Productions logo. A pyramid containing Anger's signature with MAGUS on each of its three sides appears. The credits unfold with A FILM BY KENNETH ANGER in red letters against a black background. MUSIC BY BOBBY BEAUSOLEIL follows, placing Beausoleil in a category with Jagger and Page as the only collaborators credited in Anger's films.

Volcanoes erupt at night as the soundtrack rumbles acid rock. Lava pours, there's a burst of flame. The title LUCIFER RISING ascends out of waters beneath a darkened sky. The letters of the title peer into flames that are reflected in the water.

The volcanoes once again appear, with a small island in the distance. Miriam Gibril as Isis, wearing an elaborate headdress and a costume baring her breasts, wakes. An alligator hatches from an egg. This Egyptian Mother Nature figure is shown through montage as being interested in the birth. She smiles. More alligators are seen in bluish tint. Blue, mudlike lava bubbles.

Isis removes a gold ankh from its place in stone and raises it to the sky. The music becomes tinged with spaghetti western brass.

Donald Cammell as Osiris, the paternal figure, appears before a tomb in a similarly elaborate headdress. His arms are crossed. He responds to Isis and she signals back.

They continue to signal to each other. As Osiris raises his staff, lightning, a primal female deity symbol, is intercut. The music grows doleful. One gets the impression that this ritual has been performed for an eternity. The forces of nature are aroused. An eclipse is followed by a fire inside a pyramid.

The Adept (Hayden Couts) sleeps on a two-eyed pillow. His face is bathed in red-orange hues. The Adept has longish dark hair and dark eyebrows. Elaborately colored pyramids cover his robe. In a stunning acid visual, heat waves appear when he exhales in profile.

The Adept's eyes open. He rises from a pentagram bedspread. He sees a golden dawn, a reference to the first mystical society Crowley joined. The Adept takes out a dagger with an eye of a medieval devil. The dagger leads him through darkness, past a door to a red room, through a red hallway, into a black ballroom area with black and white tiles. He passes a mirror and doesn't see himself.

The Adept places a wand at the statue of Horus. He pulls a cover off an intricate Egyptian throne and sits on it, surrounded in black. Quick cut to him nude. The Adept throws a spear at a London mod-era girl who's contorted in an uncomfortable position lying in a boat. She then walks through a forest and falls as his spear strikes her via montage.

He's suddenly covered in blood, holding a bloody spear, fading into red. The Adept approaches a bathroom with a pink triangle emblazoned with "trademark" turned upside down. It's eerily reminiscent of the pink triangle homosexuals were forced to wear in concentration camps.

Isis holds a kite. The Adept washes the blood off in the tub, submerging himself in the bloody water. Marianne Faithfull as Lilith, the kabbalistic goddess of destruction, wakes. The full moon, Crowley's symbol for females and menstruation, is seen through the clouds. She starts breathing in a sarcophagus. Destruction and bloodletting have been aroused by the Adept sacrificing the girl.

Lilith rises by the Nile, responding to the full moon. Clouds contract. She surveys a forest and it bursts into flames. Stone female figures are seen protecting the walls of Babylon. Lilith is next seen in profile as she walks in open embrace toward a phallic rock formation. She continues walking in an exquisite shot with the pyramids in the background. At this point, any scene in the film can be extracted to form a beautiful moment of artistic expression.

She reigns over a tiny pyramid, then unfolds her arms in an omnipotent pose under the sphinx. The face of Leslie Huggins as Lucifer is superimposed. The Adept walks nude through Stonehenge. A pan of his chest reveals jewelry with an especially noticeable figure of Michael the Archangel, another kabbalistic deity.

Distant fire appears. A hooded procession is interspersed with Lilith climbing an enormous staircase. The back and forth cuts of these figures walking is hypnotically sleep inducing.

Osiris exits a temple. Isis reappears. She raises her arm, greeting Osiris. Quick cut of a man's head superimposed over a statue. Three deities walk with outrageously huge headdresses.

Beausoleil's music stirs. A nude woman appears with arms outstretched. The acolytes have now taken up the ritual. The eight-armed Hindu goddess Kali appears, again emphasizing primal female instinct.

The magic circle is briefly seen. The names of characters from Crowley's *The Book of the Law* such as Nuit, Hadit, and Babalon, as well as Lucifer and Chaos, are painted within it. A large drop of water explodes.

Anger, as the Magus, descends a spiral staircase. He resembles Mickey Mouse in *Fantasia*. The smoke surrounds Lord Chaos (Sir Francis Rose), who stands in the center of the circle as little candles burn around him. He's old, hairy, and rotted.

Magus Anger wafts incense at Lord Chaos. Wearing a black and white royalty robe, Lord Chaos bitches silently and scowls. A gold volcanic landscape churns. Lord Chaos frowns, turns around, and an elephant stomps a cobra.

There's a pan down a tower back to the magic circle. The music builds. Magus Anger, now resembling Jimmy Page, is in its center, wearing a white Crowleyan robe. Nine candles surround the circle.

He begins to pace the circle. The primal Darwinistic imagery grows even more intense as a tiger powerfully swims through the water. The waters swirl. A small triangle frames the Magus's dance as bright specks, like fireflies, surround it. Shots of the ruins of Stonehenge and a red volcanic eruption ensue. On the soundtrack Beausoleil riffs wildly on guitar.

Lightning. A rainbow of colors introduces Lucifer, seen from behind displaying the multicolored "LUCIFER" jacket. As he turns around, a facial shot of Lucifer (Leslie Huggins) is intercut with the triumphant Magus, indicating that the working was successful. A volcano erupts in an orgasmic burst.

The action now shifts to a human tarot card tableaux. A medium shuffles a deck. In another room, an acolyte is seen wearing a robe and scarf around his eyes. The medium continues shuffling and then throws the cards in the air, followed immediately with an image of snow, representing come.

A red cane with a gold pentagram is removed to reveal a black wreath surrounding a facial photo of a scowling Aleister Crowley. Couts, the Adept, holds a knife underneath it. He then takes a copy of *The Equinox* and passes Crowley's portrait, as Huggins as Lucifer is seen in profile. Lucifer seems like an initiate who has been expected, while the Adept is more practiced. A symbol of the Beast 666—a satyr having intercourse with a goat—is seen in close-up as a goat grazing is intercut.

Jimmy Page, bearded as Crowley was in his mountaineering adventures, has a copy of the Stele of Revealing, which was Exhibit 666 in Cairo's Boulak Museum—the hieroglyphic tablet that inspired *The Book of the Law*—and holds it up to Crowley's portrait. Crowley's face then appears in a burst of white. It's his bald, Satanic, pre-Hitlerian pose, the photo which got him dubbed "A Man We'd Like to Hang" by the yellow press. The image of him in a magician's cap follows in another burst of light. Crowley's thumbs in this photo are adjacent to his hat, pointing upward, the symbol of Pan and an indication of creative energy. On his cap is the Jungian eye in the triangle figure.

Supporting adept lies in bed, while a fellow Crowleyite in a red costume passes a man painted black and white as the sun,

Crowley's ultimate metaphor for his "solar-phallic" religion, peers in through a side entrance. The two adepts approach Lucifer. One brings the match, the other blows it out. They present an unseen Lucifer with a spaceship cake with HAPPY BIRTHDAY LUCIFER MARK VI and little spacemen on it, and smile. An explosion of fire. A small idol reminiscent of *Pleasure Dome* appears. Sprockets of film move onscreen.

Lilith weeps into a scarf in a mod bedroom. Glass shatters in a shot visually recalling *A Midsummer Night's Dream*. A mirror table is shattered. Lilith holds a piece of bloody cloth and drops it. Stock *Wizard of Oz*–type footage of a twister approaching a farm appears, signaling destruction. Lilith continues weeping. It looks as if Marianne Faithfull is on the worst acid trip of her life. She weeps into violets as an adept looks on. She crumples the violet and throws it at him.

Costumed in blue, Lilith approaches an Egyptian temple. She's barred from it by an adept. As a flower shrinks at her touch, Isis holds a healthy flower and smiles approvingly. Lilith bows before a poppy, a clear reference to Faithfull's drug habits. Isis and Osiris begin to leave the temple together.

In the most weirdly touching scene of the movie, the word WISH appears with a clear wand and a star. On one level it underscores the Crowleyan principle that "every man and every woman is a star," that each individual is his or her own universe. On another more basic emotional level it's a reference to the old standard "When You Wish Upon a Star," with its implication of childlike dream fulfillment.

Osiris nods and smiles as he holds six Egyptian idols, and slowly drops them in the water. An excerpt from an old musical, tinted blue, follows. A devil from this film clip scoops up writhing dancers.

Lightning. The earth explodes backward. Isis and Osiris are together again. She raises her hands toward flying saucers, which Jack Parsons believed were an enigmatic engine mentioned in Crowley's *The Book of the Law*, as they pass over the Egyptian columns. In the film's trademark image, the flying saucers pass over the sphinx.

The past (gods), present (adepts), and future (space) have finally come together. Everything has been finalized and now it's just another day.

Page Wood's poster for *Lucifer Rising* is shown. "Kenneth Anger" appears in a pyramid and ends the film.

This version of *Lucifer Rising* differed from what Anger dubbed *Lucifer Rising, Part I*, the earlier cut with music by Jimmy Page. That version concentrated on proper spectacle shot in Egypt, the kind of footage Anger would screen for respectable grant sources to solicit financing. A great deal of new footage was added to the present *Lucifer Rising*, making it almost twice as long at forty-five minutes. The characters of the Adept and Lord Chaos, as well as the human tarot deck that climaxes the film, were new.

The character of the Adept unlocks the psychodramatic autobiographical element of Anger's moviemaking. It doesn't take much to see the image of Beausoleil in Hayden Couts. This pivotal figure unleashes Chaos during the invocation of Lucifer by throwing the spear at the girl. The girl looks specifically late sixties in a Carnaby Street manner, as opposed to the timeless period of the rest of the film. After Chaos is released, Anger as the Magus is able to produce the perfect, idealized Lucifer—Leslie Huggins, Beausoleil's enigmatic successor.

The image of Lord Chaos is especially startling, as he looks like a foul medieval demon. Anger had also been aware of Bruce Byron's antics, and the resemblance between the two is uncanny, a truly magical stroke.

Throughout *Lucifer Rising* Anger builds up a hypnotic rhythm in intercutting the gods and the human practitioners. As he did in *Scorpio Rising*, the cross-cutting builds to an exciting climax. Here it is the human tarot deck, a scene as visually stunning as any of the highlights of Anger's films.

As a religious movie, *Lucifer Rising* is of the top order. The genre is normally strewn with kitsch such as *The Ten Commandments* and *Mohammed, Messenger of God*, with few films of the caliber of Scorsese's *The Last Temptation of Christ* or Pasolini's *The Gospel According to St. Matthew*. On its most obvious level *Lucifer Rising* challenges the traditional Christian dogma that Lucifer is the devil and restores him to his place in Crowleyan mythology as the light-bearer. The film vividly illustrates a secretive religion, Thelema. So precise is Anger's imagery that he utilized the late Gerald Yorke, one of Britain's leading authorities on Crowley and an associate of Aleister himself, as Thelemic consultant.

The specifically Thelemic associations can make *Lucifer Rising* initially cold and inaccessible to viewers not versed in such matters, and, admittedly, the narrative is more internalized than any film Anger has made. Yet everyone can appreciate the film as a beautiful work of art in a purely visceral sense. Anger's love of movies is present throughout—in the homemade *Intolerance* sequences of the gods, the use of Eisenstein montage in extremis to carry the narrative, the integration of pop iconography, and the influence of exploitation movies like *Robinson Crusoe on Mars* as the flying saucers pass over the sphinx. Just as Anger's Magus reminds one of Mickey Mouse in *Fantasia*, a child's sense of fun and fascination is present in everything about *Lucifer Rising*. The film is also autobiographical in an abstracted and coded Crowleyan manner. In the scheme of Anger's work, *Lucifer Rising* fleshes out *Lucifer Rising, Part I* and deepens, extends, and comments on *Invocation of My Demon Brother*, another film with a highly internalized narrative.

More than any of Anger's movies, *Lucifer Rising* grows on you. At first glance it seems like something to be admired more than enjoyed, but by the tenth viewing it is totally enrapturing and spellbinding. I called it the best film of 1980 in the *Soho Weekly News*.

At the Whitney Museum press screening of *Lucifer Rising*, Larry O'Toole accompanied Anger. They stood together behind the small audience of journalists and arts organizations representatives. Both Anger and O'Toole had homemade megaphones constructed of rolled-up cardboard. They proceeded to bellow call-and-response-type statements as a live aural counterpoint to Anger's silent images.

As Isis would signal to Osiris, Anger and O'Toole would shout "Isis calling" and "Osiris responding." When Marianne Faithfull appeared as Lilith, the call turned to "Lilith responding." As

Anger danced around Sir Francis Rose in the magic circle, "Chaos, Chaos" was shouted. Leslie Huggins, seen from behind in the LUCIFER jacket, elicited an excited "LUCIFER!" from Anger. As Crowley's face flashed on the screen, Anger and O'Toole repeated, "AL." Finally, they said "Lucifer Rising" as the flying saucer hovered over the sphinx.

The ultimate effect of these shouted captions was distraction. Anger asked me what I thought of this performance art and I responded truthfully that it seemed a bit much.

"Thank you, Bill. I hoped you'd say that." He seemed relieved.

Lucifer Rising's official premiere was on December 18, 1980, at the Whitney Museum. To herald it, photos of Anger and Alan appeared in the centerfold of the *Village Voice* under the heading ANGELS. Two photos by Sylvia Plachy were featured. One was of Anger sporting a grin worthy of Al Jolson next to a campy rabbit-pattern curtain. Next to this shot was one of Alan, again in cutoffs, in a stance that is usually seen in Greyhound bus terminals. The accompanying caption billed Alan as "Al Fven," making him sound vaguely Scandinavian, and as Anger's "latest Lucifer."

Coincidentally, at the time these photos were taken, Anger and I had been discussing both Pasolini and Genet. Anger had met Pasolini in Paris and found him obsessed with rough trade and where to meet it. Anger also mentioned that he used to own a print of Genet's *Un Chant d'Amour,* a film known for its prison sex sequences. However, he had snipped out the idyllic, romantic fantasy scene because "it's two big lummoxes romping."

The *Lucifer Rising* premiere was Anger's first in a decade. The genteel art house crowd was treated to a beefcake slide show of Alan in his cutoffs as an hors d'oeuvre to the film. Anger had Alan take a bow before the audience. Alan, who was but a transient, seemed mystified by the proceedings but, nonetheless, loved the attention.

Recent photos of a still incarcerated, heavily tattooed, yet jovial Bobby Beausoleil adorned the auditorium. Bobby . . . Leslie . . . Alan . . . Anger's Lucifers were surrounding him. They were present on screen, in photo, and in the flesh. The entire Whitney premiere was an unqualified success. Everyone had a good time.

Beausoleil's soundtrack fit the movie like a warm glove. It was a first in more ways than its being a prison recording, in that it was the first soundtrack of an Anger movie to be committed to vinyl. Beausoleil did as good a job with the score as Jagger or Page. Journalists discussing the soundtrack unfortunately pressed the exotic convict button frequently, but Beausoleil ultimately got what he wanted—his music was heard. And Anger grew a little bit more infamous each time Beausoleil was mentioned in this manner.

Ultimately, Beausoleil had matured from the *Lucifer Rising* experience. He wanted to finish the job he initiated back in 1967 with Anger and he had succeeded.

I did another *Soho Weekly News* interview with Anger to tie in with covering the opening of *Lucifer Rising* in which Anger described Lucifer as "a teenage rebel. Lucifer must be played by a teenage boy. It's type-casting. I'm a pagan and the film is a real invocation of Lucifer. I'm much realer than von Stroheim. The film contained real black magicians, a real ceremony, real altars, real human blood, and a real magic circle consecrated with blood and cum. The typecasting was painstaking."

Anger announced plans to make other *Lucifer* films. He referred to the completed film as Part I, "Sign Language." Part II, "Living with Lucifer," would psychodramatize his real life and star Alan French. He wasn't yet certain as to what to entitle Part III, but "I Love Lucifer" was one giddy possibility. Its title was a pun not only on the Lucille Ball domestic comedies, but a jape on the "Lucy Furr" character in Crowley's book *Konx Om Pax*. Anita Pallenberg, as the Queen of Swords, was mentioned as a potential cast member and probable financier.

At this point Anger seemed both emotionally together and goal oriented. Besides these autobiographical *Lucifer* episodes, there were other projects he was pursuing. A documentary about fantasy-oriented old movie palaces would be palatable for resale to PBS or cable TV. It had been rolling around as an idea in Anger's head for a long time. As he'd travel across the country making personal appearances, he'd notice old movie houses that were monolithic coliseums compared to the peanut-size theaters of today.

Anger was obsessed with one in Albuquerque, New Mexico, in particular. This theater resembled a psychedelic version of the Port Authority bus terminal store, Tepee Town, with gargantuan wooden Indians scowling disapprovingly at patrons.

The other project would be a study, in Anger's words, "in very heavy fantasy," of the world's largest Mickey Mouse collection, which was owned by a friend of his. He found the early Mickeys sadistically hilarious and thought Disney later turned him into a "sissy, which was unforgivable," adding, "when I meet Walt Disney in hell I'll kick him in the balls."

Chapter 17

The Budweiser Boys

What if I killed her one day in just the same manner I had beaten her up? Such things happen.

MARCO VASSI
THE SALINE SOLUTION

You can't hold off human nature forever.

KENNETH ANGER

ike all transients, Alan left. His departure was followed by a rupture between Anger and Bobby Beausoleil. While leafing through men's mags in Tracy Prison, Beausoleil stumbled upon John Calendo's article in *Oui*. Beausoleil read about Anger repeating the mantra of his being a thief, along with Anger bragging about turning him into a toad. "It really hurt me. The whole time I was working on the soundtrack I had written to him and I said, 'Look, you know this is bullshit. STOP IT!!!' As soon as I finished the fucking soundtrack he did it again and it just broke my heart." Beausoleil parted with Anger yet again, and again not on the best of terms.

Anger's despair started to rage and he began making highly negative statements in interviews, on the attack. He complained bitterly to the British entertainment weekly *Time Out* that "money's very tight. In other words, people like Francis Coppola know I need the money. Paul Getty knows I need the money. They're millionaires. They won't give it to me. Mick Jagger's a fucking bastard. He's mean. He said, 'Oh Kenneth, you'll never finish it [*Lucifer Rising*] with help from me.' Well, I have finished it. Part of the reason was to defy him. He's over the hill. His little act is over the hill."

Michael Cooper, who shot part of *Lucifer Rising* and was the Stones' photographer, had just died. Magus Anger boasted, "He committed suicide because I bawled him out too often. I was responsible for his suicide. He was already depressed and very thin-skinned. I bawled him out and he went and took some pills."

Asked by *Time Out* whether he was annoyed or flattered that he was an influence on so many mainstream filmmakers, Anger hotly replied, "What sort of a twit do you think I am? Of course I would be annoyed. More than that, I'd put a curse on them. I have been ripped off by everybody. Scorsese is the only one who considered giving me a half-hearted apology for copying my ideas. Ken Russell uses volcanoes and things like that in *Altered States* which I think he got from *Lucifer Rising*. I know he rented *LR* because I've seen the rental receipt. I think that's shitty."

During 1981 Anger continued on this negative roll. The splits with Beausoleil, Alan, and various old friends had taken their emotional toll. It was all the more saddening because it had looked as if things would finally turn Anger's way at the *Lucifer Rising* premiere.

Anger felt pressured out of financial need to complete *Hollywood Babylon II*. He felt at a loss for additional Hollywood stories, so he actively began soliciting movie industry washups and losers for dirt on people, referring to it as real "salt mine" work.

Throwing gasoline on this pyre was the death of his father, Wilbur. Once again, there was the matter of an inheritance to be settled. When Anger's mother, Lillian, had died in 1953 she had left her house in Pacific Palisades to her three children. Anger's older brother, Bob Anglemyer, and his sister, Jean Anglemyer Roof, had given the house to Wilbur. When Wilbur died, their attorneys instructed them to contact Anger.

Bob Anglemyer wrote to his younger brother informing him of the situation. Anger told his brother that he couldn't care less that their father, Wilbur, had died and that he didn't spend any time with Wilbur before he passed away.

"Ken wrote a letter back," Bob states, "saying he'd drop the interest in the house. I gave this letter to my sister; she took it to the lawyer, and he said it wasn't good enough. So they wrote back and had him write a quitclaim deed, so that he was no longer part of the ownership of the property. Ken did it, with no ifs, ands, or buts about it.

"All we did was give him an appraisal that had been made when my mother died, what it was worth at that time [in 1953], which was $25,000. Later on, he heard that the house sold for a lot more money, so he didn't like that. He felt we had misled him.

"That's when I got all those hate letters from him. He was very abusive." Occasionally the letters would contain clippings about Anger's personal appearances. Bob thought it was ridiculous that his brother was fibbing about his age, hanging around with those much younger than himself, and that he included decades-old photos of himself in the clippings.

At this time Anger mentioned to me that he'd had no contact with his brother or sister since the making of *Pleasure Dome*, but that "I've sort of shouted at them a couple of times on the phone.

They're very conservative—incapable of understanding anything even slightly unusual."

Anger's use of LSD was on the upswing. He stated to me that he was taking three "purple pyramid" hits of windowpane acid at once for a decent trip. Each purple pyramid was equal to three hits of regular windowpane in "green pyramid" form, making Anger's trip effectively a ninefold dose. During trips his rap would veer toward the loose and the emotional. He'd be near tears, reliving childhood traumas in frightening nightmare flashbacks, saying that his parents didn't want him.

On the other hand, Anger would gleefully recall an exciting excursion to Show Palace. Like other personalities, such as Tennessee Williams when he spent time in New York, Anger was a creature of Times Square. Located right in its heart at Forty-second Street and Eighth Avenue, Show Palace presented the raunchiest of the Deuce's all-male offerings. Between showings of gay porno movies, hustlers would strip on stage and wander the audience looking for tricks.

In December 1981, after almost two decades of stalking Anger, Bruce Byron finally got up the gumption to say something to him in person. Anger was showing the "Magick Lantern Cycle" at the Millennium. Bruce parked his taxi outside and barreled in. "I says to Anger, 'Look, you promised me $10,000 if the movie made money. I know it made money. Don't you think it's time you did something about it?'

"He turned bitchy," states Byron. "He said, 'If you don't leave, Byron, I'm not going to show the movie. I don't have time to deal with you right now.'" Byron turned around and left.

In March 1982 I accompanied Anger to a screening of *The Killing of America*, a comprehensive mass murder documentary made by Leonard Schrader. After some innocuous urban travelogue shots, the movie got down to business. There were gruesome shots of chickenhawk Dean Alan Corll and teenager killer Wayne Henley's torture snuff site in Texas, followed by footage of Henley calling his mother from the police station: "Mom . . . I killed Dean." Anger found Henley good-looking and thought that his southern drawl was a turn-on.

Anger mentioned that he had "seven runaways" crashing at his pad. He said he was interviewing them for the Kinsey Institute. Shortly afterward, he was sporting a huge black eye.

The bad vibes escalated. Beausoleil got stabbed in the chest and lungs in jail. This particular dispute had been festering for almost a decade and stemmed from the same beef that left him wearing an eyepatch for a time in the early seventies. In small, enclosed places containing angry men, things tend to happen.

Anger also added a black eyepatch to his accessories to put over his own injured eye. This costume reached epic proportions when he turned up with *Lucifer Rising* in tow at the Santa Fe Film Festival on April 28, 1982. Anger was crowned with a denim tam festooned with buttons. Over the ANGER jersey hung an enormous medal and ribbon, such as one befitting an Olympic athlete or a winning racehorse. In a startling photo by Hollis Engley for *The New Mexican*, Anger is flipping his eyepatch in a salutary gesture, as if he were tipping his hat. What peeped out was a demolished blackened eye and a caved in half-face. It was shocking, like a Weegee photo of the results of a Bowery brawl. In his middle age, Anger was acquiring the looks of a weathered boxer.

He stepped up to the mike and recited a litany of woes to the fistful of Santa Fe art film buffs and students. Anger alluded to multiple eye operations to get things really right. "What I see out of my left eye resembles a film by Stan Brakhage," he quipped. Adding to the eye injury was a chipped tooth and split lip, which Anger explained away to walking down a dark street and tripping over the pavement. "I'm not letting it get me down," promised Anger. "I don't hold it against Santa Fe. I just should watch my step."

All in all, the crowd was entertained. Anger told a few anecdotes and gave a good show for art in New Mexico. As always, he mentioned needing funds for projects.

On September 21, 1982, Anger was to appear at a *Sleazoid Express* directors' forum at New York's Danceteria disco. John Waters was also on the bill, even though he was wracked by a 102-degree flu fever.

Danceteria was at its peak then. Loud, throbbing Eurodisco

music blared through multiple speakers. On the ground floor, film clips of bizarre exploitations trailers and outtakes were shown on a projector that, unfortunately, was limply malfunctioning with a fading lamp and dead sound. For the entertainment of restaurant and bar patrons on the third floor, Herschell Gordon Lewis's *Blood Feast* ran continuously on a videotape directly struck from a print. This was prior to the home video boom and the film was not yet out on tape.

People didn't care about these frills. They were there to see the directors speak. A large crowd, eager for a good time, had turned out.

Anger arrived with an entourage of flunkies. Attired in his ANGER red turtleneck and bell-bottom jeans, Anger appeared disheveled and wild-eyed. In between rubbing his sweaty, razor-stubbled face, he'd go off on a speedy tangent about "the MUSIC. It's too LOUD. Can't somebody turn it DOWN?"

The decibels of the club's sound system were fixed. Anger was repeatedly reassured that there would be no music when he spoke. His attendants, acting in a capacity similar to Howard Hughes's male nurses, brought him upstairs for a drink and a peek at *Blood Feast* to subdue him. This did nothing but exacerbate the situation. The film was a nauseating movie with blood and guts luridly wriggled at the camera. Anger's frayed nerves were shredded further.

He stormed downstairs, declaring, "I'm not going on. Don't pester me," in a high-pitched scream. He exited, plopping himself on a car directly outside the front door of Danceteria. Occasionally he'd mutter, "This is no place to give a reading, Bill . . . no place to give a reading."

Waters was in the basement dressing room, reviewing his index card notes. Suddenly, Anger broke free of the crowd, tore down Twenty-first Street and up Sixth Avenue, valise crammed with Snickers bars flying through the air. From the view down Twenty-first, he was zooming back and forth on Sixth Avenue like a pinball, before finally heading uptown.

Everyone figured he had left, but I was stuck with the task of telling an angry crowd why the star of the show wasn't going on. "Kenneth Anger can't be here tonight, because . . . " It wasn't the first time Anger had pulled a no-show; at one screening in Los Angeles he left Marjorie Cameron holding the bag as the audience walked out.

Waters was sad and disappointed that his icon had departed, but, like a trouper, he went on, coughing and sneezing his way through a talk on William Castle, which eventually became the "Whatever Happened to Showmanship?" chapter in *Crackpot*.

Whatever the amount Anger was to be paid could not have covered the cost of being Kenneth Anger for that particular evening.

The Night Shift a.k.a. the Moulin Rouge a.k.a. the Omega was notorious by reputation. It shared management with and hung over the sleazy Hollywood Theater on 777 Eighth Avenue at the corner of Forty-seventh Street, a spot so high in sex-and-drug scum quotient that it was used as part of Travis Bickle's mental inferno in *Taxi Driver*. It had a dark and filthy elevator from the street leading to two mazelike floors. The elevator was the site of weekly muggings by vicious, queer-bashing punks targeting victims they believed would not complain to the police.

When *Screw* magazine's review of all-male theaters touted the Night Shift as attracting "a motley Times Square crowd," it was an underestimation. In a room of wooden bunks, homeless black men collapsed and passed out on top of a filthy, unused pool table. Out-of-town hustlers, the cheapest, most criminally oriented white trash, were plentiful. When not visiting their drag queen wives, who were out of costume working as cashiers, they were hunting for johns. People roamed around a painted subway car called the "IRT room." Tourists, thrill-seeking suckers in Hawaiian shirts, wandered about the darkened "Central Park Ramble," a bunch of small fake trees in a row.

Those wishing to see recent hard-core porn sat on folding chairs looking blankly at a video screen. Upstairs, there was the option of real 16mm: scratchy prints of older films such as Fred Halsted's *Truck It, Confessions of a Male Groupie,* and *Leather and Things*, which was a cheap imitation of Robert Mapplethorpe's most severe work.

The Night Shift was associated with murders. The hustlers who had killed the "Junk Food Professor" had been regulars. A police sketch of a Hispanic man was posted by the cashboxes; he had stabbed another patron to death. The populace of this "theater" was perpetually stoned on anything and everything—alcohol, grass, angel dust, MDA, acid, mescaline, Christmas Tree speed pills, and heroin-cocaine speedballs. Before it was padlocked by the Board of Health, the Night Shift was a cesspool of psychosis.

On one unseasonably hot autumn evening, the second-floor elevator doors slid open to reveal Anger, valise in hand. He began making his way toward the ticket desk, past a poorly done imitation of a Tom of Finland mural. A *Casablanca*-type fan blew around putrid air that was a sludge of used-popper, Pine-Sol, and body odor.

I was working as the midnight to eight A.M. projectionist. For a break from the asphyxiating darkness of the projection booth and to get a look at the local color, I was standing at the cashbox, a glass counter containing rubber products and guidebooks.

I greeted Anger. He reeled back in horror, shouting, "You work in a scumbag whorehouse!"

"What are you doing here?" I asked.

"I'm doing research for the Kinsey Institute! Dr. Paul Cameron! I've already bought $600 worth of *those* cassettes!"

With that, Anger bolted.

The Kinsey Institute has stated flatly by letter that no Dr. Paul Cameron has ever worked for, nor been associated with, the Institute in any capacity.

Anger's rapid departure that evening was a surprise to the rest of the Night Shift staff. He had become a familiar sight there, announcing himself as an author/director sent by the Kinsey Institute. To the staff, he was merely just another eccentric customer who seemed to have a particular need to engage the Night Shift employees in conversation.

On his next visit to the Night Shift, Anger shared a candid conversation with Al, an older queen wearing a wig, who was the four to midnight cashier on the first floor. Anger complained of the robbery of his crystal ball and Valentino posters. He also whined that the culprits had left beer cans filled with warm piss all over his apartment.

"Bill's not working now, is he?" Anger inquired, about me.

"No."

"Well, in that case, I'll enter the theater."

Anger sat in the folding chair video screening room for a while, then shuffled around in the dark of the fake Central Park Ramble.

The so-called burglaries Anger was complaining of made it onto the airwaves. For years, Anger had given outrageous interviews to WBAI, a free-form listener-sponsored radio station located in New York's shabby Penn Garden district. Anger would expound on anything that crossed his mind, veering from weepy jags about actresses who had mastectomies to inflammatory statements about Hollywood actors. Verbal assaults on celebrities were unleashed.

On November 16, 1982, on WBAI, Anger gave the funniest and most detailed description of his burglary troubles. He related what he called his "paranoid tale" of being robbed by "the Budweiser Gang," a bunch of "Irish-American hoodlums" from his neighborhood.

"For four hours they had me kept, which sounds like an S&M scenario, but it wasn't very amusing, because they were after my money and not my body. They said, 'WHERE'S THE LOOT HIDDEN?' I said, 'I don't have any.' Then they found my checkbook and said, 'You go to Chase Bank on Eighty-sixth Street, don't you?' I said, 'Yes, I do.' He said, 'Well, we're going to march you down Monday morning, all sixty-five of us.' There was a gang of sixty-five. 'And you're gonna check out all your money and give it to the gang.' A contribution to the Irish-American fund or whatever it is, hoodlum fund. 'And we're gonna leave town and you're not gonna file a complaint, 'cuz if you do, we're gonna mess up your face, cut off your nose, cut off your ears, and maybe blind one eye.'"

The Budweiser Gang was, in fact, no Westies-type mob but a handful of teenage guys from the Ninety-first Street housing projects. They were known by the old white folks who still lived in the projects as local heroes who kept the area safe. For the most part, their antics involved painting their faces green on Saint Patty's Day and occasionally engaging in small gang skirmishes with Puerto Rican kids from nearby Spanish Harlem.

Anger began repeating these burglary stories to the newspapers.

He publicized a "Burglary Benefit" he was having at the Millennium in the *New York Post*, claiming that he was burglarized on Halloween, beaten, bruised, and left with a cracked rib. The thieves allegedly relieved him of various memorabilia, including a statuette of Valentino as the Sheik. "They even took a print of my *Pleasure Dome* film," Anger pouted. "They probably thought it was some porn flick."

The Burglary Benefit took place Saturday night, January 15, 1983. The Millennium was packed to the rafters. The promised reading from *Hollywood Babylon II* never happened. Anger substituted a quick thank-you and sold lots of autographed *Lucifer Rising* posters and Robert Haller monographs about himself.

Hoping to cash in again, Anger had another burglary benefit almost immediately afterward. This time about fifteen people showed, including the infamous pornographer Toby Ross. Anger rambled on, rattling off the same old stories—they were *real* sailors in *Fireworks* . . . uhhhh . . . one of the *Scorpio Rising* guys is now a wealthy prosciutto farmer upstate . . . uhhhh . . . I understand it's very good prosciutto. Anger momentarily freaked when an obscure film society's representative called out "MR. ANGER!" and rushed him and handed over some sort of award.

The final tabloid gasp of Anger's robberies finally boiled down to a Liz Smith blurb HE WUZ ROBBED in the New York *Daily News* on April 22, 1983. Anger claimed his memorabilia collection was stolen while he was in L.A. The piece also stated that "he lost to the thieves the famous crystal globe in which he liked to make predictions," referring to the same crystal ball that had supposedly been swiped six months earlier, around the time of his Night Shift forays.

Anger told the British magazine *The Face* that the manuscript for *Hollywood Babylon II* had been swiped the night he was burgled, claiming this was the reason for the book's delay. Assistants supplied by the publisher were supposedly helping him type the manuscript. Anger also mentioned that the publisher had sent him to Hollywood for a week to collect stories, complete with a driver, but it was all to no avail.

The only fruits of Anger's labors had been a chapter on British actor Lionel Atwill. "I hate the new Hollywood," Anger complained on WBAI, "and I'm having trouble finishing because I just hate everybody."

Hollywood Babylon II was belatedly put on the shelves in October 1984. The cover photo of Elizabeth Taylor with her face retouched to appear dead was all too indicative of its pointlessly mean-spirited stance. The times had caught up with and unapologetically surpassed Anger's gossip. Drug addictions, assorted terminal kinks, and the homosexuality of people long since dead were not shocking in the jaded tabloid-journalism eighties.

The original *Hollywood Babylon* emerged from an organic extension of Anger's life—tales Diggy, his grandmother's lady friend, had told him that she personally knew were true. They were part of his childhood. Anger repeatedly declared that the *Babylon* sequel was strictly for bucks. It laboriously emerged out of solicited sources or incidents of public record.

Hollywood Babylon II emphasises visuals in an attempt to compensate for the lack of sensationalism in its text. Much of the photographic content, such as home snapshots of Cary Grant and Randolph Scott, imply things that Anger seems apprehensive about overtly stating. There's a "Witch Joan" chapter about Joan Crawford that centers on old stag movie stills.

Anger had flirted all throughout the preparation of publishing *Hollywood Babylon II* about the Brando photo, but again he didn't come across. Instead, a ridiculous head shot of Brando in a Hawaiian lei was substituted.

Some chapters are merely personal vendettas in print. "Getting Gloria's Goat" is two stills of Gloria Swanson with Anger's chant of "Ding Dong, the Witch is Dead" opposite them. Anger had wailed endlessly on WBAI about his longtime legal woes with Swanson over his first book, and this display was his spitework.

Stills of the Black Dahlia's corpse are blatant snuff photos, nauseating and shocking. In this one respect, Anger anticipated a subsequent trend—graphic true crime, which is now commonplace on television in such forms as *Court TV* and *Cops*.

While the first *Hollywood Babylon* at least partially succeeded in being a manifesto of hate, this sequel is merely a symptom of a negative frame of mind.

The references to old Hollywood and the strong sales of its predecessor made *Hollywood Babylon II* an acceptable book club selection, and it received mainstream distribution. Like any gossip book, it became something old ladies and secretaries lent to their friends.

Unlike the first *Babylon*, the sequel was greeted with largely negative press. Even longtime Anger aficionado John Waters was disappointed. Waters admonished in *American Film*, "I've been a fan of your career for years, but for God's sake lighten up. True, your name isn't Kenneth Compassion but *Hollywood Babylon II* is ruined by your bitterness."

Dennis Hopper took particular offense at James Dean being called "the human ashtray" in *Hollywood Babylon II*. "When I see the name Kenneth Anger," Hopper comments, "I see filmmaker. Oh, he wrote the *Hollywood Babylon* books. Eh, not a bad guy. But when I hear stories about him I hear he's very angry and he thinks that Hollywood owes him something, that he got ripped off, I don't have to deal with that. I've heard it and ignore it. It doesn't mean anything to me."

Hopper went on to explain that "if you're in a city and the city doesn't want you and you see other people making it, you know then it must be they're against you and they're stealing from you— not that you can't get in the door and have them give you a job. You run away from that and you go live in your own world."

People magazine scrutinized Anger's personality because of the maligning nature of *Hollywood Babylon II*. His propensity for telling lysergic acid tall tales was the focus. Eccentricity that was taken as charming in an underground film director was not tolerated in a factual author expecting to be listened to or believed.

The article was one long exercise in unflattering exposure. The text depicted Anger as an author of exploitative gossip books, not the genius who had turned his back on the underground film world to which he had given birth. Anger was photographed by Harry Benson topless, crowned by a matador's hat, standing next to his half naked Boy Scout mannequin with a handkerchief around its waist. He seemed to be wailing away in mid-song, his pendulous arms raised in the air, eyes squeezed shut, lips puckered like Jolson, the LUCIFER tattoo flashing proudly.

The story opened with Anger being called "a bachelor gentleman of refined sensibilities. His apartment was referred to as a $190-per-month walkup in a dank tenement. The cherry on the cake of this circus was when Anger coyly confessed that "Lucifer" was "my nickname in the service. I was in and out of the Navy. I don't like to talk about it much." Precious, though totally lost on anyone not in the know about *Fireworks*. The *People* piece concluded by raising questions about the 1978 beating that hospitalized Anger.

Anger was on a heavy roll. A few days after the *People* story hit the stands in November 1984, he was scheduled to appear on *The Coca Crystal Show*, which was a staple of Manhattan Cable's public access programming. A good-natured anarchist chat show, it was hosted by Coca Crystal, who interviewed guests and chain-smoked joints throughout the hour-long live broadcast.

A week before, Anger had been on another public access show, *Tomorrow's Television Tonight*, which was put on by Nick Yanni, a critic for *Cue* magazine. Anger seemed disjointed, into his own head, explaining films by holding strips up to the light, but he remained subdued. This led to him being invited on Crystal's show.

When *The Coca Crystal Show* was set to air at 10:30 on Wednesday night, November 14, 1984, Anger had yet to arrive. Talent coordinator Maurine Ivice was sent downstairs to look for him. When a cab pulled up containing Anger, he demanded $20 for his fare and someone to help carry his bags.

Ivice did not have the twenty, nor did she pick up his bags. She went upstairs and announced that Anger wanted $20 for his cab. Either no one had it or no one wanted to give it. She looked at the show's director, who shot back, "Don't look at me!"

Ivice went downstairs to explain the financial situation to Anger. Hostess Coca Crystal calls this ensuing encounter "horrifying. He punched her and pulled her to the ground and slammed her to the sidewalk and tried to drag her into the taxi and acted psychotic and violent."

A friend of the show, Jim Buckley, ran downstairs, ran back up, and shouted that Anger was attempting to kidnap Ivice. The show's staff actually believed Anger was committing a kidnapping, though they didn't know why. The aging bunch of hippies charged downstairs, leaving Coca live on the air to carry the show while they struggled with Anger.

Anger finally released Ivice by throwing her to the pavement. He flung a hundred-dollar bill at the cabdriver, screaming "GET ME OUT OF HERE!"

Three days later, the incident turned up on chatty Page Six of the *New York Post*. Under the heading of "Hollywood author sparks cable TV static," the *Post* stated that Anger had "added another chapter to his own story." He was described as "an occultist who has 'Lucifer' tattooed on his chest" who "loved to reveal the tawdry secrets of the stars." The *Post*'s source for the incident claimed to be "terrified" of Anger, stating, "We don't want him going around beating women." Coca Crystal and company did not know about Anger's links to black magic or his "connection to Charles Manson through Manson family member Bobby Beausoleil." The blurb concluded by announcing that Ivice's attorney, David Lewis, planned to file assault charges and a seven-figure lawsuit against Anger.

For good or ill, this incident wound up being cable TV folklore, gossiped about from show to show years after the bout. The show's director summed it up as "Anger just went totally bonkers."

In 1985 the Robert Haller monograph about Anger appeared in the O.T.O's *Equinox* magazine, which reprinted it as a long article. It included one rarely seen still shot of Jimmy Page in *Lucifer Rising* holding a copy of the Stele of Revealing and receiving the law of Thelema.

In 1986 Anger sold the video rights to his films to the tiny outfit Mystic Fire Video, a company specializing in putting out older underground and avant-garde films on tape. The "Magick Lantern Cycle" was packaged as a boxed set of four tapes. The Haller monograph was included, its back cover now featuring a photo of a dandyish Anger superimposed over a demonic astral landscape.

Anger's final bow in New York City occurred in January 1987. The "Magick Lantern Cycle" was being presented at the Gay Film Festival. Anger issued a statement to the gay weekly newspaper the

New York Native: "My films consist of a series of idealisms reflected in the idea of beauty. Now beauty can be a terrible thing . . . beauty can be twisted and abused. I understand it within myself and try to reflect it outward in my work."

Anger made sure to mention that Rick Donovan would be his escort to the film festival. Donovan was an all-American type, reminiscent of Jan-Michael Vincent, who had appeared in popular gay porn flicks like *The Bigger the Better*.

The Kenneth Anger in New York City Show had reached the end of its run. He was tired. The city was more combative than even he could be. It was time to go home, even if Los Angeles had always been to him the land of failure and broken dreams.

Chapter 18

Going Home

To be crippled in the emotions is as real as to be crippled in the limbs. One does not say to a man with a paralyzed leg, "Why don't you run?" Then why does one ask of a man with a heart hardened through too much sensitivity shattered, "Why don't you weep?"

MARCO VASSI
THE SALINE SOLUTION

"If you think we're waxworks," he said, "you ought to pay, you know. Waxworks weren't made to be looked at for nothing. Nohow!"

TWEEDLEDEE & TWEEDLEDUM, IN LEWIS CARROLL'S *ALICE'S ADVENTURES IN WONDERLAND AND THROUGH THE LOOKING GLASS* anger moved into a small caretaker's house on the grounds of Samson De Brier's home in a Mexican section of Los Angeles. Soon the memorabilia and blood-red decor were once again in place. He set to work on a script based on *Hollywood Babylon*.

However, he continued to travel occasionally. In August 1987 Anger attended the Avignon Film Festival in France, which featured a celebration of forty years of his films. Anger mentioned to reporters that he was still toiling on the documentary capturing the world's largest Mickey Mouse collection. It was being made possible through the patronage of J. Paul Getty, Jr.

Also around this time Anger traveled to England. He did some private decorating work for Getty, putting together a screening room for him, and he appeared at a National Film Theatre lecture in London and was well received. He spoke highly of drug use, claiming it had never given him any problems.

On American Independence Day, July 4, 1988, there was an item about Anger's *Hollywood Babylon* feature in the *New York Post*. The movie was to contain rare footage and dramatic re-creation. "It will reflect the books in both subject matter and tone," said Anger, "so the film should be full of ironic black humor and feature some of the scariest moments in the history of the town." Anger was slated to direct and edit, but not appear, in the feature. A "Kenneth Anger character," the mysterious duenna of Hollywood, would be the device that would lead the audience.

Once again, the *Hollywood Babylon* movie could not be made. A stylized film without a conventional narrative structure costing in the neighborhood of $12 million was too great a risk in Hollywood terms.

Nigel Finch, a director of television films for the BBC, sought out Anger as the subject of a documentary. "It was actually my second attempt to make a documentary about him," recalls Finch. "I went to New York eight or nine years ago and visited him in his New York place because I was always influenced as a filmmaker by his films. I found him a very weird guy but nevertheless thought we should get a film together.

"We went out to L.A., and I spent a couple of weeks with him in a motel room. I'd say, 'Let's go have a look at the Hollywood sign.' We'd start to drive up the hill and he'd say, 'God—what kind of a day is it? People get lost in the hills and never come back.' So we'd never get to the Hollywood sign. He was a very strange character. And it turned out the rights to the *Hollywood Babylon* books were at that point owned by producer Ed Pressman. So we couldn't make a documentary after all, because we couldn't quote from the book.

"Then a guy who works for the BBC . . . revived the whole thing. By this time Anger had moved to Los Angeles. We went out to meet him, set most of the film up, and then went out to film it. Now he was in a complete state because he had some set-to with some local Hispanic kids. He moved from that place into another, temporarily. An apartment. It was on a very, very small block which had three or four apartments on it. Somewhere below Santa Monica Boulevard in Hollywood."

Finch explains Anger's reason for consenting to be filmed as a purely financial one. "He needed the cash. That was what did it. It was a watertight contract. I think that was the simple reason he had to put up with it, because he didn't like being filmed by me. I think he probably resented it.

"He has perfected the art of the interview. He's impenetrable. I've spent my life interviewing people. I'm used to getting a bit more out of them than I got out of him. And he's volatile to the extent that he will just explode with anger if you try. He'd get a bad day where he'd be very, very sulky. He would be moody. Eventually, you'd have to say, 'Listen, we're doing this for you, Ken.'

"It's interesting that as soon as one got anywhere near him he went absolutely bananas. At one point I said, 'I'm going to knock on the doors of the people who own the house where you lived.' He went completely berserk. 'I've never heard anything so disgraceful in my life. How dare you!'

"'But Ken, it's your home. It's where you made a film about you.'

"'It's their private life! You mustn't have anything to do with it!'

"It makes you think, well, maybe, he never lived there.

"Most of the time he was quite formal. He wore a velvet jacket.

Image is very important to him. I don't know if he's had a face-lift—it's sort of tight and he wears makeup. I think he's had a weave—there's something going on up there. I didn't want to get too close."

Finch refers to his Anger documentary for the BBC Arena series as "a subjective documentary. Ken kind of plays a character in the film. He's presiding over a funeral."

Finch's *Arena* documentary opens with a shot of a Hollywood street with heat waves rising from it. Peering through the heat waves is an old, chauffeured Cadillac hearse with Anger as its passenger. Enormous pupils envelope his eyes. He's relaxed in the sense of nerve-deadened. The scar by his right eye has become pronounced. Silent screen star makeup has been applied to his face.

The casket in the hearse suggests that Anger is going to his own funeral. Cut to a surreal parent figure—a studio head in cap and knickers, holding a bullhorn—next to a little boy in a sailor suit representing Anger as a child. The overall motif is set: Anger is being taken on a sadistic "Christmas Carol" tour of his own life.

Two gentleman embalmers talk of various stars' deaths that have passed through their funeral home. Anger begins walking toward a mausoleum. Intercut is Tyrone Power's grave. On the soundtrack an actor voices-over passages from *Hollywood Babylon*.

Anger arrives at the mausoleum wearing a bow-tie with a black and white velvet suit. He strides toward the camera in a slow, deliberate, messianic manner with palms outstretched as the sound of his shoes reverberates on the soundtrack.

Anger refers to the woman in black who visits Valentino's mausoleum as "on the brink of sanity." He visits it himself, finding Rudy's name spelled out "in the long form," disappointed at "two dinky vases. It was just Rudy and me together."

As scenes from *A Midsummer Night's Dream* unfold, Anger admits, "I was on the fringe of Hollywood." One sees the few ecstatic moments in *Midsummer* that lasted his lifetime: Anger as the Changeling Prince in a magic world, high on lacquer fumes, running after imps that fly away, being picked up by a goddess. As he watches the clips the misery on his face is heartbreaking. You remember the vulnerable human being under the cold pose.

Fine re-creations of stag films ensue. An inspired Fatty Arbuckle impersonator (Mike McCabe) appears and supplies the narration. Marianne Faithfull, looking every bit the junkie housewife in a formless, dowdy frock, is interviewed. She tells of Anger wanting her to get into Crowley and her initial apprehension. She tells of the great affection she eventually developed for Anger. Faithfull appears unkempt, arms full of collapsed veins, hair cut in a styleless butch manner. She concludes her appearance by singing a sort of dirge while accompanied on piano. However, in her 1995 autobiography, Marianne Faithfull intimates that Anger was not as wonderful as she once believed, going as far as to call him inept as a magus and film-maker. She felt her drug addictions made her a pawn for him.

Finch shrewdly integrates clips from *Scorpio Rising*, *Kustom Kar Kommandos*, *Fireworks*, *Invocation of My Demon Brother*, and *Lucifer Rising*. He doesn't let Anger control his film. As a violent clip from *Fireworks* plays, Finch asks Anger if it was a gay statement and Anger replies with pursed lips that at the time nobody was making any sort of statement.

Anger compares his *Hollywood Babylon* stories to tragedies with larger-than-life proportions. The book provides the centrifugal force to the film; Finch cannily uses it to illustrate metaphoric parallels with Anger's life and art. An especially pointed example is a fateful interview clip of Ramon Novarro, shortly before being beaten to death by rough trade hustlers, saying, "I have no friends. Only acquaintances."

Anger wanders through an empty theater to a projection booth, as if he's searching for something. He looks over nitrate-rotted film, dry ooze permeating it, his frail hands having an ever so slight nervous tremor.

At the climax of the film it all comes to death: the suicide of Peg Entwistle, leaping off the Hollywood sign.

The film's finale is two fat drag queens who give *Hollywood Babylon* a side-splitting read. Anger's gossip comes across as appropriately outrageous with the drags' acerbic wit. They go into a rap about James Dean being the human ashtray as they ponder memorabilia cutouts in a low-rent Hollywood Boulevard shop. To top it off, they do an a cappella version of Madonna's "Vogue."

Although Anger remained totally guarded throughout, Finch used him as a prop to tell his own life story. "I don't have a clue of what he thought of the film," says Finch. "He never replied when I sent him a copy. I would imagine—I would be fairly certain—that he would find it hateful. I'm sure he disliked it." Finch's film was on the mark and it cost only $150,000.

For a time, Anger continued to seek funding for his Mickey Mouse documentary. When Finch initially met Anger in 1985, he recalled seeing a four-minute pilot film of windup Mickey toys in action. This footage was never shown publicly. Anger subsequently claimed to Finch that the materials for this film no longer existed. Anger's proposed documentary about old movie palaces became a dissolving impossibility over time, since the theaters he planned to photograph had largely closed or been transformed into multiplexes.

Early in 1991 Anger moved to West Arenas Boulevard in Palm Springs. The British Film Institute had dispatched Rebecca Wood to assist him in preparing his autobiography. In his old age, Anger had become guarded. Ever since he had exposed the foibles, sexual practices, and drug addictions of individuals in *Hollywood Babylon*, it was obvious why he couldn't stand working in an autobiographical mode, and this project collapsed. This autobiographical element is intertwined with Anger's work as a filmmaker, and by this time he had also effectively abandoned making movies.

After Anger left Palm Springs he was found in a series of Odd Couple situations. For a time he stayed with Forrest J. Ackerman in Los Angeles, since 4E's wife had passed away a few years before. Curious film buffs would visit 4E's house, the house 4E calls his "Magic Castle" off Western. One would pass the robot from *Metropolis*, the toys from *King Kong*, and Anger. Anger sat resolutely as a monk.

While Anger was residing with 4E, Bruce Byron once again attempted to yank his chain. He left this acerbic message on 4E's answering machine: "This is Byron. This message is for Kenneth Anger. It's been twenty-seven years. Why don't you get your shit together? This is Richard Byron." Anger declined this invitation to conversation and ignored it.

Byron was calling from his SRO on West Eighty-third Street in Manhattan. His quarters are seven-by-eleven feet, the size of a stall in the YMCA or a room in a bathhouse. The only convenience it has is the slop sink where he keeps his pain medication.

Byron suffers pain from troublesome ankles. He has not driven a taxi for many years. Most every day is spent at a back table at a pizzeria around the corner, where he works out numerology calculations and zodiac charts.

Byron has spent his life living up to Kenneth Anger's satirization of him in *Scorpio Rising*. In true Quixote fashion, he believes this satire is heroism to be emulated. Now well into his sixties, Byron yearns to be discovered and appreciated for being one of the original cinematic icons of butchness.

Byron remains obsessed with James Dean and Marlon Brando. His SRO is filled to the ceiling with dangerously overburdened bookshelves buckling under the weight of everything from dusty editions of classics like *The Possessed* to costly film encyclopedias covering the underground movement. The massive amount of books threaten to collapse on his cot. His wives left him long ago. He has an expensive TV-VCR combo about ten inches from his cot, on which he frequently watches his scenes from *Scorpio Rising*. Byron continues to make a practice of referring to himself in *Scorpio* as "that guy in the picture." The vendetta for Anger and the wrong that he feels has been done to him is an all-consuming passion that drives his life. He has become Anger's *Pas de Chance*, weeping bitterly into the celluloid.

Anger's West Coast leading man, Bobby Beausoleil, remains incarcerated. He is forever emblazoned in people's memories as hippiedom's decadent marquis. The world has a fixed image of a Beausoleil who never ages—an Associated Press photo of the cute musician-killer nicknamed "Cupid."

Today, Beausoleil is a man nearing fifty, who has spent more than half his life behind bars. He has been married to his second wife, whom he married while in prison, for over a decade. Beausoleil writes and draws, and hopes for the day when he will be free. He no longer speaks to Anger.

As 1992 turned to 1993 *Hollywood Babylon* appeared in its first authorized adaptation as a syndicated late-night television show. Hosted by an awkwardly bewigged, ascot-sporting Tony Curtis, the show rewrote Anger's stories by constructing a verbal patchwork of his best lines. It was executed in the shoestring manner of *películas*, the UHF Spanish-language melodramas. All the sets looked like the same room barely refurbished. Its inept, unknown cast members who played out the reenactments bore scant resemblance to the celebrities they were supposed to be impersonating. Everything was padded out with newsreel footage or photos culled directly from Anger's books. The narrator had a rather somber voice, yet sometimes made vocal inflections reminiscent of Anger.

The most tasteless episodes were not derived from Anger's already published source material. One featured a bad Manson imitator in ratty wig giving an equally ridiculous hippie chick a "die for me" rap in a papier-mâché cave. This episode went on to show the kinky side of Roman Polanski, who was seen videotaping intimate swing parties. Obsure photos of Sharon Tate were interspersed to sickening effect.

During the last two minutes of the broadcasts, Curtis would slip in a quickie. "Got a minute?" he rasped, and then proceeded to give his closing rap. It was always a sleazy anecdote, such as bloodletting in the name of moviemaking, like Curtis not noticing a sword wound he had received on the set, with the punchline being that's showbiz. Others included a Peg Entwistle–type tale of an actress Curtis dated once who was soon dead, never living up to her potential. He capped that off with a chipper "another unsung hero."

Exploiting the *aesthetique du schlock* led to a void, which was the sad reality of the *Hollywood Babylon* TV series. The unauthorized Marvin Miller soft-core movie was at least blatant enough in its pornographic intentions that it avoided falling into this trap.

Anger is such a monumental artist that these trivial commercial doings are understandable. America refuses to support its artists, so it's all too obvious why Anger is forced to seek out these sort of projects for income.

Today, Anger remains very much alone. He has a huge network of relatives and their descendants among the Anglemyer family.

However, he does not look to them for emotional support. He instead gravitates toward old Hollywood friends who hold on to their own memories of what Tinsel Town used to be.

Kenneth Anger, Magus, hides behind many magickal veils and wears more than a few wizard's caps. Like his hero Jean Cocteau, he is both lowbrow entertainment and high art. His *Babylon* books have contributed their title to the popular lexicon and their sensibility to mainstream culture. Dozens of sensationalist exposés like *Nashville Babylon* and *Hollywood Babble-On* have emanated from his original idea. However, what distinguishes Anger's first *Hollywood Babylon* from its imitators is that, as Karl Marx was to capitalism, Anger was to Hollywood. He accurately depicted everything negative and dehumanizing about show business, demythologizing the popular concept that a movie star's life is a fabled, trouble-free nirvana.

As a filmmaker, Anger emerged as the premiere artist from underground film. Through his "Magick Lantern Cycle" he captured souls and revealed basic human truths within universal situations. Hermetic symbols that echo Jung's collective unconscious are passed on into a broad pop culture sensibility. Even after repeated viewings, Anger's films remain hypnotic experiences.

Anger's unique, jeweler-crafted imagery and exploration of the untold possibilities of cinema have left their imprint on directors who followed in his wake, including such extraordinary mainstream exponents as Martin Scorsese.

Anger presented a bold cinematic statement of self before homosexuality was acknowledged in society, much less on a movie screen. In this respect, he is the progenitor of the autobiographical erotic film, providing inspiration to such extraordinary individuals in that realm as Fred Halsted. Robert Mapplethorpe also took a cue from Anger's visual aesthetics and extended Halsted's conceptualization of S&M as an integral life force. The pioneering efforts of Anger, Halsted, and Mapplethorpe established a public stance on S&M that saw the love and beauty within the pain, one which could be applied to all genders. Both men and women appreciate the art of these artists because it connects with humanity.

As a fervent disciple of Aleister Crowley, Anger has acted as an archivist, proselytizer for Thelema in the media, and ultimately expressed his religious beliefs through his films, something few directors are capable of. Anger's "Magick Lantern Cycle" served to pass on Crowley's romantic reinterpretation of centuries-old occult doctrines and concepts of magick.

Anger is now an established part of the American aesthetic heritage and is revered as such. He possesses over a half-century of knowledge and has again commenced communicating it to a new generation. At a March 1994 appearance at Manhattan's Symphony Space in which he screened the "Magick Lantern Cycle," he spoke and engaged the audience for a great length of time.

As all great artists do, Anger questioned his entire being, his inward journey. What he sought to emulate in Aleister Crowley he played out for the last half-century as a life actor. He has lived by the courage of his convictions. Whatever consequences there have been on this left-hand path, Kenneth Anger has paid them.

Sources

(All interviews and conversations by Bill Landis unless otherwise specified.)

Chapter 1

Interview with Bob Anglemyer, 2/20/93
PBS Documentary, *The Great Depression*, 11/93
"Underground Man" by Kenneth Turan, 1976
Star Spangled Kitsch by Curtis F. Brown
Interview with Maxine Peterson, 7/15/91
PBS documentary, *Shirley Temple*, 5/93
Interview with Anger, 4/30–5/1/80
Conversation with Jean Anglemyer Roof, 2/5/90
Life Is Too Short by Mickey Rooney
Letter from Billy Barty, 4/22/91
"Dedication to Create Make Believe" by Tony Rayns and John DuCane,
    Time Out, 11/12–18/70
The synopses of Anger's early films exist in typescript and are reprinted in
    Visionary Film (1974 ed.) by P. Adams Sitney

Chapter 2

Interview with Bob Anglemyer, 2/5/93, 2/20/93
Interview with Maxine Peterson, 7/15/91
Interview with Marilyn Granas, 5/29/93
PBS documentary, *Shirley Temple*, 5/93
Experiment in Film, "Escape Episode" review by Lewis Jacobs is reprinted
    in *Visionary Film* (1974 ed.) by P. Adams Sitney
Interview with Anger, 4/30–5/1/80
Kenneth Anger: A Monograph by Robert Haller
Interview with Curtis Harrington, 4/28/91
Film As A Subversive Art by Amos Vogel
Underground Film by Parker Tyler
Screening the Sexes by Parker Tyler
Visionary Film (1974 ed.) by P. Adams Sitney
Sexual Alienation in the Cinema by Raymond Durgnat
A Pictorial History of Sex in Films by Parker Tyler
Canyon Films Catalogue, 1991

The Murdered Magicians by Peter Partner
"Dedication to Create Make Believe" by Tony Rayns and John DuCane,
    Time Out, 11/12–18/70
Interview with Ed Earle, 4/2/91
The History of Magic by Eliphas Levi
Transcendental Magic by Eliphas Levi
The Book of Splendors by Eliphas Levi
The Golden Bough by J. K. Fraser
The Great Beast by John Symonds
The Magical World of Aleister Crowley by Francis King
The Rites of Modern Occult Magic by Francis King
The Confessions of Aleister Crowley by Aleister Crowley
Moonchild by Aleister Crowley
Diary of a Drug Fiend by Aleister Crowley
Magick in Theory and Practice by Aleister Crowley
Leah Sublime by Aleister Crowley
The Book of the Law by Aleister Crowley
De Arte Magica by Aleister Crowley
Liber Agape by Aleister Crowley
Cocaine by Aleister Crowley
Rex de Arte Regia by Aleister Crowley
The Book of Thoth by Aleister Crowley
The Eye in the Triangle by Israel Regardie
Interview with Harry Smith by P. Adams Sitney, 6/3/77
Conversations with Harry Smith, at Chelsea Hotel, 1991

Chapter 3

Interview with Bob Anglemyer, 2/5/93, 2/20/93
Interview with Ed Earle, 4/2/91
Interview with Anger, 4/30–5/1/80
Interview with Curtis Harrington, 4/28/91
Interview with Anger by Lenny Lopay, WBAI, 10/22/84
One Arm by Tennessee Williams
"Desire and the Black Masseur" by Tennessee Williams

Chapter 4

Interview with Anger, 4/30–5/1/80
Interview with Curtis Harrington, 4/28/91
Interview with Harry Smith by P. Adams Sitney, 6/3/77

The Diary of Anaïs Nin, Volume IV, 1944-1947
Correspondence between Paul Johnston and Anger, *Film Culture* (1979)
Interview with Amos Vogel, 7/12/91
Cinema 16 program notes by Parker Tyler
Review of "Fireworks" by Lewis Jacobs
Kenneth Anger: A Monograph by Robert Haller
Stan Brakhage Lectures at the Art Institute of Chicago, 3/12/73, 4/12/73,
    5/13/75, 11/3/75
Cocteau Diaries by Jean Cocteau

Chapter 5

Interview with Bob Anglemyer, 2/20/93
Interview with Anger, 4/30–5/1/80
Underground Film by Parker Tyler
Cagliostro by Roberto Gervasio
Stan Brakhage Lectures at Art Institute of Chicago, 3/12/73, 4/12/73,
    5/13/75, 11/3/75
Moonchild by Aleister Crowley
The Book of Thoth by Aleister Crowley
Diaries of Anaïs Nin, Volume IV
Freedom Is a Two Edged Sword by Jack Parsons
Bare Faced Messiah by Russell Miller
L. Ron Hubbard: Messiah or Madman? by L. Ron Hubbard, Jr., and Bent
    Corydon
The Magical World of Aleister Crowley by Francis King
The Rites of Modern Occult Magic by Francis King
Interview with Dennis Hopper, 8/13/91
"On the Filming of *Inauguration of the Pleasure Dome*" by Samson De
    Brier, *Film Culture*, Nos. 67-68-69 (1979)

Chapter 6

Dr. Kinsey and the Institute for Sex Research by Wardell Pomeroy
"Kenneth Anger: A Profile of the Artist as a Film Maker," by Norman
    Yonemoto, *In Style*, 1985
"Was Kinsey a Fraud and a Pervert?" by Philip Nobile, *Village Voice*,
    12/11/90
Guilty of Everything by Herbert Hunke
"Lucifer Rising: Kenneth Anger's Sympathy for the Devil" by Jane Karr,
    After Dark, 12/77

"Hollywood Anger" by Mick Brown, *Crawdaddy*, 9/76
Sexual Behavior in the Human Male by Kinsey/Pomeroy/Gebhardt
Rex de Arte Regia by Aleister Crowley
The Magical World of Aleister Crowley by Francis King
The Aleister Crowley Scrapbook by Sandy Richardson
The Confessions of Aleister Crowley by Aleister Crowley
Interview with Anger by James M. Saslow, *Advocate*, 7/23/81

Chapter 7

Interview with Charles Henri Ford, 4/13/91
Stan Brakhage Lectures at the Art Institute of Chicago, 3/12/73, 4/12/73, 5/13/75, 11/3/75
Interview with Anger by Lenny Lopay, WBAI, 10/22/84
Interview with Anger, 4/30–5/1/80
"Dedication to Create Make Believe" by Tony Rayns and John DuCane, *Time Out*, 11/12–18/70
Interview with Ed Earle, 4/2/91
Hollywood Babylon by Anger (1975 Straight Arrow ed.)
Interview with Robert Dean, 7/22/91

Chapter 8

Stan Brakhage Lectures at the Art Institute of Chicago, 3/12/73, 4/12/73, 5/13/75, 11/3/75
Interview with Anger by Lenny Lopay, WBAI, 10/22/84
Interview with Gerard Malanga, 4/3/91
Interview with Bruce Byron, 6/26/91, 7/21/91
Interview with Anger, 4/30–5/1/80
"Aleister Crowley and Merlin Magick," interview with Anger (uncredited story), *Friends*, 9/18/70

Chapter 9

Interview with Amos Vogel, 7/12/91
Midnight Movies by J. Hoberman and Jonathan Rosenbaum
"Personal Traditions and Satanic Pride" by Michael Wade and "Master in Hell" by Robin Hardy, *BodyPolitik*, July 1980
Interview with Anger, *Open City News* (uncredited), 1965
Visionary Film (1974 ed.) by P. Adams Sitney
Interview with Bruce Byron, 6/26/91, 7/21/91
Hell's Angels by Hunter S. Thompson

Kustom Kar Kommando proposal exists in typescript and is reprinted in
   Visionary Film (1974 ed.) by P. Adams Sitney

"Puritanism Scores Victory: All Woman Jury Finds Ken Anger's Anti-
   Fascist Film 'Obscene'" by Seymour Stern, *L.A. Free Press*, 5/25/64

Thy Neighbor's Wife by Gay Talese

Blue Money by Carolyn See

Scorsese on Scorsese

Hollywood Babylon by Anger ("Professional Services" version), 1964

History of Eroticism by Lo Duca

Stan Brakhage Lectures at the Art Institute of Chicago, 3/12/73, 4/12/73,
   5/13/75, 11/3/75

City of Night by John Rechy

Interview with Anger in *Spider* (uncredited), *Spider #3*, 4/15/65

"13 Confusions" by Amos Vogel, *The New American Cinema*, Gregory
   Battcock, editor

"Private" (uncredited), *The New Yorker*, 1/16/65

"Anger Rising," interview with Anger by Jonathan Cott, *The Sunday
   Ramparts*, 1970

Letter to Robert Brown from Anger, 4/6/65

Chapter 10

"Follow Me into the Flower Called Nowhere," Graphics Press Program
   Notes for *The Magick Lantern Cycle*, 1966

"Scenes" by Howard Smith, *Village Voice*, 5/26/66

Interview with Bruce Byron, 6/26/91, 7/21/91

"Easeful Death" by Brendan Gill, *The New Yorker*, 4/23/66

Scorpio Rising review by Dan A. Cutiez, *Script*, 3/64

"*Brig and Scorpio* at Bleeker Street," *New York Post*, 4/8/66

"Bleeker St. Bulges" by Archer Winsten, *New York Post*, 4/20/66

Scorpio Rising review by Gold, *Variety*, 5/12/66

"*Scorpio Rising* and *The Brig*" by Edward Lipton, *Film Daily*, 7/13/66

Interview with William Klein, 2/28/91

Interviews with Bobby Beausoleil by Michelle Clifford, 7/22/91, 7/25/91,
   7/26/91, 9/30/91

"Anger Rising," interview with Anger by Jonathan Cott, *The Sunday
   Ramparts*, 1970

Shock Value by John Waters

"Aleister Crowley and Merlin Magick," interview with Anger (uncredited
   story), *Friends*, 9/18/70

Interview with Anger, 4/30–5/1/80

"Up from Underground" by Jack Kroll, *Newsweek*, 2/13/67

Conversation with Paul Morrissey, 7/15/91

"From Underground: Kenneth Anger Rising" by Elenore Lester, *New York Times*, 2/19/67

Letter from Mike Mideke, 12/21/91

Ringolevio by Emmett Grogan

The Haight Ashbury by Charles Perry

"Sex in the Cinema" series by Arthur Knight, *Playboy*, 4/67

"Lucifer Gone; Anger Offers Reward—Lucifer Lost, Strayed or Stolen but Straight" by Lenny Lipton, *Berkeley Barb*, 9/29–10/5/67

Visionary Film (1974 ed.) by P. Adams Sitney

The Secret Life of a Satanist by Anton LaVey

The Family by Ed Sanders

Helter Skelter by Vincent Bugliosi

Stan Brakhage Lectures at the Art Institute of Chicago, 3/12/73, 4/12/73, 5/13/75, 11/3/75

"Anger's Anguish" by Lenny Lipton, *Berkeley Barb*, 10/6–12/66

"A Touch for Anger" by Tom Luddy, *Berkeley Barb*, 1966

"Witchcraft by Anger" by John L. Wasserman, *San Francisco Chronicle*, 9/30/66

"Underground Movies Rise to the Surface" by Kevin Thomas, *Los Angeles Times*, 3/2/67

"In Memorium: Kenneth Anger Filmmaker 1947–1967," *Village Voice* advertisement, 10/26/67

Chapter 11

Up and Down with the Rolling Stones by Tony Sanchez

Blown Away: The Rolling Stones and the Death of the Sixties by A. E. Hotchner

Keith Richards by Victor Bockris

The Family (original 1972 version) by Ed Sanders

Helter Skelter by Vincent Bugliosi

Transcript of Anger appearance at SUNY by Neil Baldwin, *Changes*, 1978

Sinema by Kenneth Turan and Stephen F. Zito

Andy Warhol by Victor Bockris

Jagger Unauthorized by Christopher Anderson

Stairway to Heaven: Led Zeppelin Uncensored by Richard Cole with Richard Trubo

Chapter 12

The Family by Ed Sanders
Helter Skelter by Vincent Bugliosi
Transcript of Anger appearance at SUNY by Neil Baldwin, *Changes*, 1978
Interview with Dennis Hopper, 8/13/91
"Aleister Crowley and Merlin Magick," interview with Anger (uncredited
    story), *Friends*, 9/18/70
Up and Down with the Rolling Stones by Tony Sanchez
Dear Mr. Fantasy by Ethan A. Russell
"The Fabulous Anger Trilogy" advertisement, *Village Voice*, 10/9/69
"Light Up a Lucifer" by Philip Oakes, *Sunday Times* (London), 4/12/70
American Film Institute Catalogue 1961–1970
"Pretty, Sexy and Satanic" by Molly Parkin, *Times* (London), 1/17/71
"Hollywood Anger" by Mick Brown, *Crawdaddy*, 9/76
"Anger Rising" by "Osiris," *Sounds*, 10/21/76
"Gay Young Maternities," uncredited newspaper clip, 1971
Stairway to Heaven: Led Zeppelin Uncensored by Richard Cole with Richard
    Trubo
Stan Brakhage Lectures at the Art Institute of Chicago, 3/12/73, 4/12/73,
    5/13/75, 11/3/75
"Illuminating Lucifer" by Carole Rowe, *Film Quarterly*, Summer 1974
Transcript of Anger appearance at SUNY by Neil Baldwin, *Changes*, 1978
"Devil Film to Get State Aid," uncredited, *Sunday Telegraph (London)*,
    3/28/71
"At 4 AM in the Desert . . . It's Marianne Faithfull and Sphinx" by
    Alexander Walker, *Evening Standard*, 7/9/71

Chapter 13

Letters from Anger to Marjorie Keller and Camille Cook at the Art
    Institute of Chicago, 1/11/73, 1/21/73, 3/19/73, 4/2/73, 4/10/73
"*Rabbit's Moon* Review" by Marjorie Keller, *Film Culture*
"Anger Rising," interview with Anger by Jonathan Cott, *The Sunday
    Ramparts*, 1970
Variety coverage of bootleg *Hollywood Babylon* film, 7/71, 2/72, 5/73
Hollywood Babylon Pressbook, Institute for Adult Education, 1972
Hollywood Blue trailer, 1971
Life Is Too Short by Mickey Rooney
"Kenneth Anger Rising" by John Calendo, *Oui*, 10/76

"Lucifer Rising" piece, *Variety*, 2/23/72

Transcript of Anger appearance at SUNY by Neil Baldwin, *Changes*, 1978

Sinema by Kenneth Turan and Stephen F. Zito

"Cineprobe: An Evening With Kenneth Anger," Museum of Modern Art Program Notes, 3/12/74

Interview with Anger, 4/30–5/1/80

Shock Value by John Waters

"Moody-Go-Round" by Herb Caen, *San Francisco Chronicle*, 7/29/74

Chapter 14

Hollywood Babylon by Anger (1975 Straight Arrow ed.)

"Babylon Saga" (uncredited) *Publishers Weekly*, 1975

"Kenneth Anger Rising" by John Calendo, *Oui*, 10/76

"Night of the Locust" by Jack Kroll, *Newsweek*, 6/16/75

"Hollywood Babylon Review" by Michael Perkins, *Screw*, 6/15/75

"Hollywood Babylon Review" by Peter Andrews, *New York Times*, 3/31/75

"Hollywood Babylon Goes on the Road" by Greil Marcus, *Village Voice*, 10/13/75

Conversation with André Previn, 4/12/92

"Trails of Lucifer" by Robb Baker, *Soho Weekly News*, 10/28/76

"The Shiek is Chic; Greasy Kid Stuff Back by Barbar Utely, *Fort Wayne Journal Gazette*, 7/24/77

"What I Saw of Graft in the Movies" by Mrs. Rudolph Valentino (Anger Collection), *New York Times*, 3/31/75

"The Valentino Legend Stirs a Revival" by Gene Siskel, *Chicago Tribune*, 6/28/77

"Underground Man" by Kenneth Turan, 1976

"Looking Back with Anger," by Ernest Leogrande, *New York Daily News*, 6/21/76

"Return of Kenneth Anger" by Jan Hoddenfiled, *New York Post*, 6/16/76

Interview with John Calendo, 6/21/91

Interview with John Le Moss, 3/27/92

"Look Back with Anger" by John Waters, *American Film*, 1–2/85

"Yank Producer Does It with Mirrors," *Variety*, 9/23/76

Cagliostro by Roberto Gervasio

The Public Humiliation of Jimmy Page: An Interlude

"Anger Rising" by "Osiris," *Sounds*, 10/21/76

"Hollywood Anger," by Mick Brown, *Crawdaddy*, 9/76

"Trials of Lucifer" by Robb Baker, *Soho Weekly News*, 10/28/76
"Fire and Brimstone" by Jack English, *Time Out*, 12/81

Chapter 15

"Manson Follower to Score Anger Pic While in Cal Jail," *Variety*, 11/17/76
"Anger's Ten Year Trauma Ends with Lucifer Rising," *Datebook*,
    12/19/76
Interviews with Bobby Beausoleil by Michelle Clifford, 7/22/91, 7/25/91,
    7/26/91, 7/27/91, 9/30/91
Press releases from Abby Hirsch, 1976, 1977
"Hollywood Bohemia" by Ann Bardach, *Wet*, 3–4/80
Interview with Bruce Byron, 6/26/91, 7/21/91
Warhol Diaries
The Denunciation of Stan Brakhage, Puck Productions Flyer, Spring 1975
Stan Brakhage Lectures at the Art Institute of Chicago, 3/12/73, 4/12/73,
    5/13/75, 11/3/75
Conversation with Sam McElfresh, 7/20/91
"The Erotic Art of Bobby Beausoleil" by Kenneth Anger, *Puritan*, 1979
Letter from Bruce McPhearson, 3/25/91

Chapter 16

Warhol Diaries
"Hollywood Bohemia" by Ann Bardach, *Wet*, 3–4/80
Kenneth Anger: A Monograph by Robert Haller
Interview with Anger, 4/30–5/1/80
"Look Back at Anger" by Bill Landis, *Soho Weekly News*, 7/1/80
Interview with Jamie Gillis, 3/11/91
Conversation with Marc Stevens, 7/27/83
Interview with Kit Fitzgerald by Bill Landis and Michelle Clifford,
    4/30/91
Notes on *Lucifer Rising* screening at the Whitney Museum by Sam
    McElfresh, 12/15/80
Sleazoid Express, ed./pub. Bill Landis, 12/18/80
"The Sin Also Rises" by Bill Landis, *Soho Weekly News*, 12/23/80
"Angels" centerfold, *Village Voice*, 12/17–22/80
Interviews with Bobby Beausoleil by Michelle Clifford, 7/22/91, 7/25/91,
    7/26/91, 7/27/91, 9/30/91
"Grim Souveniers from Lennon Suspect," *San Francisco Chronicle*,
    12/18/80

Letter from Mark David Chapman, 6/25/91
"Kenneth Anger in 4 Film Show at the Whitney" by Lawrence Van
    Gelder, *New York Times*, 12/18/80

Chapter 17

Interview with Bob Anglemyer, 2/20/93
Interviews with Bobby Beausoleil by Michelle Clifford, 7/22/91, 7/25/91,
    7/26/91, 7/27/91, 9/30/91
"Fire and Brimstone" by Jack English, *Time Out*, 12/81
"Underground Filmmaker Struggling: Looking for backing for project"
    by Jon Bowman, *The New Mexican*, 4/28/82
Interview with John Le Moss, 3/27/92
Letter from the Kinsey Institute signed June Machover Reinisch,
    10/31/91
Interview with Anger by Lenny Lopay, WBAI, 11/16/82
Interview with Alfred Vitale, 5/31/93
"Cause for Anger" by Jay Padroff, *New York Post*, 1/13/83
"He Wuz Robbed" by Liz Smith, *New York Daily News*, 4/22/83
"A Look Back at Anger" by James Truman, *The Face*, 7/83
"Naked City" column in *Screw*, any issue from Fall 1982
Hollywood Babylon II by Kenneth Anger
"Babylon Revisited" by John Gross, *New York Times*, 11/3/84
"Babylon' Revisited" by Liz Smith, *New York Daily News*, 10/23/84
"Look Back with Anger" by John Waters, *American Film*, 1—2/85
Interview with Dennis Hopper, 8/13/91
"The Look Back of Anger" by Michael Ryan, *People*, 11/12/84
Interview with Coca Crystal, 4/11/91
Interview with William Hohauser by Michelle Clifford, 12/16/91
"Hollywood Author sparks cable TV static" by Richard Johnson, *New
    York Post*, 11/17/84
"Avant Babylon" by Vincent Aletti, *Village Voice*, 1/13/86
Anger interview in *New York Native* (uncredited), 1985

Chapter 18

Hollywood Babylon movie piece by Leonard Klady of the *Los Angeles Times*,
    New York Post, 7/4/88
Interview with Nigel Finch, 9/23/91

Faithfull by Marianne Faithfull

Interview with Bruce Byron, 6/26/91, 7/21/91

Interviews with Bobby Beausoleil by Michelle Clifford, 7/22/91, 7/25/91, 7/26/91, 7/27/91, 9/30/91

Conversation with Michelle Clifford, 11/15/93

Index

À Rebours (Huysmans), 25
Acid, 131, 162, 220. *See also* Drugs; LSD
Ackerman, Forrest J. (4E), 155, 259
Act of Seeing with One's Own Eyes, The
    (film), 66
Against the Grain (Huysmans), 76
Aigner, Hal, 195
Allman, Duane, 218
Altamont concert, 177–78
Altered States (film), 240
America, Paul, 148
American Federation of the Arts (AFA),
    216–17
American Film (Waters), 250
American Nazi Party, 128. *See also* Nazis
Anger, Kenneth. *See also* Beausoleil,
    Bobby; Crowley, Aleister; *film*
    titles; Harrington, Curtis;
    Hollywood Babylon; "Magick
    Lantern Cycle"
  arrested, 37, 39, 125
  BBC documentary, 255–59
  behavior
    at Belgian film festival, 93
    at *City* magazine, 195
    at Equinox event, 156
    at March on the Pentagon, 158
    throughout 1980s in New York,
      240–53
  and blacks, 50
  Brakhage breakup, 215–16
  and burglaries, 246–48
  childhood and family, 5–14, 19–20, 67,
    100
  drug use, 38–39, 131, 153, 162–63,
    220–21, 242, 255
    LSD and Lucifer metaphor, 140
  early films, 14, 17–18, 35
  exposé of Hollywood stars, 94–95
  film revisions at AFA, 217
  film video rights sale, 252
  filming techniques, 66–71, 79, 93, 113,
    175–76
  films, monogragh, memorabilia sales,
    218, 222–23
  films projected, but never made,
    211–12, 221
  financial and funding problems, 117,

    121, 124–26, 139, 166, 178–79,
    181–82, 218, 240–41, 259
  future projects, 204, 221, 237–38
  in Germany, 137
  Haller monograph, 223, 248, 252
  Hollywood Babylon lawsuit, 189–91, 196
  homosexuality, 15, 46–48, 50, 57, 83,
    145, 262
    police entrapment and arrest, 37, 39
  image, 202
    enfant terrible, 38, 227
  in *Invocation of My Demon Brother*,
    172–73
  and Jimmy Page, 184, 208–9
  Landis assessment of, 261–63
  Landis interviews with, 223–24,
    237–38
  lies about age and background, 203
  London, 1968, drug use and contacts,
    162–68, 170, 177–78, 181–84,
    192, 208
  London–New York commuting,
    188–207
  in Los Angeles, 100–101, 255–59
  in *Lucifer Rising*, as Magus, 231–32
  media interviews, in 1970s, 203–7
  New York
    1962, 101
    1966, 132
    1976, 203, 211
    1978 mugging, 212–13
    1980s, 220–29, 236–53
  Night Shift theater visits, 246–47
  paranoia, 220
  in Paris, 58–63, 92–94, 100, 136
  personality and character, 39, 48, 57,
    226–27, 250–51
    "if-only-I-were" type of death wish,
      50
  physical appearance
    1970, 181
    1975, 201–2, 220
    1974, aging and gaining weight,
      194–95, 204
    1980s, 222, 243, 257
    in school, 17
    at university, 38
  popularity of films in America, 165, 188

Anger, Kenneth (*cont.*)
    prizes and awards, 59, 93
    quoted
        on Beausoleil, 218
        on burglaries, 247
        on *Fireworks*, 44–46
        on Halsted, 194–95
        on *Hollywood Babylon* film, 255
        on idealism and beauty in film, 253
        on Jesus Christ footage in *Scorpio Rising*, 111
        on Kinsey's stag film collection, 86–87
        on living in Brooklyn Heights, 101
        on LSD effects, 220–21
        on Lucifer, 237
        on mainstream filmmakers, 240
        on making of *Kustom Kar Kommandos*, 126–28
        on Marianne Faithfull, 182
        on *Scorpio Rising* cast, 111–12
        on secret code in *Hollywood Babylon* book, 204–5
        on secret photo of Brando, 206–7
        on S&M, 223
        on venereal disease, 192
    renunciation of claim to mother's estate, 241
    in Rome, 63–64
    sadist doctor film, 124–25
    in San Francisco, 159, 162–63, 195
        Russian Embassy house, 141–44, 156–57, 173–75
    stationery design, 196, 215
    tattoos, 225–26
    teenage years, 14–15, 17, 35
    Thelema Abbey pilgrimage, 88–90
    underground film popularity, 188
    Valentino collection, 202
    videotape copies of films, 227–28
    Village Voice death announcement, 158, 175
    visits to Brakhage in Colorado, 125, 159–60
    Vogel, and Cinema 16, 56–57, 115
    Warhol compared to, 148, 149–50
ANGER jersey, 202, 218, 243
Anglemyer, Bob (brother), 4–5, 9, 14, 25, 37, 44, 241
    on Anger's anger, 39
    on loan, 45
Anglemyer, Kenneth Wilbur. *See* Anger, Kenneth
Anglemyer, Lillian Coler (mother), 5, 19, 66, 241

Anglemyer, Wilbur (father), 5–6, 26, 66, 241
Animation, 20–21
Anthology Film Archives, 212, 215, 223
Aquarian Age, 139, 145, 146, 155
Arabesque for Kenneth Anger (film), 101
Arbuckle, Fatty, 8, 189, 258
Arthur, Andy, 217
Aspen City News interview, 124, 125
Athletic Model Guild, 39
Atkins, Susan, 155
Atom Heart Mother (Pink Floyd), 194
Atwill, Lionel, 249
Avignon Film Festival (1987), 255

Baby Burlesks (films), 11
Back-cutting technique, 175–76
Bad (film), 214
Balin, Marty, 177
Bardach, Ann, 221
Bardot, Brigitte, 123
Barker, George, 22
Barrymore, John, 9
Barty, Billy, 13
Baskets (film), 177
Baskin, Arnold, 127
Baum, L. Frank, 10
BBC Arena documentary, 257–59
Beardsley, Aubrey, 24, 29, 49, 61, 76, 79
Beausoleil, Bobby, 142
    accused of stealing *Lucifer Rising* footage, 157–58, 160, 179–80, 204–5, 240
    Anger film for private collectors, 152
    Anger on love for, 223
    Anger's curse on, 180, 205, 240
    background and career, 142–43
    breakups with Anger, 157–58, 240
    draft evasion, 158
    erotic art, 217–18
    first meeting with Anger, 143–44
    Hinman murder, 170, 180, 191
    in *Invocation of My Demon Brother*, 171–75, 181
    and *Lucifer Rising*, 234
        Lucifer Rising premiere, 236
        Lucifer Rising soundtrack, 211, 229, 232, 237
    on Anger's film artistry, 145, 147, 152–54
    on Anger's homosexuality and character, 145–47
    on Anger's LSD use, 153
    in prison, 180, 191, 243, 260
    stationery design, 196

Bells of Atlantis (film), 55
Benson, Harry, 250
Berkeley Barb, 157
Bern, Paul, 199
Betty Page concept, 106, 155
Bickle, Travis, 245
Bigger the Better, The (film), 253
Biker films, 102–3, 175. See also *Scorpio Rising*
Bisexuality, 85–86
Blackwood, Algernon, 28
Blair, Betsy, 54
Blavatsky, Madame, 28
Bleecker Street Cinema, New York, 137, 150
Blood Feast (film), 123, 244
Blood of a Poet, The (film), 23
Bockris, Victor, 220
Bogart, Humphrey, 122–23
Book of Splendors, The (Levi), 25
Book of the Law, The (Crowley), 26, 31, 94, 140, 198, 231–33
Book of Thoth, The (Crowley), 31, 33
BORN TO RAISE HELL button, 104, 105, 106, 134
Bow, Clara, 8, 53
Boys in the Band, The (film), 47
Boys in the Sand (film), 193
Boys of the Slums (film), 193
Brakhage, Stan, 121, 192, 243
    Anger collaboration, 67
    Anger's arrest in Colorado, 125
    Anger's return to Los Angeles, 96, 100
    Anger's second visit to Colorado, 159–60
    Anger's split with, 215–16
    Newsweek article, 148
    on mainstream filmmakers, 92
    reaction to Warhol award, 121
    total abstraction in films, 215
Brakhage Scrapbook, The (Brakhage), 216
Brando, Marlon, 87, 213, 260
    making of *Scorpio Rising*, 104–6, 107, 108
    secret photo of, 206–7, 249
Brandy in the Wilderness (film), 100
Brautigan, Richard, 151
Brave New World, The (club), 142–44
Brenner, Joe, 176
Bresson, Robert, 95
Brig, The (film), 137
British Film Institute, 259
Brooklyn Heights, 101–3, 104
Brown, Mick, 206
Bruce, Lenny, 119, 121, 218

Brussels World Fair (1958), 92–93
Buckley, Jim, 251–52
Budweiser Gang, 247
Buñuel, Luis, 23, 24, 40
Burglary Benefits, 248
Burroughs, William, 30, 94, 220
"Bye Bye Baby" (Mary Wells), 188
Byron, Bruce, 112, 165, 176
    Anger's mean-spirited treatment of, 117–19, 137–39
    background, 102–3
    Hoboken melee, 139
    hounding of Anger, 242, 259, 260
    ignored, at showings of *Scorpio Rising*, 137–38, 213–14
    on machismo and sadomasochism, 99
    Playboy photo, 152
    in *Scorpio Rising*, 106–13

Cabinet of Dr. Caligari, The (film), 22, 40, 48, 73
Cable TV, 251–52
Cagliostro, Count, 77, 166, 207
Cahiers du Cinéma, 93–94
Calendo, John, 204–6, 240
California State Supreme Court, 120, 191
Cameron, Dr. Paul, 246
Cameron, Marjorie, 68, 70, 162, 199
    with Anger in Los Angeles, 100–101
    Hopper on, 72
    in *Inauguration of the Pleasure Dome*, 75–76, 81
Cammell, Donald, 181, 229
Capote, Truman, 133
Castle, William, 245
Cavett, Dick, 189
"Celluloid Heroes" (Kinks), 201
Chaney, Lon, 79
Changeling Prince, The, 12, 75
Chaplin, Charles, 189
Chapman, Mark David, 228
Charles, Ray, 107
Chelsea Girls (film), 148, 149, 150, 222
Childe, Victor, 134
Christianity, 28, 31, 164
Cimber, Matt, 191
Cinema 16, 55–56, 66, 80, 115, 117, 188
Cinema Theater, Los Angeles, 119, 128
Cinémathèque Française, 60–61, 92, 95–96, 188
City magazine, 195
City of Night (Rechy), 116, 124, 195
Clair, René, 23, 64
Clark, Claudine, 109
Clarke, Shirley, 116

Club 57, New York, 221–22, 225
Coco Crystal Show, The, 251–52
Cocteau, Jean, 15, 23, 30, 58, 217, 225
  Anger and, 24, 59
  compared with Anger, 262
  Paris showing of *Oedipus Rex,* 61–63
  surrealism, pornography, and high art,
    24–25
Coler, Bertha (grandmother), 4, 7–8, 9,
    11, 19, 52, 100
Collective for Living Cinema, 215, 221
Collins, Jess, 67
ComCo, 151, 152
"Come As Your Madness" ball, 73
Confessions of a Male Groupie (film), 245
Confidential magazine, 94
Conner, Bruce, 175–76
Connors, Chuck, 190
Constant, Alphonse Louis. *See* Levi,
    Eliphas
Cooper, Michael, 181, 240
Coppola, Francis, 240
Corll, Dean Alan, 242
Corman, Roger, 131–32, 177
Cosmic Ray (film), 175
Costello, George "Budd," 189
Couch (film), 112
Couts, Hayden, 230, 232, 234
Covert, Scott, 222
Crabbe, Buster, 10
Crackpot (Waters), 245
Crane, Hart, 134
Crawford, Joan, 249
Creative Film Associates, 20, 21, 55, 92
Crowley, Aleister, 10, 38, 150, 154, 158,
    164, 171, 184, 258. *See also*
    Crowley sex magick; Occultism;
    titles of works
  Anger influenced by, 26, 30, 33–34, 39,
    69, 83, 124, 175
  Anger's lifelong devotion to, 262–63
  Anger's proposed biopic of, 178
  audience's psychedelic trances, 135
  background, life, and philosophy,
    26–34
  Beausoleil on, 145–46
  bisexuality, 28–30
  Brakhage and, 100
  death, 34
  drug addiction, 29, 30, 34, 162–63
  and Jimmy Page, 183
  Kinsey on, 87–88
  and Lucifer, 140
  and *Lucifer Rising,* 230, 232–36
  and Nin, 55

occult concepts, 26–27, 30, 117, 132
  and *Scorpio Rising,* 113
  solar-phallic religion, 27, 32–33, 232
  in Thelema Abbey, 88–90
  and women, 28
  writing style, 29, 94, 198
Crowley, Edward Alexander. *See* Crowley,
    Aleister
Crowley sex magick, 26–33, 69, 72, 80,
    134
  followers of, and hippies, 140
  Kinsey interest in, 87–88
  those influenced by, 68
Crystal, Coca, 251–52
Curtis, Tony, 261
Curtiz, Michael, 18
Cyclops child, 128

Dadaism, 23, 149
Dale, Dick, 222
Dali, Salvador, 23
Dallesandro, Joe, 148
Danceteria disco, New York, 243–44
Dante's Inferno (film), 79
David (tabloid), 223
Davies, Marion, 123
Day, Warren, 120
De Antonio, Emile, 116
De Arte Magica (Crowley), 32–33
De Brier, Samson, 53, 68, 255
  home used as set for *Inauguration of the
    Pleasure Dome,* 74
  Hopper on, 72–73
  in *Inauguration of the Pleasure Dome,*
    76–77, 79
de Miramar, Marie Theresa, 78
de Sade, Marquis, 23, 92, 94, 217
De Sana, Jimmy, 225
Dead, The (film), 96
Dean, James, 123, 134, 203, 213, 250
  Byron obsession with, 260
  and *Scorpio Rising,* 104, 106, 108
Death in Venice (Mann), 126, 194
Deathwatch (film), 150–51
Dekker, Albert, 200
Dellenback, William, 86
Demigods (Anger film), 17–18, 35. See also
    Escape Episode
Denunciation of Stan Brakhage, The (Anger
    film), 215–16
Deran, James, 258
Derek, John, 15
Deren, Maya, 21–22, 115
"Desire and the Black Masseur"
    (Williams), 49–50

Desistfilm (film), 66
D'Este, Cardinal, 63
"Devil in Disguise" (Presley), 106
Devil's Angels (film), 150
Dianetics, 69, 155
Diary of a Drug Fiend (Crowley), 30
Dieterle, William, 11
Diggers, 151, 158
Diggy, 7, 8, 11, 17, 18, 52, 102, 249
Disney, Walt, 238
Dodds, Johnny, 104–5, 134
Dogma and Ritual of High Magic, The
        (Levi), 25
Donovan, Rick, 253
"Doors of Perception, The" (Huxley), 67
Dorfman, Bill, 105–6, 135
Dots and Loops (film), 21
Dr. Kinsey and the Institute for Sex Research
        (Pomeroy), 84
Dracula (film), 214
Drastic Demise (Anger film), 35
"Dream Lover" (Paris Sisters), 126, 127
Drugs, 21, 68, 131, 134–35, 153, 162–63,
        220, 246. *See also* Anger, Kenneth;
        Crowley, Aleister; LSD
    and hippies, 140
Druks, Renate, 68, 72–73, 75–77
Duca, Lo, 123
Duncan, Robert, 67

Earle, Ed, 37–38
    on Anger and women, 46–47
    on Anger's behavior and homosexual
        tastes, 48–50
    on Anger's voice, 94
    on casting and making of *Fireworks*,
        44–46
"Early Works" (Mapplethorpe), 105
Earp, Wyatt, 108
Eastman Kodak, 55, 67
Easy Rider (film), 175, 181
Eaux d'Artifice (Anger film), 63–64, 123,
        133, 144, 217
Echoes of Silence (film), 148
Egypt, 28, 31, 233
    filming of *Lucifer Rising*, 182–83, 218,
        234
Eisenstein, Sergei, 7, 19, 23, 55, 61, 67,
        79–80, 113, 235
El Topo (film), 175, 181, 214
Electric Light Orchestra, 81, 217
Elgin Theater, New York, 175
Elliot, Cass, 218
Empire (film), 149
Encyclopedia of the Blessed (film), 175

Engley, Hollis, 243
Entr'Acte (film), 23, 64, 93
Entwistle, Peg, 95, 258, 261
Equinox, The, 31, 232, 252
Equinox of the Gods event, 155–56
Erotikus (film), 194
Escape Episode (Anger film), 17, 35, 49, 57,
        182
"Every Man and every Woman is a Star"
        (Crowley), 94, 199, 233
Experiment in Film (Jacobs), 18
Exploitation films, 131, 201, 228

"Fabulous Anger Trilogy, The," 176, 225
Fade to Black (film), 120
Fairbanks, Douglas, Sr., 201
Faithfull, Chris, 181
Faithfull, Marianne, 163, 165, 235
    Jagger's treatment of, 192
    in *Lucifer Rising*, 181, 182, 230, 233
    on Anger, 258
Fall of the House of Usher, The (film), 20
Fantasia (film), 231, 235
Farmer's Other Daughter, The (film), 127
Farr, Florence, 28
Fast Set, The (film), 119
Faster Pussycat! Kill! Kill! (film), 131
Ferdinand the Bull (Anger film), 14, 159
Festival of the Damned Film, 58
Fields, Verna, 120
55th Street Playhouse, New York, 176,
        193
Film Culture, 115–16, 129
    awards, 121, 215
Film Exercises 1 through *5* (films), 21
Film-Makers' Cinémathèque, 116, 132
Film-Makers' Cooperative, 116, 121, 159
Finch, Nigel, 255–59
Fireworks (Anger film), 4, 39–44, 52, 96,
        106, 119, 176, 193, 195, 212, 220,
        226, 248, 251, 258
    Anger's "death wish," 50
    casting, 76–77, 111
    dedicated to Fouts, 132–33
    European screenings and prizes, 59
    Kinsey and, 83, 86
    Nin's reaction to, 55
    Playboy photo, 152
    popularity of, 66
    revivals, 150, 221
    showings and reviews in 1948, 45–46,
        57–58
Fitzgerald, Kit, 226–27
Flaming Creatures (film), 112, 121
Flash Gordon, 14

Fleischman, Stanley, 119
Fles, John, 129
Flesh (film), 148, 150
Flesh of Morning (film), 66
Florey, Robert, 20
Fonda, Jane, 137
Fonda, Peter, 131
"Fools Rush In" (Ricky Nelson), 104
Ford, Charles Henri, 53, 92, 133
Ford Foundation grants, 117, 121,
        124–26, 128
4E. *See* Ackerman, Forrest J.
Fouts, Denham, 132–33, 163
Fragment of Seeking (film), 39
France, 40, 58–59, 136–37. *See also* Paris
Frankenstein (film), 214
Fraux, Ninette, 89
Frazer, J. G., 26
Frazier, Robert, 135, 163, 164, 167
Freaks (film), 175
Freedom Is a Two-Edged Sword (Parsons),
        68
Freedom Orchestra, 211
Freemasonry, 25, 28, 32
French, Alan, 224–25, 226, 227, 236, 240
Freud, Sigmund, 26, 38, 57
Friends magazine interview, 181
From Caligari to Hitler (Kracauer), 48

"Galgolitic Mass" (Janáček), 80
Gance, Abel, 93
Gebhardt, Paul, 84
Genet, Jean, 30, 217, 236
    and Anger, 25, 223
    Deathwatch, 150–51
    Un Chant d'Amour, 58, 121, 221
Geography of the Body (film), 22
Georg (film), 100
Gerard, Jack, 143
German Expressionism, 40, 49
Germany, 48, 137, 178
    Anger TV interview, 179
Getty, J. Paul, Jr., 163, 212, 240, 255
Getz, Michael, 119
Gibril, Miriam, 229
Gilbert, John, 199
Gillis, Jamie, 225
Giorno, John, 121
Girl on a Motorcycle (film), 181
Gish, Lillian, 19
Glad Rags to Riches (film), 11
Glide Memorial Church, 151, 152
Glory Stompers, The (film), 150
Gnostic Mass, 69, 77
Godard, Jean-Luc, 92

Godot, 140–41, 143
Gold Diggers of 1933 (film), 13, 201
Golden Bough, The (Frazer), 26
Golden Grope of Marilyn Monroe, The
        (Anger collage), 136
Goldman, Peter Emmanuel, 148
Goldstein, Al, 194
Gone With the Wind (film), 52
Gospel According to St. Matthew, The (film),
        234
Granas, Marilyn, 17–18
Grant, Cary, 249
Gray, Gordon, 41, 43, 46
Great Beast, 34, 76, 79, 87, 90, 140, 183
Great Beast, The (Symonds), 26–27
Greenleaf Classics, 122
Gregory, Dick, 18
Griffin, Merv, 189
Griffin, Rick, 147
Griffith, D. W., 19, 79–80, 81, 198
Grissom Gang, The (film), 190
Grogan, Emmett, 151
Grossman, Clara, 18–19, 53
Grove Press, 115
Guns of the Trees (film), 116
Guylder, Van, 189

Hackett, Pat, 220
Hall, Jerry, 222
Hallelujah the Hills (film), 116
Haller, Robert, 223, 248, 252
Halper, Jonathan, 52
Halsted, Fred, 117, 193–94, 206, 245, 262
Hammett, Nina, 34
Haring, Keith, 222
Harlow, Jean, 199
Harper, Jonathan, 188
Harrington, Curtis, 25, 39–40, 48, 55, 68,
        73, 135
    on Anger's family, 19
    collaboration with Anger, 49, 52, 67
    and Creative Film Associates, 20–22
    on filming of *Inauguration of the
        Pleasure Dome*, 74–75
    on Fouts, 133
    Hopper on, 71–72
    in *Inauguration of the Pleasure Dome*, 75,
        78, 80
    on Kessler, 40
    in Paris, 61–63
Harris, Dare, 15
Harris, Lady Frieda, 31
Harrison, Bob, 94
Hearst, William Randolph, 123, 189
Hellfire Club, New York, 225–26

Hell's Angels, 105, 111, 134, 152
    in Britain, 168, 173, 177–78
    and *Scorpio Rising*, 118
Hell's Angels (Thompson), 120, 132
Hell's Angels on Wheels (film), 150
Hendrix, Jimi, 142
Henley, Wayne, 242
Hermetic Order of the Golden Dawn,
    27–28
Heroin, 134–35, 162–63
Hersig, Leah, 29, 89
"He's A Rebel" (Crystals), 108
Heterosexuality
    Kinsey research revelations, 85–86
    and S&M, 223–24
Hinman, Gary, 170, 211
Hippie Hollywood (film), 143
Hippies, 139
Hirschman, Ruth, 120
History of Eroticism (Duca), 123
History of Magic, The (Levi), 25, 77
"Hit the Road, Jack," 107
Hitchcock, Alfred, 52
Hoffman, Abbie, 158
Hogan, Frank, 121
Hollywood, 5, 7, 8–9, 18–19, 72, 214, 262
    Anger's exposé of stars, 94–95, 198–201
    Anger's hatred of, 11, 13, 220, 248–50
Hollywood Babble-On, 262
Hollywood Babylon (Anger), 9, 204–5, 222,
    249–50, 256
    BBC documentary, 258
    bootleg paperback, 191, 195
    Miller version of, 122–24
    Miller's film of, 188–91
    mimicry of, 218
    script based on, 255
    TV adaptation, 261
Hollywood Babylon II (Anger), 13, 198–202,
    221, 241, 248–51
Hollywood Babylone, (Anger), 93–94, 96,
    190, 202, 218
Hollywood Blue (film), 190
Holy Mountain, The (film), 214
Homosexual pornography, 39, 165, 193–94
Homosexuality, 20–21, 23. *See also*
        Homosexual pornography
    of Crowley, 28–30
    Crowley's solar-phallic religion, 33
    Kinsey on, 85–86, 90
    in *Lot in Sodom*, 20–21
    Mekas attack on underground film, 115
    myth of macho homosexual, 113
    and police entrapment, 37
    pre-gay-liberation days, 47–48

and S&M practice, 223–24
Hopper, Dennis, 71, 175, 220
    on Anger's creativity and financial
        problems, 181–82
    on Anger's hatred of Hollywood, 250
Hopper, Hedda, 18
Hubbard, L. Ron, 69–70, 155
Huggins, Leslie, 178–79, 218
    in *Lucifer Rising*, 231–32, 234, 236
Hughes, Fred, 220
Hughes, Howard, 71, 244
Hugo, Ian, 55
Human Be-In, Golden Gate Park, 146,
    151
Human Wreckage (film), 202
Hunter, Jeffrey, 111
Hustlers, 84, 245–46
Huxley, Aldous, 38, 67, 162
Huysmans, J. K., 25, 76, 154
"Hymn to Lucifer" (Crowley), 140

"I Only Have Eyes for You" (Flamingos),
    188
"I Will Follow Him" (Peggy March), 110
Image (film), 143
Images in the Snow (film), 22
Immortal Mr. Teas, The (film), 131
Impact Films, 178, 183
Inauguration of the Pleasure Dome (Anger
        film), 71, 74–81, 144, 152, 172,
        176–77, 228, 233, 248
    Electric Light Orchestra soundtrack,
        217
    print stolen, 128
    psychedelic revival, 131
    "Sacred Mushroom Edition," 76, 78,
        80, 117, 135
    three-screen version of, 93
Ince, Tom, 123
Incest (Nin), 54
Indiana University, 84–86
Indica Gallery, 135, 163, 164
Ink Spots, the, 14
Institute for Adult Education, 188, 191
Institutional Quality (film), 175
Intolerance (film), 79, 198–99, 235
Invisible Circus event, 151–52
Invocation of My Demon Brother (Anger
        film), 147, 154, 168, 170–75, 235,
        258
    homosexuality and sadism, 180–81
Isherwood, Christopher, 133
It Won't Rub Off, Baby (film), 18
Ivan the Terrible (film), 79
Ivice, Maurine, 251–52

Jacobs, Lewis, 18, 57–58
Jagger, Bianca, 183, 192
Jagger, Chris, 181–83
Jagger, Mick, 163–65, 168, 183, 192, 220, 222, 229
  Altamont concert, 177–78
  Anger's hostility toward, 192, 209, 240
  in *Invocation of My Demon Brother*, 174
  Invocation of My Demon Brother sound-track, 170–71
  Lucifer Rising film, 177, 181
  Lucifer Rising soundtrack, 229, 237
Jameson, Laura, 181
Janáček, Leos, 80
Jefferson Airplane, 177
Jensen, Kris, 109
Jesus Christ, 22, 23, 27, 31, 70–71, 113, 152
  as depicted in *Scorpio Rising*, 108–10, 111
Jodorowsky, Alejandro, 175, 181, 214
Jolson, Al, 7, 201, 236, 250
Jones, Bob, 17
Jones, Brian, 167–68
Jones, M. Henry, 222
Jung, Carl, 26, 31

Kabbalah, 25–26, 28, 136
Kable News Network, 123
Kadell, Kate, 73, 76–77
Kandel, Lenore, 151, 172, 173
Kaye, Stanton, 100, 129
Keitel, Harvey, 176
Kelly, Gene, 54
Kelly, Rose, 29
Kelly, Sir Gerald, 29
Kenneth Anger, or Film as Magic Ritual (documentary), 179, 192
Kenneth Anger's Magick (PBS documentary), 226
Kesey, Ken, 131
Kessler, Chester, 39–40, 67, 176, 204
  photo of Anger, 136
Killing of America, The (film), 242
King, Francis, 27
King Kong (film), 259
King of Kings (film), 111
Kinsey, Alfred C., 100, 162, 179, 224
  career, 83–90
  research revelations, 84–87
Kinsey Institute, 125, 151
  Anger working for, 87, 243, 246
Klein, William, 136
Knight, Arthur, 152
Knights Templars, 32, 34, 132

Knokke-le-Zoute film festivals, 59, 93
Kosloff, Maurice, 11
Kracauer, Siegfried, 48
Kroll, Jack, 148, 200
Kuchar, George, 148, 175
Kuchar, Mike, 148
Kustom Kar Kommandos (Anger film), 124, 125, 126, 131, 144, 222, 258
  Ford Foundation grant, 117, 121, 124–26, 128
  previewed in New York (1966), 132
  quest for investors, 139

L.A. Free Press, 120
L.A. Plays Itself (film), 193–94
La Bas (Huysmans), 25
La Dolce Vita (film), 94
L'Age d'Or (film), 23
Land Without Bread (film), 23
Landow, George, 175
Langlois, Henri, 61
Last Temptation of Christ, The (film), 234
Laughing Torso, The (Hammett), 34
Laughton, Charles, 123
Lautréamont, Comte de, 61
LaVey, Anton, 154–55, 159, 173, 180, 205
Lawrence, T. E., 134
Le Livre Blanc (Cocteau), 24, 217, 225
Leary, Timothy, 150, 151
Leather and Things (film), 245
"Leather Boy" myth, 112–13
Leather crowd, 112–13, 116–17, 124, 225. *See also Kustom Kar Kommandos; Scorpio Rising*
Led Zeppelin, 183, 192, 194, 208–9
Leder, Paul, 127
Lee, Arthur, 142
Leighton, Ava, 227–28
Lennon, John, 228, 229
Leogrande, Ernest, 204
Les Chants de Maldoror (Lautréamont), 61
Les Dames du Bois de Boulogne (film), 95
Les Enfants Terribles (film), 15
Lesser, Sol, 7
Lester, Elenore, 150
Let It Bleed (Rolling Stone), 170
Levi, Eliphas, 25, 27, 69, 77, 132, 154, 171
Lewis, David, 252
Lewis, Herschell Gordon, 123, 244
Liber Agape (Crowley), 32
Lickerish Quartet, The (film), 227
Life and Death of 9413, A Hollywood Extra (film), 20
Life magazine, 110

London, 59, 177. *See also* Anger, Kenneth
  drugs and celebrities, 162–63
London, Ephraim, 56
Lonesome Cowboys (film), 176
Look Back in Anger (Osborne), 204
Los Angeles, 100–101, 255–59
Lot in Sodom (film), 20
Love (psychedelic band), 142–43
Love is My Profession (film), 123
Love That Whirls, The (Anger film), 55,
  67, 125
Loveday, Betty May, 88–89
Loveday, Raoul, 88–89
Lovemaking (film), 66
Lovett, Thad, 64
Loving (film), 66
LSD, 67, 131, 134–36, 153
  Anger on potential of, 150
  Anger's use of, 140, 162, 220, 242
Lucifer, 28, 166
  antithesis of Scorpio, 145
  "bad little boy" metaphor, 140
Lucifer Rising (Anger film), 90, 139,
  229–36, 240, 252, 258. See also
  Invocation of My Demon Brother;
  Lucifer
  Anger's poster sale, 248
  Beausoleil soundtrack, 211
  British government funding, 182
  and Cagliostro Mirror, 207
  casting of, 141–43, 165, 178–79, 181,
    183, 224
  Egyptian shots, 182–83, 218
  further Lucifer films, 237
  Jagger for lead role, 164–65
  Jagger soundtrack, 170–71, 192
  missing footage, 157–58, 160, 179–80
  new Lucifer for, 224–25
  Page soundtrack, 192, 208
  publicity for, 147–48
  screening and premiere, 229, 235–36,
    241
  shown at university, 191–93
LUCIFER tattoo, 181, 218, 225, 226, 250
Lumière, August, 24, 61

Maas, Willard, 22, 101, 115, 131
McCabe, Mike, 258
McDaniels, Gene, 109
McDarrah, Fred, 139
McLaren, Norman, 21
McQueen, Butterfly, 202
Madame Blavatsky's Theosophical
  Society, 28
Madonna, 258

Magical World of Aleister Crowley, The
  (King), 27
Magick Circle (LaVey's), 155
"Magick Lantern Cycle," 132, 218, 228,
  242
  1966 program and psychedelic drugs,
    133–35
  at Club 57, 221–22
  at Gay Film Festival (1987), 252–53
  revelations and sex magick, 262–63
  video package of four tapes, 252
Magick Powerhouse of Oz (band), 145,
  153, 155, 173
Magnuson, Ann, 222
Mailer, Norman, 158
Main, Jerry, 128
Malanga, Gerard, 101, 108
Maldoror (Anger film), 92, 93
Mann, Kurt, 134
Mansfield, Jayne, 122, 191, 198, 205
Manson (film), 225
Manson, Charles, 166, 170, 205, 211, 252
Manson family, 155, 180, 195
Mapplethorpe, Robert, 41, 105–6, 245,
  262
March, Peggy, 110
Marine Corps, 103, 104, 106
Markopoulos, Gregory, 112, 121, 128,
  150
  Newsweek on, 148
Marquis, Yvonne, 52–53, 79
Masonic order, 28, 32, 34
Master Therion, 134, 183
Masturbation, 32, 66
  and conception of homunculus, 69–70
Matelots en Menottes (unmade Anger film),
  212
Mathers, S. L. "MacGregor," 28, 33
Mathiesen, Paul, 55, 68, 72–73, 75–79,
  135
Mattachine Society, 121, 176
Maugham, Somerset, 87
Mazursky, Paul, 151
Mekas, Adolfas, 115, 116
Mekas, Jonas, 115, 121, 137, 166, 215
  underground film outlet, 116
Méliès, Georges, 24, 61, 79, 149
Menken, Marie, 22, 92, 101–2
Menzies, William Cameron, 52
Merseer, Mary, 61
Meshes of the Afternoon (film), 22
Metasex, 139–40
Metropolis (film), 48, 259
Metzger, Radley, 119, 227
Meyer, Eve, 131

Meyer, Russ, 131, 189
MGM, 11
Mickey Mouse, 235, 238, 255, 259
Mideke, Mike, 141
Midnight Cowboy (film), 138
Midnight cowboys, 102. See also *Scorpio Rising*
Midsummer Night's Dream, A (film), 110, 174, 190, 203, 233
    Anger's role in, 11–13, 94
    in BBC documentary, 257
    costumes and set, 60, 75, 79, 188
Millennium, New York, 215, 218, 242, 248
Miller, Henry, 30, 54–55, 75, 119
Miller, Marvin, 121–23
    Hollywood Babylon film and lawsuit, 188–91, 198, 220, 261
Milligan, Andy, 112
Minault, Slim, 151–52
Moby Dick (film), 9
Mohammed, Messenger of God (film), 234
Mondo Cane (film), 225
Mondo Hollywood (film), 143
Mondo Trasho (film), 123
Monroe, Marilyn, 189–90, 221
Montage technique, 23–24, 79, 113, 235
Moonchild (Crowley), 28, 69, 172
Morrissey, Paul, 148, 150
Morrow, Vic, 151
Motor Psycho (film), 131
Movie, The (art house), 117, 118, 124, 131
Murnau, F. W., 199
Murray, Mae, 199–200
Museum of Modern Art, New York, 194, 216
"My Boyfriend's Back" (Angels), 105
My Hustler (film), 148, 149, 165
Mystery of the Leaping Fish, The (film), 201
Mystic Fire Video, 252

Napoleon (film), 93
Narcissism, 23, 195
Nashville Babylon, 262
National Film Finance Corporation (British), 182
National Film Theatre, 255
Navy, United States, 43, 44, 159
Nazis, 48, 110
    Anger's interest in, 136–37
Ned Kelly (film), 164
Nelson, Ricky, 104, 120
Nest, The (Anger film), 15, 17
Neuberg, Victor, 29

New American Cinema Group, 116
New York, 221. *See also* Anger, Kenneth; *names of clubs and theaters*; Times Square
    Anger's home in, 212
    Brooklyn Heights, 102–3
New York Daily News, 203–4, 248
New York Post, 137, 203, 248, 252
    on film of *Hollywood Babylon*, 255
New York Times, 150, 200
New Yorker, 137
Newsweek, 148, 150, 200
Newton, Helmut, 96
Night of the Living Dead (film), 214
Night Shift (all-male theater), 245–47, 248
Nimoy, Leonard, 151
Nin, Anaïs, 54–55, 68
    at "Come As Your Madness" ball, 73
    on Anger's loneliness, 92
    in *Inauguration of the Pleasure Dome*, 75, 78–81, 152
Novarro, Ramon, 200, 221, 258

Occultism, 21, 25, 68, 117, 124
    Anger and LaVey, 154–55, 159
    Crowley's magick and, 26–27, 30
    and Jagger, 164
    Parsons, Cameron, Hubbard and, 69–71
    in San Francisco, 180
Oedipus Rex (film), 61
Offen, Murray, 165
"Oh, What A Night" (Dells), 188
Oliver, Stephen, 131
Olympia Press, 122
Olympiad (film), 48, 137
Ondine, 149, 222
"One Arm" (Williams), 49
120 Days of Sodom (film), 23
"One Star in Sight" (Crowley), 135, 199
Ono, Yoko, 229
Orkustra, 143, 151
Osborne, John, 203–4
Osco, Bill, 190
O.T.O. (Ordo Templis Orientis), 31–32, 252
    Agape Lodge, Pasadena, 33, 69–70
O'Toole, Larry, 227, 235–36
Oui magazine, 204, 240
Our Gang comedies, 11
Outlaw Motorcycles (film), 150
Oz books (Baum), 10–11

Pacific Film Archive, Berkeley, 201
Page, Charlotte, 208

Page, Jimmy, 183–84, 231–32, 252
    Anger's attempt to humiliate, 208–9,
        211
    soundtrack for *Lucifer Rising*, 184, 192,
        194, 229, 234, 237
Pallenberg, Anita, 163, 166–67, 174, 229
    and Anger, 178, 181
Palone, John, 105
Paris, 59–96
Paris Sisters, 126
Park-Miller Theater, New York, 176–77
Parsons, Jack, 33, 134, 162, 233
    career and Crowley magick, 68–71
    death of, 71, 124
Parsons, Louella, 18
Partch, Harry, 80–81
"Party Lights" (Claudine Clark), 109
Pasolini, Pier Paolo, 234, 236
Patchen, Kenneth, 39
Patton, Richard, 141
Pauvert, Jean Jacques, 94, 122, 190
Pentagon, March on the, 158
People magazine, 250–51
Performance (film), 164, 181
Performing Garage, SoHo, 222
Perkins, Michael, 200
Peterson, Maxine, 14–15, 17
Petit, Roland, 59
Physique Pictorial, 39, 42
Picture Post magazine, 89–90
Pink Flamingos (film), 195, 214
Pink Floyd, 194
Pink Narcissus (film), 13
Plachy, Sylvia, 236
Playboy, 136, 152
Plaza Art burlesque, Chicago, 119
Plymouth Brethren, 27
Poe, Edgar Allen, 20
"Poem for Perverts" (Kandel), 172
"Poem of Ecstasy" (Scriabin), 35
"Point of No Return" (McDaniels), 109
Pol, Talitha, 163
Polanski, Roman, 261
Polk, Brigid, 149
Polly Tix in Washington (film), 11
Pomeroy, Dr. Wardell D., 84
Poole, Wakefield, 193
Pornography. *See also* Homosexual
        pornography
    Fireworks, 39–45
    hard-core, 214
    and Kinsey, 86
    Scorpio Rising, 119
Portrait of Jason (film), 116
Posada, Juan Guadalupe, 73

Pour Vous magazine, 203
Power, Tyrone, 123, 200, 257
Powers, Jim, 112, 119, 134, 135
Presley, Elvis, 106, 120
Pressman, Ed, 256
Previn, André, 203
Prevost, Marie, 199
Prisoner of Mars (Anger film), 14, 182
Prix de l'Age d'Or, 93
Prix du Cine-Club Belge, 93
Prix Henri Chomette, 59
Professional Services, Inc., 122, 189
Prok. *See* Kinsey, Alfred C.
Provincetown Playhouse, New York, 56
Puce Moment (Anger film), 52–54, 78–79,
        117, 188
Puck Productions, 196, 215, 229

Quartet (film), 87
Que Viva Mexico! (film), 7–8, 23, 61

Ra, eye of, 171, 173, 174
Rabbit's Moon (Anger film), 60, 188, 217,
        226
Raging Bull (film), 227
Ramrodder (film), 170
Rebel Without a Cause (film), 203
Rechy, John, 116, 195
Red Kimona, The (film), 202
Reed, Rex, 200
Reed, Wallace, 202
Reflections of Youth (film), 193
Reinhardt, Max, 11
Resnais, Alain, 92
Resnick, Marcia, 220, 221
Revenant, Claude, 60
Rex de Arte Regia (Crowley), 33, 87
Richards, Keith, 163, 166—67, 174, 178,
        181
Riefenstahl, Leni, 48, 137
Ringolevio (Grogan), 151
Rite of Spring, The (Stravinsky), 62
Ritt, Martin, 119
Road to Jerusalem, The (film), 108–9
Robinson Crusoe on Mars (film), 235
Rocco, Alex, 131
Rocco, Pat, 165
Rockefeller Foundation, 84, 90
Rogosin, Lionel, 178
Rolling Stones, 163, 164–68, 170, 175
    Altamont concert, 177–78
Rome, 63
Roof, Jean Anglemyer (sister), 4–5, 9, 14,
        66, 241
Rooney, Mickey, 13, 110, 174, 190, 201

Rose, Sir Francis, 231, 236
Rosemary's Baby (film), 69
Rosicrucian philosophy, 10, 25, 32
Ross, Toby, 134, 193, 248
Rossett, Barney, 115
Runt Page, The (film), 11
Russell, Ken, 240
Russian Embassy house, Haight-Ashbury,
        141–46, 156–57
    footage in *Invocation of My Demon
        Brother*, 173–75

Sadomasochism (S&M), 193, 194, 212,
        225. See also *Scorpio Rising*
    Byron and, 103
    in *Fireworks*, 41–43
    heterosexual/homosexual differences,
        223
    as integral life force, 262
    in *Rabbit's Moon*, 60
Salome (Wilde), 24
Salvatorelli, Carmillo/Carmilla, 63
San Francisco. *See also* Russian Embassy
        house, Haight-Ashbury
    Anger's home in North Beach, 117
    drug scene, 162–63
Sanchez, Tony, 166–68, 170
Santa Fe Film Festival (1982), 243
Satanis—The Devil's Mass (film), 180
Satanism, 27, 63, 154, 159
Satie, Erik, 23
"Scarlet woman" symbol, 28–29, 68, 69,
        76–79, 89
Scented Garden, The (Crowley), 88
Scharf, Kenny, 222
Schellerup, Henning, 189
Schrader, Leonard, 242
Scientology, 69
Scorpio. *See* Byron, Bruce
Scorpio Rising (Anger film), 14, 102–13,
        123, 128–29, 132, 144–45, 176,
        193, 195, 225, 226, 234, 248, 258
    ad for, 131
    Byron and, 213, 260
        Byron's crack-up at showing, 137–38
        Byron's photo in *Playboy*, 152
    casting and analysis, 103–4, 111–13
    characters in, 134–35
    cinematic technique, 175–76, 193
    Club 57 crowd and, 222
    exploitation film copies, 150
    Hopper and, 175
    Invocation of My Demon Brother com-
        pared to, 174
    mainstream acceptance, 137

    1966 program notes for, 134–36
    obscenity case and verdict, 119–20
    prints sold at Film Expo, New York,
        218
    screenings of, 116–17, 136
Scorsese, Martin, 67, 227, 234
    Anger's influence on, 120, 240, 262
    Anger's technique, 176
Scott, Randolph, 249
Screening the Sexes (Tyler), 20–21
Screw (tabloid), 194, 200, 223, 245
Scriabin, Alexander, 35
Seal of Solomon, 171, 173
Sebring, Jay, 143
Sedgwick, Edie, 149
Seltzer, Bill, 42
Senators in Bondage (Anger film), 212
Sensually Liberated Female, The (film),
        191
Sex, John, 222
Sex Garage (film), 193–94
Sex magick. *See* Crowley sex magick
Sexploitation films, 119, 137, 155, 165–66
Sexual Behavior in the Human Male
        (Kinsey), 83, 85, 88
Sexuality. *See also* Crowley, Aleister;
        Crowley sex magick;
        Heterosexuality; Homosexuality;
        Kinsey, Alfred C.
    and Anger's childhood, 10
    aspects in *Scorpio Rising*, 103
    Crowley's writings on, 30
    in underground films, 20
Sher, Lou, 119
Sherpix, 119, 176, 180
Show Palace, New York, 242
Siamese "honeymoon films," 87
Siegel, Bugsy, 199
Silent films, 18, 79, 149
Sinatra, Nancy, 131
Singing Fool, The (film), 7
Sleazoid Express director's forum, 243–45
Sleep (film), 149
"Sleepers Awake on the Precipice"
        (Patchen), 39
Sloane, Mel, 119
Smith, Harry, 21, 34, 54, 67
Smith, Jack, 112, 121, 128–29
Smith, Liz, 248
Smooth Silk and Raw Velvet (film), 218
Snofox (Beausoleil's dog), 142, 172
Society of Spartans, 134
Soho Weekly News, 225–26, 235
    Anger interviews, 223–24, 237–38
Solar-phallic religion, 32

Song Remains the Same, The (film), 208, 209

Sontag, Susan, 95

Soubeyran, André, 60

Sounds (newspaper), 208

Spector, Phil, 108

Spider magazine, 125–26

Split-screen technique, 93

Spring Equinox 1966, 132–36

Stag film collection, 86–87

"Stairway to Heaven," 208–9

Stars and Stripes (film), 21

State University of New York (SUNY), 192–93

Steichen, Edward, 179

Stevens, Marc, 225

Stone, Lewis, 200

Story of O, The (Anger film), 95–96

Straight Arrow Press, 122, 198

Straight Theater, San Francisco, 157

Stravinsky, Leopold, 61–62

Streetcar Named Desire, A (film), 87

Sturges, Mary D'Este, 29

Sturges, Preston, 29

Submission (De Sana), 225

Sun Ra, 143

Superimposition technique, 21

Surfaris, 110

Surrealism, 23–24, 40, 92

Swanson, Gloria, 249

Symbolism, 25, 27, 58

Symonds, John, 26–27

"Sympathy for the Devil" (Rolling Stones), 164, 192

Symphony Space, New York, 263

Tarot cards, 28, 31, 33, 60, 117

Tate, Sharon, 200, 261

Tattoo parties, Hellfire Club, 225–26

Tavel, Ronald, 149

Taxi Driver (film), 245

Taylor, Elizabeth, 249

Tchelitchew, Pavel, 133

Temple, Shirley, 11, 17

Ten Commandments, The (film), 234

Thelema Abbey (Anger film), 90

Thelema Abbey, Sicily, 88–90, 162, 178

Thelemic mythology, 31, 75, 80, 146, 150, 175, 235, 252

"There's a Moon Out Tonight" (Capris), 188

Thiel, Reinhold, 179

Thompson, Hunter S., 30, 119, 132

Thunder Over Mexico (film), 7–8, 23, 55

Time Out magazine, 240

Times Square, 107
    Hell's Kitchen, 137
    hustlers and Kinsey researchers, 84–85
    Night Shift Theater, 245
    Tenderloin district, 102, 225

Tivoli Fountains, 63

Tomorrow's Television Tonight (TV show), 251

Too Young to Die (film), 218

"Torture" (Jensen), 109

Tower, Whitney, 220

Trash (film), 148

Trent, Sandy, 126–28, 132

Trick, The (film), 177

Trip, The (film), 177

Trip to the Moon, A (film), 24

Triumph of the Will (film), 48, 137

Tropic of Cancer (Miller), 120

Truck It (film), 193, 245

Truffaut, François, 61, 92

Twice a Man (film), 112

2001 (film), 24

Tyler, Parker, 20, 53, 81, 117, 133, 158
    Cinema 16 screenings, 56

Un Chant d'Amour (film), 58, 121, 221, 236

Un Chien Andalou (film), 23, 40

Under a Glass Bell and Other Stories (Nin), 54

Underground film, 20–22
    Anger and Brakhage productions, 66–67
    Anger as premier artist of, 262
    at Brussels 1958 World Fair, 92
    Cinema 16 distribution, 55–56
    demise of Cinema 16, 115
    Kinsey and, 83
    Mekas control of, 166
    new distribution outlets, 115–16
    new publicity for, 148
    in porn circuit, 176
    replaced by cult and pornographic films, 214–15
    Scorpio Rising elevated above, 137
    sexploitation market, 119

Underground film-makers, 66–67
    superimposition technique, 21

Unholy Rollers (film), 120

Universal Pictures, 178

Unknown Marilyn, 221

Up and Down with the Rolling Stones (Sanchez), 166

Uribe, Madeline, 141

USC (University of Southern California), 38, 44, 48

Valence, Nadine, 60
Valentino, Nazimova, 52
Valentino, Rudolph, 8, 18–19, 52, 127,
    149, 189, 200, 257
  Anger on, 94
  memorabilia, 246, 248
Van Meter, Ben, 156, 172
Vapors (film), 112
Varda, Agnes, 92
Variety, 137, 188, 189, 190, 191, 207, 211
Vassi, Marco, 139–40
Vaughn, Betty, 74
Vaughn, Jimmy, 178–79, 182–84
Veidt, Conrad, 22–23
Velez, Lupe, 95, 199
Venereal disease, 192
Vidal, Gore, 133
Videotapes, 227–28
Vietnam War, 158, 164
Village Voice, 176, 236
  Anger's death announcement, 158, 175
  on Byron's Hoboken melee, 139
Vincent, Jan-Michael, 253
Vinyl (film), 222
Violent World magazine, 199
Visual Variations on Noguchi (film), 22
Vito and Szou (Godot's parents), 140–41,
    143
Vogel, Amos, 55–57, 115, 116
  on Anger's personality and character,
    57
Von Stroheim, Erich, 189, 200

Waite, Arthur, 28
Wald, Jerry, 71
War Babies (film), 11
Warhol, Andy, 72, 101, 112, 176, 183
  compared with Anger, 148–50
  film awards, 121
  homosexual films, 165–66
  on Anger's hostility, 220
  sexploitation films, 214
  superstars, 137–38, 213, 222
Waters, John, 123, 195, 206, 243–45
  Hollywood Babylon II review, 250
Watson, James Sibley, 20, 78

Watson, Ted, 195
WBAI, New York, 247–49
Webb, Spider, 225
Webber, Melville, 20, 78
Wein, Chuck, 149
Wet magazine interview, 220
"When You Wish Upon a Star," 233
White Stains (Crowley), 30, 88
Whitney, James, 21
Whitney, John, 21
Whitney Museum, 235–36
Who Has Been Rocking My Dream Boat
    (Anger film), 14
Who's Afraid of Virginia Woolf? (Albee),
    101
Who's That Knocking at My Door? (film),
    176
Wild Angels, The (film), 131, 150, 177
Wild One, The (film), 105, 107
Wild Rebels, The (film), 150
Wilde, Constance, 28, 33
Wilde, Oscar, 24, 33, 59
Williams, Tennessee, 87, 224, 242
  homoerotic fiction, 49–50
  on *Fireworks*, 58
Wilson, Dennis, 166
"Wind-Up Doll" (Ran-Dells), 104
Window Water Baby Moving (film), 66
"Wipe Out" (Surfaris), 110
Wolfe, Warren I., 119–20
Wood, Page, 234
Wood, Rebecca, 259
World War II, 35, 48

Yale, Joey, 194
Yanni, Nick, 251
Yeats, William Butler, 28
Yippies, 158
Yorke, Gerald, 235
Young and the Evil, The (Tyler and Ford),
    53, 133
Young Man and Death, The (Cocteau bal-
    let), 59

Zahed, Eliphas Levi. *See* Levi, Eliphas
Zimmerman, Vernon, 120